Virginia Colonial Abstracts
Vol. #3

Northumberland County, VA.
Records *of* Birth
1661-1810

Abstracted by:
Beverly Fleet

Southern Historical Press, Inc.

This volume was reproduced from
an 1938 edition located in the
publisher's private library,
Greenville, South Carolina

Please Direct all Correspondence & Orders to:

Southern Historical Press, Inc.
P.O. Box 1267
375 West Broad Street
Greenville, S.C. 29602-1267

Originally published: Richmond, VA., 1938
Reprinted: Southern Historical Press, Inc.
Greenville, S.C.,
ISBN # 0-89308-389-5
Printed in the United States of America

Preface.

This is the Register of St. Stephen's Parish, Northumberland County, Virginia.

Intimidated by the meticulous, I am sending forth this transcript bereft of it's own name. The difficulty is in that it seems that the original is both more and less than it is marked by it's makers. When the early records of Northumberland County were brought to the Department of Archives, in the Virginia State Library, in Richmond, most of them in sad condition, there appeared this worn and disordered book, marked St. Stephen's Parish. The entries date from 1661, long before there was a St. Stephen's Parish. Those from the beginning to the middle of the 18th century, a period of over ninety years, are all in the same handwriting. This hand is that of an educated gentleman. He wrote of these happy events with style. We would assume that the book was made up from other records, now long lost. The entries in the seventeen fifties and afterwards are in different handwritings, or rather in most indifferent handwritings. Now we have sary, susaner and fillize, written by those who were more familiar with the hoe than the mighty quill. Occasionally there appears a single entry in a good firm hand. Perhaps some father having started the incident was determined to see it properly recorded. But I think the aristocrats as a whole, had then left St. Stephen's Parish.

Perhaps not more than 2000 of these upwards of 5000 recorded innocents survived their second year.

A few deaths are also recorded.

Northumberland was a well established community before the Law and Gospel were put upon the people. Many entries in this register go to show that the Church of England never quite caught up with the inhabitants of colonial Northumberland. One of the early ministers was so heedless as to allow himself to be caught and convicted of adultery. His example as well as his precept is reflected here.

Mr. Morgan Portiaux Robinson, Miss Estelle Bass and Mrs. James Claiborne Pollard of the Department of Archives, in the Virginia State Library in Richmond, have been, as they always are, most kindly, patient and helpful.

This transcript has been checked back twice. As a proposition the work has been about the dullest I've ever undertaken. Had it not been for the interest and faithful work of my daughter, Charlotte Reol Fleet, I can assure you that we would not have this register as Vol. III in this series.

Beverley Fleet.

Richmond, Virginia.
June 1st 1938.

St. Stephen's Parish.

Dr. G. MacLaren Brydon, Historiographer, Diocese of Virginia, in his "Report on Parish Lines in the Diocese of Virginia", 1827. gives us the following regarding St. Stephen's Parish.

page 148. Northumberland, an original County, is first mentioned in statutes in 1644/5 (Hening I. 294). It was represented in 1645, November, and by Act of Assembly in 1648 was formerly admitted as a county: described as "Chickcoun and other parts of the neck of land between Rappahannock and Potomack River" (Hening I. 352).
In 1649, (Hening I. 362) "It is enacted, That the inhabitants which are or shall be seated on the southside of Potomacke River shall be included and are hereafter to be accompted within the county of Northumberland".

page 190. Chickacoan Parish. Northumberland County. One of the earliest parishes (probably the first), in Northumberland County, established upon the first settlement. Centered around Chickacoan, now Coan, River. Name changed to Fairfield Parish in 1664. Later became. or was incorporated into St. Stephen's Parish.

page 21. Boutracy Parish. Northumberland County. Combined with Fairfield Parish to form St. Stephen's Parish before 1724. Not mentioned in list of 1680, 1702 or 1714.

page 189. St. Stephen's Parish. Northumberland County. The earliest of a parish of this name in Northumberland is found in Order Book #2, page 3 in 1704, when St. Stephen's Parish is mentioned in Leonard Howson's will. George Cooper bequeathed land to St. Stephen's Parish in 1711. At some time in the colonial period the name of Fairfield Parish was changed to St. Stophen's Parish, or else the territory of Fairfield, Boutracy and St. Stephen's was combined into the one parish of St. Stephen's.

- - - - - - - -
- - - - - - - -

Note Concerning this Register as Genealogical Authority.
"Is it accurate ?". A question that sooner than later must come up. Let me state immediately, NO, it is not. Not a comforting thought for the genealogist. However there are many apparent errors in the original. Then my own transcription is open to question. While every reasonable care has been taken, I am positive that many corrections can still be made. Here the human element enters. The late depression has shown us that many financial statements prepared by the most astute and conscientious accountants were but deceptive folly. So what are we to accept ? The answer is-not very much. Please therefore do not presume to accept my interpretation of these miserably written entries as final. It could not be final.

Beverley Fleet.

Original in Department of Archives, Virginia State
Library, Richmond, Virginia.
Marked "Church Record of Births (with a few deaths) Northumberland
County. Limiting dates 1661-1810. "

page 1.

-on Atkison Daughter Thos Atkison was born	Date worn away.
Thomas Ashburn Sone to Thos Ashburn was born	Feby year worn away.
-rael Apleby Daughter Jo'n Aplebey was born	Feby " " "
-hos Atkeson Son to Thos Adkeson was Born	Jany " " "
Eliza Armstrong Daughter to Hen'y Armstrong	
was born	Ootr 2 " " "
Tabitha Armstrong Daughter to Do was born	Jany " " "
Henry Armstrong Son to Do was born	Jany " " "
Hannah Ashburn Daughter to Jo'n Ashburn was born	Ootr " " "
John Ashburn Sone to Do was born	Jany " " "
Sarah Allen Daughter to Jo'n Allen was born	Jully " " "
James Allen son to Thos Allen was born	Jany " " "
John Armstrong Son Adam was born	Nov 20 " " "
Samuell Aires Son to Jo'n born	Ootr 20 " " "
Thos Aires son to Do born	Feby 20 " " "
Mary Allen Daughter to Thos was born	Feby 10 " " "
James Allen Son to Do was born	March 10 " " "
Wm Ashburn Sone to John was born	Deomr 24 " " "
John Adkeson Sone to Thos was born	Aug " " "
Thos Allen Son to Thos was born	Augt 18 " " "
Thos Ashburn Sone to John was born	Nov 22 " " "
Eliza Anderson Daughter to Susanah born	Feby " " "
Rebeokah Armstrong Daughter to Adam was born	Novr 10 " " "
Elliner Armstrong Daughter to Do was born	Maroh " " "
Adam & Eliza Armstrong Twins born	Jany 18 " " "
Wm Aderson Sone to Robt was born	Jully 15 " " "
Wm Algood son to Jo'n Algood was born	Augt 14 " " "
Jo'n Algood son to Do was born	Maroh 2 " " "
Leanah Aires Daughter to Josh.u born	Maroh " " "
Ann Atkins Daughter To Jean Atkins was born	Jany 3 " " "
Sarah Adkins Daugh'r to William was born	Decemb " " "
Jo'n Armstrong son to Hezekiah born	Deoem " " "
Bette Allin Daug'r to Thos was Born	Jany " " "
Bethsheba Allin Daugh'r to Do was born	Jany 2 " " "
John Aires sone to Jo'n was born	Deor " " "
Mary Algood Daug'r to Mary & Jo'n Algood was born	Sept " " "
Jo'n Algood Sone to Do was born	Date missing.
- - Adkin son to William was born	" "

page 2.   headed   "- Stephens Parish"

- - Daug'r To Thos was borne	Jany	6	1723
- - Daug'r to John was born	Jany	9	1739
- - Sone To John was born	Apl	8	1739
- -son Sone To Wm was born	Augt	2d	1740
- -derson Daug'r To Rich was bern	Maroh	25	1741
- Aplebey Daug'r To Jo'n was born	Nov'r	10	1740
- Anderson Sone To Robt	Maroh	6	1737/8

page 2 (continued)

- - Anderson Daug'r To Rich was born	March	4	1742/3
- - Allexander Daug'r To Jo'n was born	Ootr	8	1737
- - Allexander Sone to Do was born	Feby	19	1739/40
-rah Aplebey Daug'r To John was born	Nov	15	1743
-Ann Adair Daug'r to James was born	Ootr	20	1743
- - Allen Sone To Elliza'th was born	Feby	28	1743/4
- Alderson Daugr To Rich was born	Marsh	17	1744/5
- Hobson Adair Daug'r To James was born	Jany	23	1745/6
- Alderson sone to Richd & Sayrah his wife Born	Aug	18	1748
- Alderson son To Richd & Sarrah his Wife Born	Jully	8	1751
- Ashburn Sone To Thos & Leannah born	Jully	27	1742
-ey Ashburn Daug'r To Thos & Leannah born	Ootr	28	1743
-enah Ashburn Daug'r To Thos & Lean'h born	Aug'st	14	1746
-anah Ashburn Daug'r To Thos & Lean'h his Wife born	Apl	25	1747
- - Ashburn sone To Thos & Lean'h was born	Feby	27	1744
-ge Ashburn sone To Thos Lean'h (sic) was born	Decemb'r	15	1749
- - Ashburn sone To Peter & Sarah was Born	Nov'r	20	1747
- - Ashburn Daug'r To Peter & Sarah was Born	March	14	1750
-an Aplebey sone to Jo'n & Eliza was born	May	11	1746
- - Aires Daug'r To Thos & Win: Born	Apl	2	1753
- - Airs Daug'r To Thomas & Winifred was Born	Apl	22	1754
- - Airs Son To Do was Born	June	15	1755
- - Alderson Daug'r To Richard & Sarah was Born	July	13th	1755
- - Alexander son To James was Born (sic)	Ootr	21	1747
- - -r Daug'r To Do was Born (sic)	March	25	1747

(Note: One of the above entries, perhaps that of March 25th 1747, iseither the record of a miracle or is in error, which further goes to show that this book was compiled. about the middle of the 18th century from other written sources. Beverley Fleet.)

- - - - Do was Born	Janry	12	174-

page 3. (This page mutilated and contains at least one error. B.F.)

-ent Aldridge Son to Clement Was Born	Sep	-	-
-d Aldridge Daughter to Do was borne	Mar	-	-
-oe Aldridge Daughter to Do was borne	Oct	-	-
- - Aldridge Son to Do was Borne	Feb	-	-
-aao Aldridge Son to Do was borne	S-	-	-
-hn Aldridge Son to Do was borne	Feb	-	-
- - - Wm Adams was born	Feb	-	-
- -threne Adams was borne Daur to John (Sic)	Oot	-	-
- - Ann Allin Daur To Do was born (Sic)	Feby	-	-
John Allin Son to Do was born	June	9	-
Eliza Allin Daughter to Do was born	June	23	-
Thos Ashburn son to Thomas Ashburn was baptoz'd	Jully	-	-
Jo'n Ashburn son to Charles Ashburn was bap	Jully	-	-
Joyce Ashburn Daughter to Do was born	Ootr	-	-
Thos Ashburn son to Do was born	Augr	10	-
Isabella Ashton was born	Sept	9	-
Elliz'a Ashton was born	June	15	-

page 3 (continued)

William Adams Was born	Feby	27	-
Catherine Adams was born	Ootr	25	-
Eliz'a Adams Daughter to Richd Adams was born	May	27	-
Edward Algood sone to Wm Algood was born	March	24	-
William Algood son to Do was Born	Nov	30	-
Sarah Algood Daughter to Do was born	Oct	-	-
Ann Algood Daughter to Do was born	March	-	-
John Algood sone to Do was born	Oct	-	-
John Algrue son to Nicholas Algrue bap'd	June	-	-
Ailce Anderson Daughter to William bap'd	Ap-	-	-

page 4 (mutilated)

- - -aught'r to William Anderson was born	-	-	-
- - - - Allins Twins to James were Born	May	13	-
- - - son to John Atkins was born	May	19	-
- - - -ns Son to Do was born	July	8	-
- - - -s sone to Do was born	May	13	-
- - - -kins son to Do was born	Jany	12	-
- - - - Daughter to Joseph Ame was Born	March	21	16-
- - - - Daughter to Do was born	Nov	12	16-
- - - - Daughter to Do was born	May	6	16-
- - - - Daughter to Richd Adams was born	May	27	169-
- - - -one Daughter to Garvis Alistone was born	June	23	169-
- - - Daughter to John Allene was Borne	June	23	169-
- - -ton Daughter to Joseph Auston Bap'd	May	8	169-
- - Atkins son James Atkins was born	Sept	10	169-
- - Adamty sone to Oneale Adamty was Borne	Sept	3	1696
- - -amty Daughter to Do was born	Sept	8	16-
- - - Ame Daughter Joseph Ame was born	Jully	21	169-
- - -burn Daughter to Thos Ashburn Bap'd	Ootr	19	170-
-n Aldridge sone Wm Aldridge was born	May	16	170-
-n Ashburn Sone to Thos Ashburn Bap'd	Feby	10	170-
- - -ins sone James Atkins was Borne	Jany	21	170-
- - Atkins Sone to Do was borne	Apl	23	170-
-n Anderson Daughter Wm Anderson Bap'd	May	23	17-
- - -plebey sone to John Aplebey was borne	Ootr	6	17-
- - Aplebey Daughter to Do was born	Feby	30	17-
- - Aplebey sone to Do was borne	Jany	2	170-
- - Aplebey Daughter to Do was Borne	Jully	17	171-
- - Aplebey sone To Do was Borne	May	29	17-
-n Atkins son to Ann was Born	Feby	20	17-
-s Atkins sone to Thos Atkins was Bap'd	Decem'r	16	17-
- - Armstronge sone Hen'y Armstrong Bap	Apl	18	17-
- - -ton Daughter to Charles Ashton Borne	Ootr	20	17-
- - -ton Son to Do was born in	Augt		17-
- - Ablin Daughter to Hen'y Abline borne	June	13	17-
- - -n Sone to John Allen born	March	11	17-
- - eson Daughter to Thos Atkeson born	March	12	17-
- - -son Sone to Do was born	Novr	1	17-
- - - Daughter to Do was born	Feby	-	17-

page 5. headed "Northberl'd County A".

Hannah Alexander Daugh'r To Do was Born	July	22	1752
-etty (prob. Letty) Alexander Daugh'r To Do was Born Sept		29	175-

(Note: When this book was deposited in the Department of
Archives in Richmond, the pages were worn, torn and disordered. When it was restored, unfortunately pages 3 and
4 were bound out of place. The numbering of the pages is
modern, due to the fact that many of the pages of the
original (transcript) were missing. Hence Hannah Alexander
born July 22nd 1752 and her sister -etty born Sept 29th
175- were daughters of James Alexander. See last three
items on page 2 of the original.   Beverley Fleet.)

-nos (prob. Amos) Alderson Son to Richd & Sarah Alderson was born	May	9th	1758
-lly Allin Son to Thos & Susannah Allin was born	Aug'st	2	1750
-ry Airs Daughter to Thos & Winny Airs was born	March	17	1757
-amuel Airs son to Thos & Winny Airs was born	Jan'ry	25	1759
Presly Anderwigg Son to William & Mary Anderwigg was born	June	26	1757
Thomas Aires Son to Thomas and Winny Aires was born	Jan'ry	18	1760
Betsey Anderwigg Daugh to Wm and Mary Anderwigg was born	Octr	28	1760
Betty Aires Daughter to Thomas & Winny Aires was born	Jany	20	176-
Billy Alverson Son to William and Grace Alverson was born	Feby	22	1759
Thomas Aires Son to Thomas and Winny Airs was born	Novem	30	176-
Mary Alexander Daughter to Jesse & Mary Alexander was born	Septem	30	175-
Hannah Alexander Daughter to Jesse & Mary Alexander was born	Feby	6	176-
Lucretia Anderwigg Daughter to William and Mary Anderwigg was born	May	8	1764
William Airs Son to Thomas and Winny Airs was born	April	17	1766
Jeanie daughter of William & Molly Anderwick was born	April	13	1767
-llis son of John and Sarah Armstrong was born	March	18	1767
- Roystin Alexander son to Jesse & Mary - Alexander was born	April	11	1760
James Alverson son of William and Sarah his wife was Born	december	5	1769
-linor Alverson Daughter of William and Elizabeth his wife was Born	Septmbr	9	1771
-tty Ashburn the Daughter of William & Mary his wife was born	March	24	1773
Thomas Ashburn Son of Thos & Hannah his wife was Born	May	27	1773
-y Alexand (sic) Daughter of Rawley & Mary his wife was Born	Aprill	1st	1773
-illiam Anderson Son of John & Letty Was Born	January	18	1773
-lley Armstrong Daughter of John & Jeane his wife was born	Febry	22	1773
Nancy Ashburn daughter to George & Sary his wife was born	Octobr	16	177-
Hannah Alexand (sic) daughter of William & Darke his wife was born	Novmbr	10	1773

page 5 (continued)

Thomas Ashburn Son of thos & hanner his wife ws bn   May   27 177-

-en Airs son to Thomas Airs & Winne his wife was Born Septemb 13 1773

Hannah Airs Daughter to James Airs & Ann his wife
   was Born   Febr   28 1774

William White Appelbee son of Normun & Molle his
   wife born   Octobr   16 1773

Hannah Ashburn Daughter to William & Mary his wife
   was born   November 8 1774

-liam Nelms son of Aron Nelms was Broh (sio)   June   24 1774

-y Ashburn Daughter to Thos & hannah his wife was
   born   May   2 1774

-ttey Beacham Daughter to William Alurson and
   Elizabeth his wife was born   January 17 1775

-ooah Astin Daughter of George & Winne his wife
   was born   July   14 1774

-hey Shelton Ashburn son of George and Sary Ashburn
   his wife was born   Oor   29 17-

- - Astin Daughter of George & Winne his wife was
   born   June   29 -

- - Anderson son of John was born   May   10 -

- - ~ - Daughter of John Born   May   - -

page 6.

John Appelbe son of Normun & Elizabeth his wife
   was born   March   22 1777

Jonathan Abbey son of John & Easther his wife was
   Born   March   20 1769

Hannah Ashburn Daughter of Thomas & Hanner his wife
   was Born   Sept   17 1777

Sarah Alexander Daughter of Roughley and Mary his
   wife was Born   February 26 1778

Salley Airs Daughter of James & Ann his wife was
   born   March   8 1778

Haynie Ashburn son of George & Sarah his wife
   was Born   March   12 1778

Thomas Appleby son of Norman and Elizabeth his wife
   was Born   Janr   3 177-

Benjamin Aspray son to Burshaba Aspray was born   June   18 177-

Mime Astin Daughter to George & Winney his wife
   was born   July   16 1778

Hannah Christopher Ashburn Daughter to William and
   Maryan his wife   Oot   9 1778

William Ambros son to Joseph & Mary his wife was
   born   Deom   29 1778

Izates Anderson son to John & Judith his wife was
   Born   Feb   7 1779

Elizabeth Angel Daughter to William & Judith his
   wife was born   April   7 1779

George Ashburn son to Thomas & Hannah his wife
   was born   Augt   27 1779

Judith Astin Daughter to George & Winnah his
   wife was born   June   21 1780

Nansoy Ashburn Daughter to George & Salley his wife   July   20 1780

Christopher Ashburn son to William & Maryann his
   wife was born   May   4 1781

page 6 (continued)

Mary Ambrose Daughter to Joseph & Mary his wife was born	Sept	26	1781
John Ambrose son to Ditto & Ditto was born	July	7	1775
Molley Ashburn Daughter to Thomas & Hannah his wife was born	March	17	1782
George Astin son to George & Winney his wife was Born	Novm	4	1782
Fanney Anderson Daughter to William & Ann his wife was born (sic)	Aril	23	1783
John Ashburn son to William & Maryann his wife was born	Feb	28	1784
Bettey Shelton Ashburn Daughter to Thomas & Hannah his wife was b'n	Feb	17	1784
Elizah (Elijah ?) Ambruse son to Joseph & Maryann his wife ws b'n	Decem	15	1783
Yewell Alexander son to Thomas & Fanney his wife was born	Feb	3	1784
Winney Frit Boggess Daughter To John McAdam Winneyfrit his wife was Born	Janr	27	1784
Salley Astin Daughter To William Astin & Ann His Wife was Born	May	27	1784
Edwin Astin son to George & Winney his wife was Born	Feb	22	1785
James Anderson son to John B Anderson was born	March	25	1785
Ann Anderson daughter to William and Ann his wife was born	May	4	1785
John Anderson son to William & Ann his wife was born	Apr	5	1787
Fanney Pitman Astin Dauahter to John & Sarah his wife was Born	Augt	1	1787
Samuel Ashburn son to Thomas & Hannah his wife was Born	March	28	1788
William Anderson son to William & Ann his wife was Born	March	31	1789
Samuel Anderson son to William & Nancey his wife was Born	Feb	14	1792

page 7, headed "A Northumber Land County Ss't Parrish 1770"

Winne Astin Daughter of George & Winne his wife was born	January	16	1770
Thos Anderson son of John Anderson & Lette his wife Born	March	29	1770
Salley Ashburn Daughter of Thos Ashburn and Hannah was born	Aprill	5	1770
William Ashburn the son of Wm & Maryan Ashburn his wife was born	April	6	1771
Milley Ashburn Daughter of Thomas Ashburn & Hannah his wife was Born	June	9	1771
Mary Anderwig Daughter to William & Mary his wife was Born	May	17	1771
John Ashburn Son of Thos & Margit his wife was Born	March	10	1771
Alloway Son of John & Elizabeth his wife was Born	August	18	1771

page 7 (continued)

Molle Astin Daughter of George & Winnefrit his wife was Born	January 6	1772
Bettey Ars (sic) Daughter of James Airs & Nancy his wife was Born	January 12	1772
John R Abbay son to Jonathan & Margaret alies Peggy his wife was Born	Augt 22	1792
Jonathan Abbay son to Jonathan & Marget his was Born (sic)	March 27	1795
William Ashburn son to Thomas Ashburn & Rachel his wife was Born	October 20	1796
-ley Ashburn Daughter to Thomas & Rachel his wife was Born	October 7	1798
-n Tiffy son to Austin Tiffy & Rebeccah his wife was Born	September 17	1798
William Ashburn son to William & Rachel his wife was Born	October 20	1796
Henry Ashburn son to Thomas & Rachel his wife was Born	- 26	1800
Betsey Ashburn Daughter to Thomas & Rachel Ashburn his wife was Born	Septemb 26	1802
Neddey Ashburn son to Ditto & Ditto his wife was Born	April 10	1805

page 8, headed "St Stephen B Parish"

Katherine Bagguss Daug'r To Henry Borne	Octr 15	1671
(Note: The Boggess family moved to Frederick County, Virginia, and prospered there. B.F.)		
Henry Bagguss son to Do Born	Jany 26	1680
Benet Bagguss sone to Henry borne	Augt 16	1703
Henry Bagguss son to Do born	Decr 6th	1705
Robt Bagguss sone to Do born	Decr 1	1707
Mary Bagguss Daug'r To Do born	Augt 13	1710
Thos Bagguss sone to Do borne	Decr 21	1713
Ruth Bagguss Daugr to Do born	June 18	1717
John Boze sone to John Bozze born	May 9	1675
John Bradley sone to Robt was born	Novr 30	1676
James Bradley sone to Do was born	Apl 5	1679
Robt Bradley sone to Do was borne	May 10	1682
Thos Brown son to Dav'd was born	Decem'r 18	1683
Richd Booth sone to Adam Booth born	- -	1681
Eliza Bean Daughter to William was Born	Octr 11	1675
John Bean Son to Do was born	Sep'r 21	1682
Jayles Beshan sone to William was born	Apl 20	1675
Catherine Beshan Daughter to Do was born	Augt 4	1677
Andrew Beshan Son to Do was born	March 7	1679
Thos Beshan son to Do was born	Augt 6	1682
Sarah Beshan Daugr To Do was born	May 6	1684

page 8 (continued)

John Bridgman son To John Born	May	12	1686
Mosses Bridgman son to Do was born	Apl	24	1700
Judith Bridgman Daug'r To Do was born	Sept	16	1706
Yearet Bridgman Daug'r To Do Born	March	28	1704
Winifrid Bridgman Daug'r to Do born	-	-	1710
Thos Bryant son To Thos was born	Jully	12	1689
Robt Bryant Son To Richd was born	Octr	10	1686
Ann Bushrod Daug'r To Thos was Born	March	16	1694
John Barcroft son To Thos was Born	March	31	1696
Richd Bushrod son To Thos was Born	Feby	10	1690
Sarah Bessick Daughter To John Born	Feby	10	1674
John Bessick Son To Do Born	Feby	24	1679
Eliza Bessick Daug'r To Do was Born	Novr	24	1682
Mary Besick Daugr To Do was Born	Jany	28	1684
Arther Bridgman son To John was Born	Jany	12	1679
Mary Bridgman Daugr to Do was Born	June	31	1675

    (Note: Well Mary got here anyway regardless of when
    she came.   B.F.)

Hannah Bridgman Daug'r To Do Born	Jun	14	1680
Eliza Bridgman Daug'r To Do Born	Jany	15	1683
Francis Britaine Daug'r To Francis Born	July	10	1679
Mary Butler Daugr To Hen'ry was Born	Sepr	9	1685
John Butler son To Do was Born	June	2	168-

page 9, headed "St Stephens Parish B"

Mary Buller (Butler ?) Daugr to Henry was Born	Jan'ry	28	1677
Wm Buller (Butler ?) son To Do was Born	Feby	14	1685
Eliza Bee Daugr To John was Born	Feby	16	1674
Mary Bee Daugr To Ditto was Born	Jany	29	1679
Sarah Bee Daugr To Do was Born	Jully	13	1676
Aquila Bee Daug'r To Do Born	Octr	8	1687
Lois Bee Daug'r To Do Born	March	25	1688
Ann Bennet Daugr To Edward was Born	Sepr	20	1676
John Bennet Son To Do was Born	Decem	15	1678
Cuthbard Bennet Son To Do was Born	Jany	15	1680
Eliza Bennet Daugr To Do was Born	Decem'r	10	1662
Dorathy Bennet Daugr To Do was Born	Jany	30	1684
Edward Bennet Son To Do was Born	March	27	1687
Thos Berry Son To Thos was Born	Jany	9	1683
William Berry sone To Thos was Born	May	13	1691
James Berry Son To Do was Born	June	8	1694
Mary Barns Daug'r To Thos Born	March	29	1679
James Barns Son To Do was Born	Jany	19	1681
Jean Barnes Daug'r To Do was Born	Sepr	15	1697
Eliza Barnes Daug'r To Do was Born	March	25	1703
Sarah Barnes Daug'r To Do was Born	Augt	2d	1706
John Baylie son To John was Born	March	21	1681
Ann Bayle Daugr To Do was Born	Nov'r	16	1683
John Baley son To Do was Born	June	22	1679
John Blandle son To Wm was Born	June	22	1679
Sarah Blandle Daugr To Do was Born	Feby	16	1683
John Banister son To Richd was Born	Jully	26	1691
Ann Blandle Daugr To Wm was Born	Augt	28	1684
Patience Blandle Daugr To Do was Born	Jany	31	1689
Jeane Blandle Daugr To Do was Born	March	31	1691

page 9 (continued)

Lazarus Bowley son To Simion was Born	December	29	1691
William Bowley Son To Do was Born	June	28	1694
Sarah Bowley Daug'r To Do was Born	May	28	1710
Eliza Bridgman Daugr To Thos was Born	Augt	16	1681
Mary Bridgman Daug'r To Do was Born	Apl	23	1682
Hannah Bridgman Daugr To Do was Born	Novr	17	1688
John Bridgman Son To Do was Born	Apl	22	1686
Sarah Bridgman Daugr To Do was Born	March	22	1690
Jean Bridgman Daugr To Do was Born	Jully	22	1693
Thos Butcher Son To John was Born	May	1	1692
Catherine Butcher Daugr To Do was Born	May	14	1700

page 10, headed "St Stepens Parish B"

Ann Baile Daug'r To Jo'n Baile was Born	Jany	30	1708
Rich Bryant Son to James was Born	Apl	10	1709
Eliza Bradley Daugr To Robt was Born	June	8	1707
Ann Bradley Daugr To Do was Born	June	8	1716
Robt Bradley son To Do was Born	Feb	21	1717
Richd Brown son To Manley was Born	March	16	1689
Mary Brown Daug'r To Do was Born	March	16	1692
Charles Brown Son To Do was Born	Decr	6th	1695
Manley Brown Son To Do was Born	Decr	8	1699
Thos Brown Son To Do was Born	Novr	23	1701
Hester Brown Daugr To Do was Born	Oct	18	1707
Susana Brown Daugr To Do was Born	Oct	13	1710
John Broadley (sic) Son To Edward was Born	Jully	13	1707
Isaac Broadey (sic) Son To Edward was Born	May	18	1705
Benj'n Bussell son To Benj'n was Born	Oct	3	1708
Winfret Britt Daugr To Wm was Born	Sepr	9	1708
Edward Benn Son to Cuthbert Bap.	Nov	25	1708
Hannah Brill Daugr To Hen'y was Born	March	21	1705
Ann Bennett Daugr To Edwd was Born	Aug	25	1707
Joseph Bennet son To Do was Born	Decr	3	1709
Frances Booth Daugr To Jo'n Booth was Born	Feby	12	1710
Richd Booth Son To Richd Booth was Born	Aug	25	1706
Eliza Booth Daugr To Do was Born	June	15	1709
John Booth Son To Do was Born	Apl	13	1712
Samuell Blackwell son Sam'll was Born	Jany	19	1710
William Blackwell Son To Do was Born	Apl	25	1713
Joseph Blackwell Son To Do was Born	Jully	9	1715
Eliza Blackwell Daugr To Do was Born	Jany	9	1717
Hannah Blackwell Daug'r To Do was Born	Mar'h	30	1720
Corbell Brown Son To Wm was Born	Feby	3	1710
Eliza Brown Daug'r To Do was Born	Apl	5	1705
William Brown son To Ditto was Born	Apl	29	1713
Jacob Baylie son To Jacob was Born	Feby	17	1711
Sarah Bayle Daugr To Do was Born	Jany	9	1713
Penolope Barrat Daugr To Hester Barrat was Born	May	5	1711
James Bilingham Son To Frances was Born	Oct	14	1712
Francis Bilingham Daugr To Do was Born	Aug	14	1714
George Baylie Son To Peter James was Born	Jany	11	1712
Joseph Bayle Son To Do Born	Decr	13	1714
James Borling Son To Thos was Born	Nov	16	1714
William Badger son To James was Born	Apl	8	1706

page 11, headed "Northumberland B County"

Mary Barton Daugr To Robt was Born	Sepr	9	1677
John Butcher Son To John Bucher was Born	June	14	170-
Sarah Butcher Daug'r To Do was Born	Feby	23	170-
Mary Bonnet Daugr To Daniell was Born	Sept	4	1692
Thos Baile Son To Jessee Baile born Apl (sic)	Apl	30	1688
Jesse Baile Son To Do was Born	Apl	30	1698
Margrit Baile Daughter to Do Born	Dec'r	4	1700
Mulraine Baile son To Jesse Baile was Born	Novr	14	1703
Dav'd Baile son To Do Born Jully (sic)	Jully	4	1706
Marcy Baile Dau'r To Do Born	Septr	15	1709
Jo'n Baile Son To Do was Born	May	15	1712
Ann Belsher Daur To William was Born	Jun	11	1693
Marcy Belsher Daug'r To Do was Born	March	15	1695
Eliza Belsher Daugr To Do was Born	Jany	26	1689
Wm Belsher Son To Do was Born	May	17	1702
Wm Betts Son To Charles was Born	Jany	21	1687
Mary Betts Daugr To Do was Born	Septr	28	1688
Charles Betts Son To Do was Born	Feby	21	1699
Eliza Betts Dau'r To Do was Born	June	13	1693
Jonathon Betts Sone To Do was Born	May	3	1702
Hanah Betts Daug'r To Do was Born	Jully	7	1706
Francis Bickley Son To Ralph was Born	Feby	22	1701
John Bickley Son To Do was Born	Decem	10	1703
Eliz'a Bickley Daur To Do was Born	Jully	12	1708
Ann Bickley Daugr To Do was Born	June	29	1711
Ralph Bickley Son To Do was Born	Octr	7	1716
Wm Bickley Son To Do was Born	Augt	28	1719
Spencer Bickley Son To Do was Born	Nov'r	20	1721
Thos Blackabey Son To James was Born	June	21	1696
Wm Benawaay Son To Wm was Born	Apl	10	1698
Martha Bercroft Daugr To Thos was Born	Aug	8	1701
Eliz'a Barton Daug'r To Robt was Born	Apl	5	1702
Samuell Blackwell Blackwell Son To Joseph was Born	Sep'r	23	1680
Dav'd Brown Son To Dav'd was Born	Jully	29	1687
Manley Brown Son To Do was Born	Sepr	3	1677
Nathaniell Barrat Son To George was Born	May	19	1702
George Barrat Son To Do was Born	March	5	1704
Wm Barret Son To Do was Born	Mar'h	28	1708
Mary Ann Baily Daugr To John was Bapd	Jully	27	1706

page 12, headed "Northumb: County B"

William Badger Son To James was Born	Apl	8	170-
-iz'a Badger Daug'r To Do was Born	Feby	10	1707
Spencer Ball Son To Joseph was Born	March	14	1707
Rich'd Ball Son To Do was Born	Octr	25	1710
Joseph Ball Son To Do was Born	March	8	1712
-rah Ball Daugr To Do was Born	March	10	1714
-lliam Barnes Son To Edward was Born	Apl	13	1715
Edward Barnes Son To Do Born	Novr	4	1717
-liz Biddle Daugr To Jacob Born	Decemr	13	1716
Ann Biddle Daugr To Do Born	Sep'r	16	1718
Penelope Bayles Daugr To Thos Born	Nov'r	11	1718
John Boles Son To Solomon Born	June	16	1714
John Boggust Son To Hen'y Born	Aug	30	1720

page 12 (continued)

Elij'a Betts son To Wm was Born	Augt	21	1720
Eliz'a Bankes Daug'r To Robt was Born	Oct'r	19	1707
John Brodey sone To Jonathan was Born	Feby	21	1720
William Blundle Son to John was Born	Augt	22	1721
James Bradley Son To Robt was Born	June	9	1722
John Baker Son To John was Born	Decembr	7	1722
Eliz'a Baker Daughter To Do was Born	Decr	7	1722
John Beacham Son To Daniell was Born	Sepr	24	1715
Mary Beacham Daug'r To Do was Born	May	5	1719
Ann Beacham Daughr To Do was Born	Octr	12	1721
Ann & Eliz'a Baggust Twins To Hen'y Born	Jully	5	1723
Rebeckah Bell Daugr To John was Born	Decembr	25	1721

       (Note: Our colonial grandmothers seem to have been able
       to stand any and everything, including our grandfathers
       in at least, according to this register,   recorded
       silence. But is it not a little too much when John is
       given entire credit for this gift ?   B.F.)

John Bell Son To Ditto was Born	Jany	2	1723
John Blundle Son To John was Born	Jany	21	1723
Lowles Bennit was Born	Jany	1	1716
Samuel Bonnum Son To Samuell was Born	Jully	22	1723
Daniell Betts Son To Wm was Born	Augr	8	1723
Wm Bean Son To William was Born	Decr	9	1721
Eliz'a Bean Daugr To Do was Born	Novr	25	1723
Robt Bean Son to Do was Born	Jany	13	1725
Elijah Blundle son to John Born	May	13	1726
William Berrey Son To Georg was Born	March	11	1727
John Berry Son To Ditto was Born	Decemr	25	1728
Sarah Bowley Daugr To Simon was Born	Nov	1	1726
Nanne Bowley Daugr To Do was Born	May	3	1728
Winefred Bowley Daugr To Do was Born	Jany	20	1729
Judith Bell Daugr To John was Born	Novr	2	1727
Footman Brown Son To Thos was Born	March	7	1730
Margret Berry Daugr To George was Born	Nov	19	1730
Judey Bennet Daugr To Edward was Born	Mar	16	1730
Winefred Bennet Daugr To Ditto was Born	Feby	2	1732
Winefred Brown Daugr To Elliza Do was Born	Octr	24	1727
Thomas Brown Son To Do was Born	Apl	5	1732
Simon Peter Boolley Son To Simon	Apl	17	17-
Thomas Berry son To George Was Born	March	-	-

page 13,   headed "St Stephens Parish B"

Frances Buckley Son To Francis was Born .	Apl	27	1733
William Buckley son to Jo'n was Born	Decem'r	26	1733
Judith Betts Daugr To Charles was Born	Augt	3	1732
Hannah Betts Daugr To William was Born	Decr	29	1728
Winefred Betts Daugr To Do was Born	May	10	1730
Daniell Betts Son To Do was Born	Octr	7	1731
Spencer Betts Son To Do was Born	May	29	1734
John Bennet Son To Edward Born	Octr	14	1734
Mary Bowley Daugr To Simon was Born	Octr	7	1734
Judith Ball Daugr To Spencer Ball was Born	Jany	17	1735
Mary Betts Daugr To Charles Born	March	31	1735

page 13 (continued)

Spencer Morgan Beekley son To Francis Born	Decr	17	1735
John Beekly Son To Jo'n Born	May	10	1735
Cuthbert Buford Son To John Born	Sepr	15	1736
Spencer Mattrom Ball Son To Spencer Ball Born	Sepr	9	1736
William Bowley Son To Symon Born	Jully	16	1737
Eliza Betts Daugr To Charles was Born	Feby	18	1736
Joseph Beekley Son To Francis was Born	Jany	31	1739
Jedeah Betts Daugr To Charles Bett was Born	March	23	1739
Esther Brade Daugr To Charles was Born	Apl	6	1740
Charles Beekley Son To Ann Born	Oct	27	1735
Eliza Bigbey Daugr To George Born	Apl	20	1741
Samuell Blackwell Junr Born	Nov	20	1731
John Blackwell son - Born	Feby	18	1732/3
Wm Blackwell - - Born	Aug	16	1736
Eliz'a Blackwell - - Born	March	25	1741
John Burch Son To Jo'n was Born	Octr	1	1740
Wm Bridgman Son To Joseph was Born	Octr	4	1737
Hanna Bridgman Daugr To Do was Born	Feby	15	1740
Morgain Beekley was Born	Jully	18	1741
Sarah Betts Daugr To Charles was Born	Decr	3d	1741
Smith Barrat Son George was Born	Apl	12	1741
Hanna Fallin Buford Daugr To Margaret was Born	Jully	14	1741
Amelia Brown Daugr To George Born	Jany	29	1736
Juliann Daugr To George Brown Born (1738)	Sepr	26	1738
William Brown Son To Do was Born	Decr	25	1742
Richd Bigbey Son To Georg was Born	Sepr	19	1742
Joseph Bridgman Son To Joseph was Born	Decr	18	1742
Spencer Bowlen (or Bowlin) Son To Mary was Born	Sepr	4	1744
Joseph Blundall Son To William was Born	Sepr	20	1744
Winefred Brigman Daugr To Joseph	June	8	1745
Jesse Beekley Son To Francis was Born	Sepr	24	1745
Jesse Bowlin Son To Mary was Born	Decr	25	1746

page 14.

-stan Betts Son To Charles was Born	Augt	12	174-
-liam Betts Son To Do was born	Sepr	26	174-
-es Blackwell Son To Samuell was Born	March	28	1743
-rge Blackwell Son To Do was Born	March	31	1745
-n Bickley Daugr To Ralph & Margarett Born	Sepr	30	1746
-hill Bryant Daugr To Wilfrey & Eliza was Born	Jany	6	1738
-ary Bryant Daugr To Martha a Bastard was Born	May	17	1746
-oseph Blackwell Son to Sam Blackwell & Elliz Born	Apl	20	1738
Ann Blackwell Daugr To Samuell Blackwell & Elliz: was Born	Feby	2	1747
Isaac Bekley Son To Ralph & Margaret was Born	Jully	13	1748
Thos Bridgman Son To Joseph & Grace was Born	March	29	1748
John Blundell Son To Jo'n & Ruth was Born	May	18	1750
Latty Bekly Daugr To Francis & Eliz'a was Born	Mar	4	1750
Betty Beekly Daugr To Spencer & Sara Ann was Born	Sepr	6	1751
Judith Blackwell Daugr To Sam'll & Eliz was Born	Jany	8	1751
William Bransdon Son To Jo'n & Jane was Born	Mar	25	1748
Jo'n Bransdon Son To Do was Born	Jully	1	1751
Saml Barns Son To Margaret was Born	Aug	12	1744

page 14 (continued)

Betty Bonnam Daugr To Jo's & Sara was Born	Sepr	9	1751
Hanah Bryant Daugr To Thos & Ann was Born	Apl	16	1751
Georg Ball Son to Joseph & Hanna Was Born	Jully	16	1750
Joseph Ball Son To Do was Born	March	14	1752
Winifred Beekley Daur To Spencer & Sara Ann was Born	Feby	28	1753
John Betts Son To Charles & Jeddaeh was Born	Jany	9	1748
Chas Betts Son To Do was Born	March	20	1760
Ann Dogget Brown Daugr To Geo: Leaz: and Betty was Born	May	30	1748
Betty Brown Daur To Do was Born	Deer	10	1752
James Booth Son To James & Eleanor was Born	March	16	1740
Richard Booth Son To Do was Born	March	20	1742
Eleanor Booth Daugr To Do was Born	Deer	9th	1745
John Blundel son to Elijah was Born	Febry	13	1753
Elijah Blundel Son To Elijah was Born	Sepr	4	1754
William Bussel son to Matthew and Martha was Born	Febry	14	1740
Judith Bussel Daugr To Do was Born	Deer	3	1743
Katherine Bussel Daugr To Do was Born	May	13	175-
George Betts Son To Charles & Jedidah was Born	June	22	1753
Katherine Bayles Daugr To John & Sarah was Born	Octr	21	1754
Rosannah Ball Daugr To Thomas & Betty was Born	June	16th	1754
Duanner Blincoe Daugr To John was Born	Janry	6	1755
Nancey Beekley Daugr To Spencer & Sarah was Born	Feb	3	1755
Betty Beekley Bastard of Martha was Born	Deer	23	175-
Aquilla Snelling Beekley Bastard of Do was Born	Feby	14	175-
Winefred Bryant Daugr To Thomas & Ann was Born	Sept	2	175-
Isaac Beacham Son To Isaac and Susannah was Born	Apr	7	175-
-tty Betts Daugr To Daniel was Born	Novr	29th	-

page 15, headed "B"

Elisa Bush Daugr To John & Susannah was Born	April	23	175-
Betty Blackorby Daugr To Joseph was Born	Deer	4th	175-
Gidelhon Blackerby Son To Do was Born	March	10th	175-
William Brown Son To George Leazure Brown and Betty his wife was Born June 2d 1755 and died July 9th 1755			
Eliza Beacham Daugr To Abraham was Born	July	25th	1755
Ann Bailey Daugr To William & Jeane was Born	Deer	13	1746
Stephen Bailey Son To Do was Born	Feby	8th	1749
Dorcas Bailey Daugr To Do was Born	Febry	16	1753
William Bailey Son To Do was Born	Septr	21	1755
Judith Betts Daugr To Elisha & Mary Ann was Born	Augst	12th	1755
Ann Barnes Daugr To William & Mary was Born	Sept	30th	1755
Hannah Boyer Daugr To Henry & Hannah was Born	Deer	31st	1755
Joseph Brown Son To Joseph was Born	Janry	30th	1756
John Burrows Son To Charles was Born	Augst	22d	1752
Charles Burrows Son To Do was Born	Augst	25th	1755
Spencer Ball Son To Thomas was Born	April	15th	1756
Winder Brown Son To John was Born	July	18th	1756
Daniel Bennet Son To Eleanor was Born	Augst	-	1756
Charles Allen Burrows Son To Charles Died	Octr	10th	1766
John Bussell Son To Matthew & Martha was Born	Novr	15th	1756
Peter Boyer Son To John & Mary was Born	Deer	30th	1756
Sally Beelley (sic) Daugr To Spencer & Sarah was Born	Deer	27th	1756
Leannah Bussel Daugr To Philip & Eliza was Born	Augst	31	1747

page 15 (continued)

Mary Bussel Daugr To Do (Philip & Eliza) was Born	Novr	1st	1748
Adam Bussel Son To Do was Born	Janry	27th	1750
Hannah Bussel Daugr To Do was Born	Octr	24th	1752
Eliza Bussel Daugr To Do was Born	Janry	15th	1757
Presly Barecroft Son To John & Mary Born	Dec	3d	1756
Wm Brown Son To Geo Leasure Brown	March	7th	1757
Joseph Beekley Son To Francis Born	March	13th	1756
Hannah Boyer Daugr To Henry was Born	Sepr	27th	1757

page 16, headed "B".

- - Blackwell Son To John & Hannah was Born	March	24	1754
- -l Blackwell Son To Do was Born	April	4th	175-
David Ball son to Joseph & Hannah Ball born on Saterday	Novem	23d	1754
Grace Ball Daughter to Joseph & Hannah Ball was born on Sat	June	18th	1757
Billy Beekly Son to Francis & Eliza Beekly was born	June	23rd	1754
John Blewford Son to George Blewford Junr & Eliza his wife was born	January	28th	1758
William Blundell Son to Elijah Blundel & Judith his wife was born	Febry	12th	1756
Betty Blundell Daughter to Elijah & Judith Blundell was born	March	1st	1758
Thomas Blackwoll son to Saml Blackwell Gen't: & Eliza his wife was born	September	15th	1752
David Blackwell Son to Sam'l Blackwoll Gen't: & Eliza his wife was born	November	27	1753
Elizabeth Blackwoll Daughter to Sam'l Blackwell Ju'r & Sarah his wife was born	June	10	1756
Saml Blackwell son to Saml Junr and Sarah Blackwell his wife was born	March	25th	1758
William Betts son to Elisha and Maryan Betts his wife was born	March	29th	1757
John West Beacham son to Abraham & Leasure Beacham was born	July	2nd	1758
Eli Bayly son to Ann Bayly a bastard was born	January	17th	1758
Kezia Barcroft Daughter to Martrum Barcroft & Alice his wife was born	Novemb	17th	1758
William Blewford son to Mary ann Blewford a bastard born	March	26th	1754
John Beekly son to Francis & Judith Beekly was born	Jany	18th	1759
John Barcroft son to John & Mary Barcroft was born	Octbr	12th	1758
Spencer Betts son to Elisha and Maryann Betts was born	April	6th	1759
James Boyer son to John & Mary Boyer was born	March	10th	1759
Ann Berry Daughter to William & Eliza Berry was born	Octobr	6th	1758
Nelly Brown Daughter to Thomas & Winefred Brown was born	October	9th	1759
Sarahan Barecraft Daug to John and Mary Barecraft was born	March	6th	1760
Margret Beekley Daughter to Spencer & Sarah Beekley was born	Decemb	11th	1758
Elisha Beekley son to Frances and Judith Beekley was born	March	13th	1761
Katy Barecraft Daughter to Matrom & Alice Barecraft was born	April	17th	1761
George Berry son to William & Elizabeth Berry born	January	12th	1761
Samuel Blundell son to Elijah & Judith Blundell born	May	16	1760
Nancy Betts Daughter to Elisha and Maryann Betts was born	April	24	1761

page 16 (continued)

Lucretia Nelms Barecraft a bastard Daughter to Winefred Barecraft born	Decemb	18	1757
Billy Blewford son to George and Eliza Blewford was born	Augst	10	1760
Peter James Bayly son to Charles and Sarah Bayly was born	Febry	19	1761
Molly Beekly Daughter to Spencer and Sarah Ann Beekley born	Decem	25	1760
Elisha Betts son to Elisha and Mary ann Betts was born	March	1st	1763
Betty Bryant Daughter to Thomas and Ann Bryant was born	Octobr	7	1762
Molly Beekly Daughter to Joseph & Dianna Beekly was born	Septem	18	1763
Molly Bayly Daughter to Charles and Sarah Bayly was born	Novem	9	17-
Charles Beekly son to Charles Jones and Winefred Beekly was born	June	10	17-
William Bush son to John & Susannah Bush was born	March	12	175-
Joseph Blackwell son to Joseph and Hannah Shapleigh Blackwell was born	April	27	1764
William Betts son to Winefred Betts a bastard was born	August	26	1753
Betty Dawson Betts Daughter to Winefred Betts a bastard was born	April	11	1754
Judith Betts Daughter to Winefred Betts a bastard was born	July	20	1757
Hannah Betts Daughter to Winefred Betts a bastard was born	February	10	1760
Ralph Beekley son to Spencer & Sarah ann Beekley was born	Decemb	29th	1760
John Beekley son to Spencer and Sarah ann Beekley was born	March	11	1765
Jane Ball Daughter to Joseph and Hannah Ball was born	Septem	29	1761
Hannah Ball Daughter to Joseph and Hannah Ball was born	Novem	24	1764
Spencer Morgan Beekly son to Joseph and Dianna Beekly was born	March	18	1766

page 17

Thomas Berry son to John and Judith Berry was born	May	6	1766
George Beekly son to Charles Jones Beekly and Winefred his wife was born	October	25	1765
Hannah Betts Bastard Daughter to Millicent Betts was born	April	9	1759
Reuben son of John and Phillis Boyd was born	Janr	4	1767
Rodham Neale son of George and Susannah Bearcraft born	Feb	28	1767
James son of Abraham & Leazur Beacham was born	Feb	19	1767
John son of Joseph and Hannah Ball was born	March	6th	1767
Lindsay son of Sarah Blueford was born	Septr	2nd	1766
Sarah Blackwell Daughter to Cap: Saml: and Sarah Blackwell was born	Jany	9	1763
Eleanor Blackwell Daughter to Cap: Saml: and Sarah Blackwell was born	October	17	1766
Sarah Berry Bayly Daughter to Charles and Sarah Bayly was born	Decem	19	1767

page 17 (continued)

Margaret Berry Daughter to John and Judith Berry was born	January 23	1769
George Blewford son to George and Elizabeth Blewford was born	January 14	1763
Nancy Blewford Daughter to George and Elizabeth Blewford was born	August 19	1765
Giles Blewford son to George and Elizabeth Blewford was born	May 22	1768
Hannah Bridgman Daughter to William and Frances Bridgman was born	August 2	1762
Joseph Bridgman son to William and Frances Bridgman was born	Novemb 5	1765
William Bridgman son to William and Frances Bridgman was born	January 10	1768
Elizabeth Bickly Daughter to John and Sarah Bickly was born	Febry 18	1769
Molley Bailey Daughter of Stephen and Elizabeth was Born	October 21	1771
Nance Blackelee Daughter of frances & Thos Glasscock was Born	August 5	1771
Elennor Baley Daughter of Spencer & Sary his wife was Born	August 26	1771
Spencer Morgin Beekly son of George & Lette Bluford born	October 22	1771
Molley Bearcroft Daughter of John & Mary his wife was born	January 16	1772
John Bush son of Rubin Bush Born	Apr 7	1772
Dannel Baley son of Danel & frances Baley his wife was Born	May 19	1772
Cannaday Bluford son of Sary Bluford Was Born	April 14	1772
Jesse Bryant the son of Johnnathan & Elizabeth his wife was born	January 26	1773
Rostin Betts Son of William & Mille his wife was born	January 3	1773
Sally Beetley (sic) Daughter of John Was Born	Septem 7	1772
Charles Baley son of Charles & Sary his wife was born	March 25	1773
Spencer Boyed son of John & fillizs was Born	March 24	1773
John Betts son of Betty Covington was born	Decembr 16	1773

page 18, headed "B".

Mary Beacham & Elizabeth twins daughters to Parker & Susanna Beacham was Born	Novmbr 22	1763
Ruth Daughter to Do was Born	July 4	1766
Susanna Daughter to Do was Born	Septembr 23	1768
Mary Beacham Daughter to Do was born	January 19	1771
Iigas Bell Daughter of Elias Bell & Joanna his wife was Born	Siptembr 8th	1769

(Note: The handwriting here is very poor. It is impossible to decide just what these people attempted to name this child.B.F.)

Rebecke Buckly daughter of Joseph Buckley and Elizabeth his wife was Born	Novembr 29	1769
William Ball Son to Joseph Ball and Hannah his wife was Born	Decembr 12th	1769
William Beattey the son of Joseph Beattey & Dianner his wife was Born	february 14	1770

page 18 (continued)

Judith Brown Daughter to Wm Brown & Mary his wife
was Born   May   12   1770
Jean Bailey Daughter of Stephen & Elizabeth his wife
was Born the   October   30   1769
John Bets son of John & Elizabeth his wife was Born January 29th 1770
Margaret Baly Daughter of Charles Beley was born   March   13th 1770
Judith Beacham Daughter to John & Elizabeth his
wife was Born   June   23   1770
Salloy Bluford Daughter to Sarah was Born   December   4   1769
Charles Bell the Son of Thomas Bell & Rebecah Bell
was Born   Novembr   20   1770
John Booth the son of James Booth & Sary was Born   January   12   1771
John Bell the Son of William Bell & Sarah his wife
was Born   January   25   1771
Martrom Bearcraft Son of Martrom & Alsee his wife
was Born   March   20   1771
Salley Blundon Daughter of William & Winnefrit
Blundon was Born   March   3   1771
John Booth Son of John Booth & Winnefrit Hudson A
Bastard Child was Born   May   16   1767
Sary Blincoe Daughter To John was Born   August   7   1771
Jean Brumbly Daughter to Dannel & Bette his Wife
was Born   Septembr   4   1771
Isaac Beacham son of Abraham & Leasure Beacham his wife
was Born   february 19   1773
Charlotte Bets the Daughter of John & Elizabeth his wife
was Born   Jan'ry   13   1772
Ellen Bridgman Daughter of Joseph & Mary his wife was
Born   Decembr   12   1771
Keziah Bearcraft Daughter of Martrom & Alis his wife
was Born   Novembr 17th 1758
Caty Bearcraft Daughter to Do Was Born   Aprill   17   1761
William Bearcroft Son to Do Was Born   May   8   1763
Jeanne Bearcroft Daughter to Do Was Born   february 20th 1766
Thomas Bearcroft Son to Do Was Born   Aprill   17   1768
Aley (or Aliss) Bearcroft Daughter to Do Was Born   Octobr   12   1773
Nancey Bearcraft Daughter of Martrom & Alse his wife
was born   Novembr   21   1775
Mary Boyd Daughter to John & Phillis his wife was Born Sept   6   1769
wis Lewis Boyd son to John & Phillis his wife was Born April   17   1777
John & William Brown twins sons to Vincent & Salley
his wife w's B'n   May   28   1791
Fanney Bryant Daughter to Jonathan & Elizabeth his wife
w's Born   Augt   19 179-
                                    (appears to be 1791)

page 19, headed "B".

Antony Sidnor Booth son to John & Winney his wife
was Born   May   21   1792
Lewis Brumbley son to Samuel & Elizabeth his wife
was Born   July   20   1792
William Self Betts son to John Betts & Nancey his
wife was Born   Janr   23   1793
Presley Self Blincoe son to George C Blincoe & Mary
his wife was Born   Sept   1   1792

page 19 (continued)

Nancey Oldham Brown Daughter to Vincent Brown & Salle
   his wife w's Born   Jan'r   3   1793
Kenner Blincoe son to Mark Blincoe & wife was Born   June   8   1793
Josiah Burris son to William H Burris & Mary his
   wife was Born   October 1   1794
Betsey Blincoe Daughter to George & Mary his wife
   was Born   Feb   25   1796
Fanney Booth Daughter to John Booth & Bettey his
   wife was Born   April 28   1796
   (Note: Most unfortunately the 'Ts' are not crossed in the
   name appearing in the original as that of Mrs. John Booth.
   We feel sure that descendants will pardon our insistence
   that this name is 'Bettey' although it is certainly not
   like that in the original.   B.F.)
Jean Middleton Beacham Daughter to John Beacham & Betsy
   his wife w's Born   October 18   1796
William Ashburn son to William Ashburn & Rachel his
   wife was Born   October 20   1796
Fanney Booth Barnes Daughter to William Barnes &
   Molley Barnes his wife was Born   December 6   1796
James Oliver Brumbley son to Samuel Brumbley & Winney
   his wife was Born   August 11   1798
John Booth son to James Booth & Susannah his wife
   was Born   May   20   1798
Joseph Eidson Brumley son to Samuel Brumley &
   Winnefret his wife was Born   Septemb 22   1799
Nancey South Booth Daugr to James Booth & Susannah
   his wife was born   February 14 1800
William Booth son to John Booth & Bettey Booth his
   wife was Born   November 21 1797
Milley Pullin Booth Daughter to Ditto & Ditto was
   Born   Decembr 8   1799
Leroy Pullin Booth son to Ditto & Ditto was Born   March   12   1802
Elizabeth Booth Daugr to James Booth & Susannah
   Booth his wife was Born   January 20   1802
Susannah Blincoe Daughter to George Blincoe & Mary
   his wife was born   January 20   1803
Milley Webb Blincoe Daughter to Mark Blincoe & Salley
   his wife was born   Feb   24   1803
Hannah Brinnen Booth Daughter to James Booth & Susannah
   Booth his wife was Born   March   6   1804
Mary Booth Daughter to James & Susannah his wife was
   Born   March   4   1806
John Booth son to John Booth & Bettey his wife was
   Born   Janr   25   1804
George Booth son to John Booth & Bettey his wife was
   Born   July   27   1806
David Crenshaw Booth son to James Booth & Susannah
   his wife was Born   October 1   1808
William Booth son to Joseph Booth & Salley Booth his
   wife was born   Decem 31   1804
Hiram Robuck Booth son to Ditto & Ditto was Born   Decem 17   1806
Walter Booth son to Ditto & Ditto was Born   Decem 23   1808
Thaddeuse Mitchie Booth son to Frederick & Loannah
   was Born   August 31   1809

John Beacham son of Thomas & Ann Beacham his Wife was born	July	8	1773
Catey Bearcraft daughter of Samuel & Ann Bearcraft his wife was born	May	20	1774
William Blundel son of John & Bettey his Wife was Born	Novemb'r	29	1773
Nancy Bailey Daughter of Stephen & Elizabeth his wife was born	January	3	1774
Rebeckah Bell the Daughter of Thos & Rebeckah his wife was born	June	3	1774
James Buckley son of Joseph Buckley & Elizabeth his wife was born (Beekley ?)	December	29	1773
Jeremiah Brown Son of Elizabeth Brown a bastard child Born	August	29	1773
Hannah berry Daughter of John & Judah his wife was born	Octobr	20	1773
Griffin Brin son of Joshew & Pegge his wife was born	Agust	3	1773
Winne Blueford Daughter of Cloe bluford was born	Novembr	25	1773
fanne Devenport Betts Daughter to John & Elizabeth his wife was Born	March	23	1774
Mary Blincoe Daughter of John & Mary his Wife was Born	November	3	1773
Billie Hainnice (or Hainniu or Hainnin ?) burrus son of Josias Burrus & Milley was born	March	10	1774
Thomas Bell Son of Thos & Rebeckah his wife was Born	Decembr	20	1768
Betsey Bush Daughter of Rubin Bush was born	Decembr	2	1774
Dannell Brumley Son of Dannell & Bettey his wife was born	January	14	1775
Jorden Betts Son of Mary ann Alexander bastard child was Born	April	6	1759
John Butler the son of Thos Butler & Susannah Butler his wife was born	Sept	27th	1752
Caty Cole Butler Daughter of Do Was Born	Mar'h	29	1761
Susannah Butler Daughter of Do Was Born	May	27	1766
James Butler the Son of Thomas & Susannah Butler was Born	April	23	1769
Ann Blackwell Daughter of George was Born	November	29	1772
Mary Briser (Bruer ?) Daughter of William & Susanner his wife was born	December	8	1774
George Leasure Beacham & Griffin twins to Abraham & Leasure Beacham his wife was Born	October	10th	1774
John Beacham son to Parker & Susaner his wife was Born	Aprill	19	1775
Bettey Morgan Beetley (?) Daughter to Jesse & Winnefrit his wife was born	Decembr	28	1774
James Berkley Son to John & Sary Berkley his wife was born	february	22	1775
Thos Smith Beekley Son of Joseph & Dianner his wife born	Feby	4	1775
Rebecca Breen Daughter of Josheway & Margit his wife was born	Januay	7	1775
William Golds Bery Son of Robert & Margit his wife was born	Novembr	9	1775

Lucy Wadde (or Wodde) Betts Daughter of William
   Betts was Born   May   30   1774
Grigg Blackeby Glascock son of Frances Blackeby
   a bastard Child was born   Aprill   29   1774
Nancey Ballentino Daughter to Mottrum & Leanner
   his wife was born   Octobr   28   1775
Winno Bearcraft the Daughter of Samuel & Ann his
   wife was Born   Febur   27   1776
Presly Burton son of Wm Burton & Ann his wife
   was Born   April   7   1776
Willim Baily son of Stephen and Betty Baily his
   wife was Born   January 27   1776
Elizabeth Bell the Daughter of Thos & Rebeckah
   his wife was born   February 8   1776
Thomas Blincoe Son of John & Mary Was Born   Octobr   21   1776
Bettey Blincoe Daghter of John & Mary his wife
   Was Born   february 16   1761
Mark Blincoe Son of John & Mary his wife Was Born June   27   1766
Ann Keen Blincoe and George Conley Blincoe Son and
   Daughter Twins was born
   son & Daughter to John & Mary   Novembr 18   1768
Nancy Brown Daughter of Charles & Susanner his wife
   was born   Septembr 1st 1776
Ann Trussell Beacham daughter of Thos & Ann - -
   was born   Jany   1   1777
   (Note: There is a faded out word following the name Ann.
   I cannot see whether this is a proper or a common noun. B.F.)

page 21,   headed "B".

Charles Betts son to William was Born   June   29   1776
Nancy Beetley Daughter of John & Bette his wife
   was born   february 21   1775
Cud Baley Born the   March   28   1776
Alexander & Thomas Bridgman twins sons to Thos was
   Born   September 11 1775
Sammuel Ball the son of Joseph & Hannah his wife born June   2   1776
Elisha Betts son of Wm & Judith his wife was Born Jany   7   1776
Frances Beattey son of William & Salley his wife was
   Born   May   3   1777
Charles Betts son of John & Elizabeth his wife was
   Born   May   6   1777
Jean Blewford Daughter of Cloe Blewford was Born   April   1   1777
William Anderson Buckley son of Joseph & Elizabeth his wife
   w's born   Dec'm   23   1776
Samuel Bearcraft son of Samuel & Ann his wife was Born
                                                      July   17   1777
Thomas Butler son of John & Mary his wife was Born June   28   1777
Billey Betts son of William was Born   August   9   1777
Russel Barrick son of George & Nancey his wife was Born May 24 1777
Mary Bisker Bransil Daughter of John & Susannah his
   wife was Born   August   4   1777
Josiah Burris son of Josiah and Milley his wife was
   Born   March   15   1778

page 21 (continued)

Thomas Taylor Brim son of Joshua Brim and Pegga his wife was Born	Dec'm	19	1777
Nancy Blackerby Daughter of Francis Blackerby was Born	March	9	1778
Martha Bearcraft Daughter of Motrom and Alse his wife w's borne	March	2	1778
John Ballentine son of Mottram and Leanner his wife was Born	Octobr	6	1777
Hannah Ball Daughter of George (and) Molley his wife was Born	March	11	1778
George Blackwill son of George and ~ ~ (wife's name omitted) was born	April	26	1778
Nancey Taylor Beetly Daughter to Jesse and Winnefret his wife w's born	May	28	1778
William Trussel Beacham son to Parker and Susannah his wife w's born	June	25	1778
Martha Hall Beacham Daughter to Ditto was born	June	25	1778
William Betts son to William & Milley his wife was born	May	22	1778
Mark Blincoe son to John & Mary his wife was born	June	27	1766
George Blincoe & Ann Keene Blincoe twins son & Daughter to John & Mary Blincoe his wife was born	Nov'm	18	1768
Jeremiah Bailey son to Stephen & Elizabeth his wife was born	August	12	1778
George Lucas Broun son to Joseph & Sarah his wife was born	Sept	12	1778
Samuel Lamkin Beacham son to Abraham & Leasur his wife w's born	Sept	17	1778
Samuel Garner Barnes son to Edwin & Hannah his wife w's born	Dec'm	13	1778
John Berry son to John & Jude his wife was born	Dec'm	28	1778
Winnefret Betts Daughter to William & Bettey his wife was born	Nov'm	15	1778
James Blewford son to Elijah & Alse his wife was born	Decem	1	1778
Ann Bennitt Bush Daughter to Bennitt & Ann his wife was born	March	4	1779
John Barecraft son to Samuel & his wife was born	March	18	1779
George Williams Brown son to Richard & Sarah his wife was born	Jan'r	9	1779
William Burton son to William & Ann his wife ws born	April	29	1779
Jimme Beatley son to John & Elizabeth his wife ws born	May	16	1779
Rebeckah Blincoe Daughter to John & Mary his wife was Born	Nov'm	13	1779
Peggey Brin Daughter to Joshua & Peggey his wife was Born	June	3	1780
Hollon Thomas son to Sarah Bean Thomas was born	Nov'm	15	1779
Salley Barnes Daughter to Neddey & Bettey his wife w's born	June	22	1780

page 22 (continued)

Richard Haynie Bearcraft son to Motrom & Ailsey his wife was born	Feb	9	1781
Jean Bailey Daughter to Stephen & Elizabeth his wife was born	Nov'm	1	1780
Meridia Barns son to Edwin & Hannah his wife was born	June	9	1781
Salley Brown Daughter to Charles & Susannah his wife was born	Octobr	8	1781
Vincent Brown son to Vincent & Sarah his wife was born	Octobr	12	1781
Thaddey Brown son to John & Roda his wife was Born	Feb	19	1778
Chloe Brown Daughter to Rawleigh & Sarah his wife was born	Jan	6	1781
Judith Bryant Daughter to Jonathan & Elizabeth his wife was born	April	3	1782
John & Winnefrit Brin twins son & daughter to Joshua & Pegga his wife was born	June	24	1782
John Blincoe son to John & Mary his wife was born	Augt	6	1782
Rodman Math Barnes son to Neddey & Elizabeth his wife was born	Decm	28	1782
Molley Bryant Daughter to Peter & Ann his wife was born	March	3	1783
Charlotte Betts Daughter to Jordon & Nancey his wife was born	March	14	1783
Anne Bush Daughter to Elizabeth a Bas. child was born	Oct	17	1782
Aphia Boush Daughter to Bennet & Ann his wife was born	March	29	1783
Vincent Barns Son to William & Winnefrit his wife was born	May	24	1783
Molley Brown Daughter to Vincent & Sarah his wife was born	Sept	5	1783
David Butlear son to James & --- (wife's name omitted) was born	May	25	1783
Salley Bryant Daughter to Joseph & Franckey his wife	Janr	13	1784
Ann L. Brumley Daughter to Samuel & Bettey his wife was born	Janr	14	1784
John Burton son to William & Ann his wife was born	Oct	9	1781
Betsoy Burton Daughter to Ditto & Ditto was Born	April	11	1784
Hannah Brown Daughter to Charles & --- (wife's name omitted) ws born	Oct	4	1784
Rubin Bryant son to Jonathon & Elizabeth his wife was born	Sept	10	1784
Elizabeth Tarpley Bennot Daughter to Thomas T. Bennet was Born	Oct	18	1784
Rostin Betts son to Jordon & Nancy his wife was born	Dec	2	1784

page 22 (continued)

Oston Barns son to Edwin & Hannah his wife was born	Feb	17	1785
Betsey W. Butler Daughter to James & Mary his wife was Born	March	17	1785
Ailsey L. Bailey Daughter to Stephen & Elizabeth his wife was bn	April	12	1785
Reuben Bennett son to Thomas T. Bennett & Ann his wife was born	Novmbr	29	1782
Burges Brown son to John & Betsey his wife was born	Oct	9	1785
Alfred Barnes son to Neddey & Elizabeth his wife was born	June	6	1786
Fallon Barnes son to William & Winney his wife was born	March	18	1786
Richard Coelman Brin son to Marget Brin a bastard chd was born	May	14	1786
Nancey Crelley Blincoe Daughter to Mark & Mary his wife was born	Decm	19	1786
Mary Ann Bennett Daughter to Thomas T. Bennett & Ann his wife was born	Apr	8	1787
Salley Bayliss Daughter to William & Molley his wife was born	June	16	1787
Milley Betts Daughter to Jordon & Nancey his wife was born	Feb	18	1787
Samuel Brumbley son to Samuel & Elizabeth his wife was born	Sept	4	1787
Morton Barns son to Edwin & Hannah his wife was born	Nevm	14	1787
Nancey Rowbuck Booth Daughter to John & Winney his wife was born	Novm	25	1787
Fleat Barnes son to William & Cloey his wife was Born	Novm	20	1787
Elizabeth Brown Daughter to Thomas & Elizabeth his wife ws bn	Feb	29	1788
Alisce Barns Daughter to William & Winney his wife was born	April	8	1788
Stephen Bailey son to Stephen & Elizabeth his wife was Born	Janr	31	1788
Alpheus Barns son to Neddey & Elizabeth his wife was born	Augt	15	1788
Botsey Holland Daughter to Ruth Beacham a bastard child was Born	Decm	22	1788
John West Beacham son to John W. Beacham & Ann his wife was Born	Feb	4	1789
Nancey Bryant Daughter to Jonathon & Eliz his wife was Born	April	7	1789
James Beacham son to William & Sarah his wife was Born	October	22	1788
Hannah McFarlane Beacham Daughter to Thomas & Jean his wife was Born	Decm	11	1788
Luccy Ball Daughter to Edmond & Salley his wife ws Born	May	2	1789
Baptized	Augt	23	
George Brown son to Charles & Susannah his wife was Born	March	1	1787

age 23 begins

Nancey Betts Daughter to Jordon &
  Nancey his wife was born   Decm   11   1789
Betsey Brumbley Daughter to Samuel
  & Elizabeth his wife was Born   Decm   16   1789
Ann Edwards Barns the Daughter of
  Edwin & Hannah his wife ws Born   January 13   1790
Thomas Baylis son to William & M°lley
  his wife ws Born   May   24   1790
Samuel Jackson Booth son to James Booth
  & Magdalane his wife was Born   April   28   1790
Fanna Brient daughter to Joseph & Frankey
  his wife was born   Augt   20   1790
Isaac Edward Baless son to Samuel & Sarah
  his wife was born   July   13   1790
Judith Robuck Booth daughter to John &
  Winney his wife was born   Augt   23   1790
Polley Middleton Wroe Bryant daughter of
  Rachel Bryant & Tho Wroe born   May   4   1790
Austin Ball son to Edmund & Salley his
  wife was Bn   June   7   1790
John Owins Baley son to Hugh Baley &
  Judith his wife ws Born   January 23   1791
Elizabeth Brown Daughter to Charles &
  Susannah his wife ws Bn   Decm   11   1790
Hallar Crane Beatley son to John Jones
  Beatley & Saraan his wife ws Bn   Novm   9   1790
John Brown son to Thomas & Elizabeth
  his wife was Born   March   17   1791
Charles Betts son to John & Nancey his
  wife was born   March   17   1791
Betsey Stone Burten Daughter to Thomas
  Burten & Molley his wife was born Feb   28   1792
Asslon Barcraft son to Mottrom & Fanney
  his wife was Born   April   28   1794
Alfred Barcraft son to Ditto & Ditto was Born Dec'm 30   1796

page 24, headed "St.Stephens 'C' Parish".

Philip Clues son to John was Born   Novr   16   1681
Eliza Clues Daugr to Ditto was Born   Decr   16   1683
Samuell Churchwell son To Samuell Born   Octr   19   1670
Sarah Churchwell Daughter To Do was Born March 16   1675
Richd Churchwell Son To Do was Born   Apr   29   1673
Livey Churchwell Daugr To Do was Born   June   25   1676
Simon Churchwell Sone To Do Born   March 17   1681
Joseph Churchwell Son To Do Born   Novr   10   1684
Charles Croe Son To Charles was Born   Jully   15   1679
Hannah Christopher Daugr To Robt Born   June   27   1688
George Craffourd son To Jo'n Born   Jan'y 26   1689
Pitts Curtice son To Walter Curtice Born Jan'y 16   1674
Eliza Curtice Daugr To Do was Born   Jan'y 26   1681
John Craffourd Son To Jo'n Born   Jully 13   1685
Rich'd Craffourd Son To Do was Born   Octr   16   1692
Mary Clarke Daug'r To Tho Clark was Born Apl   25   1679
Thos Clark son To Do was Born   Jany   22   1682
Peter Clark son To Do was Born   Novr   15   1685
Daniell Clarke Son To Do was Born   Jully 17   1692

Rebeckah Clark Daugr To Rich'd was Born	Nov'r	6	1687
Mary Clark Daugr To Do Born	Jan'y	5	1685
Sarah Clark Daugr To Do Born	Jan'y	1	1692
Rich'd Clarke Son To Ditto Born	Dec'r	11	1695
John Conaway Son To Dennis was Born	Jan'y	15	1673
Thos Conaway Son To Do was Born	Jan'y	15	1680
Lazarus Conaway Son To Do was Born	Jully	20	1682
Christopher Conaway Son To Do was Born	May	3	1684
Allex'r Cummins Son To Wm was Born	Dec'r	10	1677
Edw'd Cole sone To John Cole was Born	Jan'y	2	1683
John Cole son To Do was Born	Oot'r	23	1685
Peter Comoday son To Peter was Born	Novr	14	1683
John Cockrell Son To Jo'n was Born	Nov'r	22	1669
Eliza Cockrell Daug'r To Do was Born	Nov'r	21	1671
Hannah Cockrell Daugr To Do was Born	Feby	20	1680
Edward Cockrell Son To Do was Born	Dec'r	29	1674
Rich'd Cockrell Son To Do was Born	De'r	3	1683
Clement Carbell son To Jo'n was Born	June	7	1687
Mayre Crosbey Daug'r To George Was Born	June	28	1676
Sarah Crosbey Daug'r To Do was Born (1679 ?)	Ap'l	4	1677
Georg Crosbey Son To Do was Born	Oot'r	27	1681
Daniell Crosbey Son To Do was Born	March	6	1684
Tho's Cole son To Charles was Born	Jully	28	1692
Edmond Cole Son To Do was Born	March	1	1695
Mary Cole Daug'r To Do was Born	Feb'y	28	1687

page 25, headed "C".

Eliza Carr Daug'r To Joseph was Born	Oot'r	2	1692
Thos Carr Son To Do Bap'd (1693)	Jan'y	7	1693
Mary Cassiday Daug'r To William was Born	Oot'r	29	1693
Stephen & Hannah Chockalet Twins To Stephen Born	March	4	1693
Margaret Collin Daug'r To Hugh Bap'd	Aug't	5	1694
James Collin Son to Do was Born	Ootr	2	1700
Nicolas Collin Son Do Bap'd	Augt	26	1703
Eliza Collin Daugr To Do Bap'd	Sep'r	6	1706
John Cockrell Son To John Jun'r Bap'd	Nov'r	24	1695
Thos Cockrell Son To Do was Bap'd	Oot'r	22	1699
Peter Cockrell Son To Do was Bap'd	March	13	1700
Wilabey Cockrell Son To Do was Bap'd	-	-	1702
Presley Cockrell Son To Do was Bap'd	Dec'r	10	1704
John Coleman Son To John Bap'd	Jully	19	1698
Eliza Cliffurd Daug'r To Robt was Born	Apl	5	1702
John Cliffourd Son To Do was Born	Feby	13	1706
Peter Cornish Son To Wm was Born	Nov'r	3	1702
Elliner Cornish Daug'r To Do was Born	Oot'r	30	1707
Rich'd Cornish Son To Do was Born	Dec'r	5	1709
Wm Cornish Son To Do was Born (1717)	June	12	1717
Clevey Churchwell Daug'r To Samuel was Born	Ootr	16	1707
John Carnegie Son To John was Born	May	24	1707
Mary Crump Daug'r To John Bap'd	Feb'y	20	1708
John Claughton Son To Jas was born	Feb'y	20	1708

Millard Camell Daug'r To Hugh Bap'd	Nov'r 20	1709
Eliner Cheetwood Daug'r To Mathias Bap'd	Aug't 12	1712
Wm Creel Son To Charles was Born	Ap'l 17	1712
Stephen Crane Son Jas was Born	Jully 29	1709
Isabela Crane Daug'r To Do was Born	Jully 12	1710
Winee Crane Daug'r To Do was Born	March 8	1714
Jas Crane Son To Do was Born	Jun 19	1716
Georg Conway Son To Dennis was Born	Nov'm 30	1706
Eliza Conway Daug'r To Do was Born	March 9	1709
Winifred Conaway Daug'r To Do Born	Dec'r 28	1711
Judith Conaway Daug'r To Do Born	June 21	1714
Dennis Conaway Son To Do Born	Feby 15	1716
Stephen Colman Son To Stephen Bap'd	Sep'r 28	1707
John Coppidge Son To Wm was Born	Jan'y 31	1710
John Cockrell Son Rich'd was Born	Sep'r 23	1715
Sarah Curtice Daug'r To George Born	Ap'l 12	1717
Eliz'a Clyton Daug'r To Rich'd Born	Sep'r 13	1709
Eliz'a Christo'r Daug'r To John was Born	Sep'r 6	1720
Mary Ann Creel Daug'r To Charles Born	Oct'r 4	1717
Charles Creel Son To Do was Born	Dec'r 5	1715

page 26,   headed   "C".

Betty Creel Daug'r To Georg was Born	Feb'y 28	1719
Hanah Creel Daug'r To Char's was Born	Feb'y 17	1721
Wm Curtice Son To Georg was Born	Nov'r 24	1720
Nanny Christopher Daug'r To John Born	Dec'r 1	1722
James Farnet Cole To Robt was Born	Feb'y 19	1722
Georg Curtice son To Georg Born	June 22	1723
Joseph Cooper Son To Wm was Born	Dec'r 26	1713
Rebeckah Cooper Daug'r To Do was Born	Aug't 30	1717
Wm Cooper Son To Do was Born	Aug't 25	1721
Eliza Crump Daug'r to Joh'n was Born	Oct'r 19	1717
John Crump son To Do was Born	Aug't 21	1720
Susannah Crump Daug'r Do was Born	Jully 11	1723
Wm Cols son to John was Born	Sept'r 8	1720
Eliza Cols Daug'r To Do was Born	May 23	1723
John Cralle Son To Tho's Cralle Born	Sep'r 8	1724
Tho's Cottrell Son To Jo'n was Born	Dec'r 1	1724
Winifred Curtice Daug'r To Henry Born	March 13	1725
Judey Corbell Daug'r To Jo'n Born	Jan'y 2	1725
Jane Curtice Daug'r To George Born	Ap'l 5	1725
Hannah Curtice Daug'r To Do Carp'r Born	Aug't 9	1725
Spencer Corbell Son To Clement Born	Oct'r 22	1719
Peter Corbell Son To Do Born	Ap'l 18	1724
John Campbell Son To To's Born	Aug't 22	1726
Judey Cockrell Daug'r To John Born	Jully 24	1724
Tho's Cockrell Son To Do Born	Dec'r 24	1725
Lucretia Cottrell Daug'r To Jo'n Jun'r was Born	Ap'l 26	1727
John Corbell Son To John Born	Dec'r 3	1727
John Cottrell Son To And'w Born	Nov'r 15	1728
Sarah Conre Daug'r To John	Ap'l 18	1729

Lucretia Cottrell Daug'r To And'w Born	May	13	1730
Rebecka Cooper Daug'r To Wm Born	Dec'r	23	1728
Wm Corbell son To John Born	Jully	1	1730
Betty Curtice Daug'r To George	Oct'er	20	1730
John Corbell Son To Winefred Born	Feb'y	26	1726
Else Condre Daug'r To John Born	Nov'm	24	1731
John Cotrell Son To And'w Born	Jan'y	28	1732
Clement Corbell Son To Jo'n Born	Aug't	3	1732
Lucretia Cottrell Daug'r To And'w	March	3	1734
John Cole Son To Edward - - -	Sept'r	22	1734
John & Cath'rn Condry Twins of Jo'n Born	Jun	18	1735
Samuell Cole Sone To Edmund	Jun	25	1736
Winifred Cottrell To Daniell Born	Dec'r	15	1736
Eliza Corbell Daug'r To John Born	June	9	1737
Wm Condry Son To John Born	Feb'y	16	1738
Robt Clark Son To Rob't Jun'r Born	May	28	1737
Eliza Clark Daug'r To Do Born	Jully	14	1738
Eliz Cotrele Daug'r To Daniell was Born	Jan'y	26	1738

page 27, headed "C".

Hanah Clark Daug'r To Rob't J'r Born	Dec'r	15	1740
-ffellah Cole Daug'r To Edmund Born	Feb'y	13	1739
Stephen Corbell Son To Jo'n Born	Jan'y	14	1741
Samuell Carpender son To John Born	Nov'r	8	1730
Tho's Carpender Son To Do Born	Feb'y	11	1734
Absolom Carpender Son To Do Born	Sep'r	9	1737
Eliz Carpender Daug'r To Do was Born	Feb'y	8	1741
John Cottrell Son To Daniell Born	Nov'r	10	1741
John Conway Son To John & Susana Born	Nov'r	26	1702
James Conway Son To John Born	Seprr	26	1728
Mary Conway Daug'r To Do Born	Nov'r	19	1730
Ann Conway Daug'r To Do Born	Aug't	26	1732
Winifred Conway Daug'r To Do Born	Nov'r	19	1734
John Span Conway Son To Do Born	Jan'y	15	1738
Richd Conaway Son To Do Born	Nov	11	1740
Thos Cole Son To Edmond Was Born	Oct'r	28	1741
Robert Clark Son To Rob't Jun'r was Born	May	26	1742
Hannah Carbell Daug'r To Spencer Was Born	Nov'r	23	1742
Winorvey Conner Daug'r To Ja's was Born	Jully	27	1743
John Collins Son To Timothey was Born	Dec'r	7	1744
William Cottrel Son To Daniell Born	Mar'h	8	1744
John Coner Son To James Coner Born	Mar'h	13	1745
William Cornish Son To Rich'd & Nanne Born	Nov'r	21	1745
Tho's Cottrell Son To Daniell & Eliza Born	Feb'y	20	1746/7
William Collins Son To Timothy Born	May	19	1747
Samuel Cockrell Son To Ann Born	May	22	1734
Blendell Curtice Son To George & Eliz Born	Oct'r	20	1744
Margaret Curtice Daug'r To Do & Do Born	Sept	25	1746
Sarahann Curtis Dau'r To Do & Do Born	Oct'r	16	1748
John Cornes Son To Rich'd & Nanny Born	Feb'y	8	1747
Cha's Colston son To Travers Colston & Alce Corbin Born	May	31	1736
Eliza Griffin Colston Daug'r To Do & Do Born	Sep'r	23	1738
Travers Colston Son To Do & Do Born	Nov'r	10	1740
William Colston Son To Do & Susanna Born	Oct'r	10	1744

page 27 (continued)

Rauleigh Colston Son To Travers & Susanna Born	May	11	1747
Samuell Colston Son To Do & Do	Nov'r	21	1749
Danill Cottrell Son To Danill & Eliza Born	Jully	9	1740
John Corbell Sone To Spencer Born	Jully	29	1747

page 28, headed "C".

Joanna Lewas Corbell Daug'r To Spencer Born	Feb'y	9	1750
Sarah Corbell Daug'r To Spencer Born	Dec'r	19	1752
Margaret Curtice Daug'r To George & Eliza Born	Sep'r	7	175-
Robert Conway Son To John & Francina was Born	May	10th	1749
Joseph Conway Son To Do was Born	Janry	9th	1754
William Corbel Son To John & Betty was Born	July	17th	1752
John Cockrell son To John Was Born	Dec'r	23	1752
Rich'd Cockrell Son To Do was Born	Aug't	10	1750
William Conner Son To James & Judith was Born	March	24th	1748
Elizabeth Conner Daug'r To Do was Born	Janry	5th	1750
Susannah Daug'r To Do was Born	July	2	1752
Presley Clark Son To Robert was Born	Febry	25th	1745
Charles Clark Son To Do was Born	Octobr	4th	1746
Robert Clark Son To Do was Born	March	5th	1748
Katherine Clark Daug'r To Do was Born	Oct'r	9th	1750
William Clark Son To Do was Born	Oct'r	4th	1752
James Claughton Son To Pemberton & Griffifelo was Born	Nov'r	6th	1754
Patrick Connolly Son To George & Frances was Born	Nov'r	21st	1754
Judy Croswill Daug'r To William was Born	March	18th	1752
John Croswill Son To Do was Born	Oct'r	13th	1754
William Christopher Son To Robert was Born	Feb	24th	1755
Ann Claughton Daug'r To John and Sarah was Born	Feb	9th	1755
Presley Cockrel son To Presly & Sarah was Born	July	7th	1754
Francis Siner Conway Daug'r To James was Born	April	25th	1755
Spencer Corbell Son To Spencer & Joannah was Born	June	2nd	1755
Ann Clarke Daug'r To Robert was Born	Febry	16th	1755
James Conner Son To James was Born	Dec'r	20th	1755
Edward Cockrell Son To John & Elizabeth was Born	Nov'r	20th	1755
		(or 28th)	
George Connolly Son To George was Born	March	26th	1756
Sally Churchill Daug'r To Willoughby was Born	May	16th	1756
John Lamkin Crute Son To Richard & Hannah was Born	May	1st	1756
John Crallie Son To John & Judith was Born	Sept	16th	1756
John Craine Son To Stephen was Born	Nov'r	19th	1756
Ann Clarke Daug'r To Robert was Born	Febry	16th	1755
Samuel Clarke Son To Do was Born	Decr	30th	1756
Winney Christopher Daug'r To Robert Born	April	6th	175-
Betty Cockarel Daug'r To Thomas Born	Nov'r	17th	175-

page 29, headed "C".

Dennis Conway Son To Dennis Was Born	Septr	6th	1757
Sarah Curtis Daughter to Wm & Prudence Curtis was born	July	17th	1747
Hannah Curtis Daughter to Wm & Prudence Curtis was born	Septm	7th	1749

page 29 (continued)

Betty Curtis Daughter to Wm & Prudence Curtis was born	Nov:	20th	1756
Edward Coles Son to John & Winifred Coles was born	May	6th	1755
John Coles Son to John & Winifred Coles was born	Novm	2d	1756
William Coles Sons to John & Winefred Coles was born	March	6th	1758
Susanna Cookeril Daughter to Presly & Sarah Cookeril was born	Decemb	22nd	1755
Judith pincord Cookaril Daughter to Presly & Sarah Cookaril was born	June	8th	1758
Millecent Chilton Daughter to Stephen & Judith Chilton was born	March	26	1749
Fleet Chilton Son to Stephen & Judith Chilton was born	March	5	1751
Molly Chilton Daughter to Stephen & Judith Chilton was born	June	3	1753
John Chilton Son to Stephen & Judith Chilton was born	Octob	10th	1755
William Chilton Son to Stephen & Judith Chilton was born	March	12th	1758
Stephen Crain Son to Stephen & Sarahann Crain was born	January	5th	1759
John Christopher Son to John & Mary Ellin Christopher was born	May	9th	1759
Winefred Corbell Daughter to John & Sarah Corbell was born	June	15th	1751
Sally Corbell Daughter to John & Sarah Corbell was born	Novem	8	1753
Nancy Corbell Daughter to John & Sarah Corbell was born	Decemb	31	1755
William Curtis Son to Betty Curtis a Bastard born	Septem	22	1759
Mary Claughton Daughter to James Claughton born	April	13th	1758
Susanna Claughton Daughter to James Claughton born	Aug't	18th	1760
Susannah Crane Daughter to James & Rebeckah Crane born	April	9th	1743
Mary Crane Daughter to James & Rebekah Crane born	May	2	1745
Elisabeth Crane Daughter To James & Rebeckah Crane was born	April	28	1747
Rebeckah Crane Daughter to James & Rebeckah Crane was born	Septemb	11th	1749
John Crane Son to James & Rebekah Crane was born	March	10th	1752
Sally Crane Daughter to James & Rebekah Crane was born	April	11th	1754
James Crane Son to James & Rebekah Crane was born	March	28th	1756
Thomas Crane Son to James & Rebekah Crane was born	January	19th	1759
Francinah Coles Daughter to John & Winefred Coles was born	July	19th	1760
Thomas Christopher son to John & Mary Ellen Christopher was born	March	20	1762
John Claughton son to James & Susannah Claughton was born	Novemb	1	1762
Edward Coles Conway Son to James & Alice Conway was born	April	28	1763
Henry Curtis son to George Ju'n & Millecent Curtis was born	April	9	1762
Littleton Cookarill Son to John & Elisabeth Cookarill was born	June	14	1760

page 29 (continued)

Joshua Cookarill Son to Do was born	Decemb	8	1762
Richard Conway Son to James & Alice Conway was born	Febry	18	1765
Maryann Campbell Daughter to Thomas & Winifred Campbell was born	Novem	9	1762
Charles Campbell Son to Thomas & Winifred Campbell was born	Janry	4	1764
Winny Campbell Daughter to Thomas & Winifred Campbell was born	March	24	1765
William Chapman Son to Peter & Mary Chapman was born	March	2d	1765

page 30. headed "C".

Lukey Curtis Daughter to William & Prudence Curtis was born	Janua	14	1759
William Hayes Curtis Son to William & Prudence Curtis was born	Novem	29	1762
Molley Curtis Daughter to George and Millecent Curtis was born	May	15	1763
Jane Curtis Daughter to George and Millecent Curtis was born	October	7	1766
Molly Corbell Daughter to John and Betty Corbell was born	May	16	1756
John Corbell Son to John and Betty Corbell was born	Octob	15	1758
Clement Corbell Son to John and Betty Corbell was born	Octob	21	1761
Fleet Corbell Son to John and Betty Corbell was born	Septem	10	1764
Gilbert Corbell Son to John and Betty Corbell was born	August	21	1766
Nanny Blundell Curtis Daughter to William and Prudence Curtis was born	Decemb	26	1766
William Son of John & Maryhelen Christopher was born	Feby	1	1767
Stephen son of Stephen & Judith Chilton was born	Feby	28	1767
Martrom son of John Cralle Jun'r & Sarah his wife was born	Feb	17th	1767
Mary Daughter of Pemberton & Behatheland Claughton was born	March	17	1767
Samuel Son of John and Duannah Carter was born	March	29	1767
Richard Smith Corbell Son to John & Sarah Corbell was born	January	12	1763
John Corbell Son to John and Sarah Corbell was born	April	30	1766
Peter Claughton Son to James and Hannah his wife was Born	July	25th	1768
Susanner Christefer Daughter of Hennery & Sary was Born	Septmbr	13	1771
Peter Christefer the Son of John & Mary his wife was Born	February	28	1772
William Kennon Son of John & Sary Kennon his wife was Born	June	7	1772
Nancey Kennon Daughter of tho's & Sary his wife was Born	June	14	1772

(Note: The old pronunciation of this name was 'Cannon'. B.F.)

Aimme Churchwill Daughter of Willebe & Mary his wife was Born	August	15	1772
Winnefret Cole Daughter of Samuel Cole & Ann Coles his wife was Born	Februry	3	1773
Salley Curtis Daughter of George & Sisse (or Lesse) his wife was Born	December	15	1772
Charles Coleman Dau of Charles & Nancey his wife was Born	Aprile	28	1773
Zeakel Cookman Son of Rich·* & Hannah his Wife was born	March	21st	1773
Winnefrit Cretcher Daughter of Richard & Jeane his wife was Born	Februry	17	1774
Susannah Cookrill Daughter of William & Molle his wife born	Septm	12	1773
Jesse Crouther Son Robert & Hannah his wife was Born	April	28	1774
William Crouther Son to tho's & Ann his wife was Born	Januy	29	1774
Christofer Cornish Son of William & Judith his wife was born	May	11	1773
Mary Crowder Daughter to John & Elizabeth his wife was Born	March	26	1774
William Christefor Son of Hennery & Sary his wife was born	Novembr	10	1773
John Carpenter Son of Charles & Mary his wife was Born	October	9	1773
Dannel & frances Corbill twins Son & Daughter to William & Sary his wife w. b.	February	10	1774
Robert Christefor Son to John & Mary his wife was born	Novembr	26	1774
Stephen Crouther Son of John Crouther was Born	June	7	1774
Jeremiah Cookman Son of Rice* & hannah his wife was Born	Aprill	14	1775
Salley Cole Daughter of Sammuel & Ann his wife was born	March	31	1775
Samuel Churchwill son of Willibay and Molley his wife was born	Augt	2	1775
Alse Nelms Clark Daughter of Robert Clark Jun'r was born	July	9	1775

page 31,   headed "C".

Richard Cretcher Son of Richard & Jean his wife was born	february	27	1776
Sammuel Clark Son of Robert Clark was Born	March	13	1777
Richard Booth Son of Salley Churchwill was Born	June	22	1776
Thomas Claughton Son of Thos & Mary his wife was born	April	19th	1777
John Crouther Son of John & Judith his wife was born	febry	9	1777
Catesby Tho's Son of Thom Thomas & Dorous his wife was Born	June	1	1776
William Cauender Son of James & Susanner his wife was born	Novmbr	27	1776

* Rice Cookman

Nancy Cristefer Daughter of Hennery & Sarah was Born	Decembr	3	1776
Caty Cornish Daughter of William & Judith his wife was born	May	23	1775
Presley Coleman Son of Joseph & Clery his wife was Born	July	8	1776
Molley Carpenter Daughter of Charles Was Born	Januay	20	1776
Peter Christopher son of John & Mary his wife was born	June	20	1777
John Crowther son of Thomas & Ann his wife was Born	Decm	3	1776
Robert Delap Crowther son of Robert & Hannah his wife was born	Augt	15	1777
Francis Clark Daughter of Robert Jun'r - - his wife was Born	Augt	23	1777
John Christopher son of Henry Christopher & Sarah - - was Born	October	30	1777
James Claughton son of Richard and Priscilla his wife was born	Novm	19	1777
George Cole Born (Note: See entry below. B.F.)	Feb	1	1778
Winnefret Corbin Daughter of Daniel & Francis his wife ws born	Novm	10	1777
George Cole son to Samuel & Ann his wife was born	Feb	1	1778
John Sims Cavender son to James and Susannah his wife ws bn	May	20	1778
George Betts Curtis son to george & Millicent his wife was born	Sept	26	1777
Hannah Kenner Cralle Daughter to John & Sarah his wife ws born	July	31	1778
Jean Churchwill Daughter to Williby & Mary his wife was born	July	21	1778
Elizabeth Claughton Daughter to James & Hannah his wife	July	29	1778
Lucey Coelman Daughter to Thomas & Bettey his wife ws born	March	1	1759
Richard Coelman son to Ditto & Ditto was born	Apr	22	1761
Bettey Coelman Daughter to Ditto & Ditto was born	Janr	26	1763
Thomas Coelman son to Ditto & Ditto was born	June	30	1770
Robbin Coelman son to Ditto & Ditto was born	Aug't	15	1772
Sarah Coelman Daughter to Ditto & Ditto was born	May	19	1775
James Coelman son to Ditto & Ditto was born	Jan'y	4	1778
Lucoy Cornish Daughter of William & his wife was born	July	15	1778
Bottey Hopson Chilton Daughter to John was born	Apr	2	1778
(Note: This child's name was Elizabeth Hobson Chilton. B.F.)			
Cyrus Payne Connolly son to James & Catherine his wife ws bn	Novm	17	1778
John Coles son to Edward & Rhoda his wife was born	Novm	16	1778
Thomas France Cretcher son to Richard & Jean his wife was born	Decm	12	1778
Samuel Clarke son to William & Elizabeth his wife ws born	Decm	17	1778
Sarah Cain Daughter to Ellin Cain was born	Novm	3	1778
Judith Coles Daughter to William & Sara his wife was born	Feb	10	1779
Thomas Cottrell son to John & Sirah his wife was born	Mar	5	1779

Thos Claughton & William Claughton twins sons of
Richard and An his wife was Born   May   3   1770
William Cornish Son of John Cornish & ann his wife
was born   April   5th 1770
William Coleman Son to Charles & Ann his wife was
Born   June   2   1770
Archable Couper was born   June   8th 1770
Bettey Parker Corbell Daughter of John Corbell &
Sarah his wife was Born   October 11   1770
Salley Claughton Daughter of James & Hannah
Claughton his wife was Born   October 29   1770
Joan Corbin Daughter of Danell Corbin & Francis
Corbin was born   September 10 1770
Jeanne Claughton Daughter of Pemberton Claughton
Juner & Bohathalan his wife was born   February 26 1771
Winnifret Cole Daughter of John Cole & Winnifret
his wife was Born   March   30   1771
Richard Cornish Son of William & Judith Cornish
his wife was Born   March   29   1771
Lucresha Cottrell Webb Daughter of John & Molle
his wife was Born   December 5   1771
Vincent Critcher Son of Richard & Jean his wife
was Born   February 5   1772
Elizabeth Cox Claughton Daughter of James & Hannah
Claughton was Born   January 11th 1773
Pemberton Claughton Son of Pemberton & Behatheland
his wife was born   May   7th 1776
Jean Griffin Claughton Daughter to John Claughton
& Nancey his wife was Born   April   12   1792
Christapher Clark son to William & Lucey his wife
was Born   March   14   1792
Richard Presley Coles son of Edward Coles & Rhoda
his wife was Born   September 29 1791
Polley Sydnor Cookman Daughter to George Cookman
& Nancey his wife was Born   April   30   1796
George Christopher Clarke son to William Clarke
& Lucy his wife was Born   April   13   1796
Lindsey Crowther son to John Crowther & Nancey
his wife was Born   July   24   1794
Kenner Cralle son to Kenner Cralle & Nancey his
wife was Born   October 6   1785
Elizabeth Hallow Cookman Daughter to George Cookman &
Nancey his wife was Born   January 21   1798
Elizabeth Dunlop Crawther Daughter to Jesse Crowther
& Ann his wife was Born   September 3 1798
Poley Flinton Crowther Daughter to Jesse Crowther
& Nancey his wife was Born   November 7   1800
John Cookman son to George Cookman & Nancey Cookman
his wife was Born   July   4   1800
Hanah Haynie Crowther Daughter to Jesse Crowther
& Nancey his wife was born   December 15 1803
Ledey Pue Cookman Daughter to George Cookman & Nancey
his wife was Born   September 28 1802
Jenney Singer Cookman Daughter to Ditto & Ditto
was Born   January 30   1805
Jeremiah Cookman son to George Cookman & Nancey
his wife ws born   March   20   1807

page 34 headed "C".

Charles Coleman son to Joseph & Cloe his wife was born	April	9	1779
Lucy Crowther Daughter to Thos & Ann his wife was born	May	15	1779
Judith Bell Crowther Daughter to John & Judith his wife was born	Augt	1	1779
Vinson Clarke son to William & Catherine his wife was Born	Nov	11	1779
Molley Coelman Daughter to Thomas & Bettey his wife was born	Apl	23	1780
Elizabeth Sydnor Coelman Daughter to Richard & Lucey his wife was born	Sept	15	1780
James Cox son to James & Molley his wife was born	May	22	1780
Nelley Sharp Christopher Daughter to John & Mary Ellen his wife was born	Nov	14	1780
George Crutcher son to Richard & Jean his wife was born	Jan'y	23	1781
Harrison Connolly son to John & Mary his wife was born	Novm	2	1780
Nancey Griffin Claughton Daughter to Thomas & Molley his wife was born	May	28	1781
Aisley Claughton Daughter to James & Hannah his wife was born	May	7	1781
Jane Clark Daughter to Charles & Cynthia his wife was born on monday about 8 oclock in the morning	July	6	1772
Elizabeth Clarke Daughter to Ditto & Ditto was born Tuesday about 2 oclook in the morning	April	18	1775
Susanna Hancock Clarke Daughter to Ditto & Ditto was born on tuesday about 5 oclook in the morning	March	25	1779
Septimus Clarke son to Ditto & Ditto was born monday about 2 oclock in the Evening	Sept	10	1781
Peter Griffin McClanham son to James & Elizabeth his wife was Born	Jan'y	27	1782
William Fleet Christapher son to John Christopher & Dolley his wife w.b.	March	3	1782
Salley Christopher Daughter to Henry & Sarah Betts was born	April	6	1782
John Clarke son to John & Elizabeth his wife was Born	Aug't	15	1782
Sarah Clarke Daughter to William & - - his wife was born	Sept	30	1782
George Connolly son to John & Mary his wife was Born	Aug't	13	1782
Elizabeth Claughton Churchill Daug't to Willoby & Salley his wife ws bn	Novm	8	1782
Lucey Rautt Coelman Daughter to Richard & Lucey his wife ws bn	Decm	25	1782

page 34 (continued)

Thomas Crouther son to Thomas & Ann his wife was born	Decm	24	1781
Molley Claughton Daughter to Thomas & Mary his wife was born	Augt	29	1779
Thomas Claughton son to Ditto & Ditto was born	Feb	7	1783
Griffethello Claughton Daughter to John & Nancey his wife was born	Sept	7	1783
James Claughton Gill son to William Claughton & Salley Gill was born	Decm	10	1784
James McClanaham the son of James & Elizabeth his wife was born	Feb	16	1785
Hannah Claughton Daughter to James & Hannah his wife was born	May	9	1785
John Connolly son to John & Mary his wife was born	March	14	1785
Randolph Crowther son Thomas & Ann his wife was born	May	8	1785
Thomas Crowther son to Thomas & Ann his wife was born	Decm	24	1782
Betsey M Coal Daughter to Andrew & Hannah his wife was born	March	8	1785
John R. Clarke son of Charles Clark & Cynthia his wife was born 10 oclock at night	November	17	1784
Thaddeus Clark son of William & Lucy his wife was born	July	5	1785

page 35 headed "C".

Elizabeth Clark Daughter to William & Elizabeth his wife was born	Jan'y	19	1787
Anne Pemberton Claughton Daughter to John & Nancey his wife ws born	Decm	25	1785
Anna Ceckman Daughter to Rice & Hannah his wife ws Born	April	20	1781
James Campbell son to Pryse & Sarah his wife was Born	March	20	1780
Charles Campbell son to Ditto & Ditto was Born	Oct	11	1782
Robert Campbell son to Ditto & Ditto was Born	Jan'y	10	1785
Pryse Campbell son to Ditto & Ditto was Born	Decm	25	1786
Betsey Connolly Daughter to John & Mary his wife was born	Apr	6	1787
John Lewis Claughton sone to John & Nancey his wife was Born	Aug't	16	1787
Charles Marmeduke Berkly Clarke son to Charles Clarke & Cinthia his wife was Born on Thursday about 4 oclock in the morning	Aug't	16	1787
Christian Pinkston Campbell Daughter to Pryse Campbell & Sarah his wife was born	Novm	5	1788
Pemberton Claughton son to John & Nancey his wife was Born	March	16	1789
Williamson Connolly son to John & Mary his wife ws Born	July	8	1789

page 35 (continued)

Thaddeus Coelman son to Thomas & Ann his wife was born	May	21	1791
Charity Ann Coleman Daughter to Ditto & Ditto was born	Febr	21	1793
Judith Clark Daughter to William & Catherine his wife was Born	Oct	14	1793
Nancy Coleman daughter to Thomas Coleman and Clarisa his wife was born	May	27	1792
Thomas Bouchell Coleman son to Do & Do was born	Febr	4	1794
Ledy Pue Cookman Daughter to George Cookman & Nancy his wife was Born	September	28	1802

page 36. headed "D".

Christopher Dawson son to Wm Born	Jan'y	16	167-
Wm Dawson So To Do Born	Jully	7	1675
Frances Dawson Daug'r To Do Born	Feb'y	5	1680
Jane Dawson Daug'r To Do Born	Feb'y	15	1683
Hugh Dermett Son To Owen Born	Sep't	3	1681
John Donook Son To Patrick Born	Sep'r	28	1684
John Dawson Son To Hen'y Born	Apl	27	1671
Sarah Dawson Daug'r To Do Born	May	21	1676
Hen'y Dawson Son To Do Born	Jully	24	1679
Eliz'a Dawson Daug'r To De Born	June	2	1683
Susana Dawson Daug'r To Do Born	Jan'y	28	1684
Walter Deves Son To John Born	Jany	22	1686
Mary Dunaway Daug'r To John Born	Dec'r	19	1689
Frances Dunaway Daug'r To Do Born	Oct'r	29	1668
John Dunaway Son To Do Born	Jan'y	29	1670
Samull Dunaway Son To Do Born	Mar'o	8	1676
Hanna Dunaway Daug'r Born	March	31	1678
Abraham Dunaway Son To Do Born	Dec'r	1	1680
Daniell Dunaway Son To Do Born	March	15	1682
Sarah Dunaway Daug'r To Do Born	Feb'y	22	1686
Thos Davis Son To John was Born	Nov'r	10	1682
John Davis Son To Do was Born	Aug't	17	1691
Katherin Dearem Daug'r To Morris Born	Nov'r	25	1681
Margaret Dearem Daug'r To Do was Born	Nov'r	5	1684
Elliza Downing Daug'r To Wm Born	Dec'r	30	1679
Ambros Davis Son To John Born	June	5	1694
Ann Davis Daug'r To Wm Born	Dec'r	31	1702
Sarah Davis Daug'r To Ja's Bap'd	May	5	1701
George Davis Son To Do Born	March	1	1702
Wm Davis Son To Do Born	Jully	31	1700
Hen'y Dawson Son To Hen'y Born	Feb'y	8	1708
Christopher Dawson Son To Francis Bap'd	May	18	1707
Mary Duke a Bastard was Born	Jully	28	1704
Wm Denny Son To Katherine Bap'd	Dec'r	10	1704
Mary Dauhety Daug'r To Wm Born	Ap'l	25	1704
Robert Davis Son To Wm Born	May	20	1706
Wm Danity (Dauity ?) Son To Jervis Born	Jan'y	16	1708
John Deanny Son To Katherine Born	March	27	1709
Wm Daniel Deliney Son To Anthony Born	Dec'r	9	1712

page 36 (continued)

George Dawkins Son To Wm Bap'd	Decem	10	1712
George Duke Son To Wm Bap'd	March	30	1714
Mary Dameron Daug'r To Joseph Born	March	1	1714
Wm Dollins Son To John Born	Nov'r	16	1709
Jo'n Dollins Son To Do Born	Oct'r	13	1712
Sarah Dollins Daug'r To Do Born	Ap'l	7	1715

pago 37 headed "D".

Rich'd Dallins Son To John Born	March	26	1718
Ann Dallins Daug'r To Do Born	Feb'y	27	1720
John Dawkins Son To George Born	Nov'r	11	1705
Mary Dawkins Daug'r To Do Born	March	10	1708
Ann Dawkins Daug'r To Do Born	Nov	5	1710
George Dawkins Son To Do Born	June	10	1713
Pinly Dawkins Son To Wm Born	May	17	1714
James Duke Son To John Born	Dec'r	11	1700
John Denny Son To Rich'd Born	Jan'y	2	1715
Ann Denny Daug'r To Do Born	March	11	1717
Wm Dawkins Son To Wm Born	June	25	1718
Eliza Dawson Daug'r To Eliza Born	June	23	1719
Lucrecey Davis Daug'r To Charles Born	March	2	1719
Tho's Dawkins Son To Wm Born	March	27	1721
Hannah Devis Daug'r To Rob't Born	Nov	18	1721
Charles Davis Son To Ch's Born	Feb'y	17	1721
John Dun Son To Wm Born	Oct'r	10	1719
Margaret Davis Daug'r To Cha's Born	May	31	1716
Winifred Davis Daug'r To Do Born	Dec'r	11	1717
Mary Denny Daug'r To Dav'd Born	Jan'y	10	1720
Rich'd Denny Son To Do Born	Feb'y	3	1722
Eliza Dawkins Daug'r To Wm Born	Oct'r	23	1723
Presly Dollins Son To John Born	March	8	1724
Hester Dun Daug'r To Wm Born	Oct'r	22	1724
Sarah Doged Daug'r To Wm Born	Jan'y	20	1722
Ann Doged Daug'r To Wm Born	March	21	1725
Winif'd Davis Daug'r To Rob't Born	Dec'r	20	1722
Samuell Davis Son To Do Born	Nov'r	27	1725
Bettey Denny Daug'r To Rich'd Born	July	10	1718
Edmond Denny Son To Do Born	Dec'r	14	1721
Rich'd Denny Son To Do Born	March	2	1723
Winif'd Dun Daug'r To Wm Born	Dec'r	21	1727
Ann Dohety Daug'r To John Born	March	24	1728
Wm Denne Son To Rich'd Born	Feb'y	12	1729
Rob't Davis Son To Rob't Born	Dec	11	1726
Sarah Devis Daug'r To Do Born	Feb'y	21	1728
James Dohety Son To John Born	March	8	1730
John Dudly Son To Rich'd Born	March	23	1730
Winif'd Dinne Daug'r To Rich'd Born	Dec'r	6	1724
Edmond Dinne Son To Do Born	Jully	20	1727
Dav'd Dinne Son To Do Born	-	-	-

Eliz Downing Daug'r To Edward was Born	Jan	20	1731
Mary Dunaway Daug'r To John Born	Dec'r	24	1715
Samuell Dunaway Son To Do Born	Sep'r	14	1719
Moses Dunaway Son To Do Born	Dec'r	15	1729
Hannah Dunaway Daug'r To Do Born	Jully	12	1732
Hannah Douning Daug'r To Edw'd Born	Dec'r	11	173-
Samuell Douning Son To Wm Born	Jully	29	1730
Sarah Daughity Daug'r To Jo'n Born	Dec'r	10	1734
Hannah Daughity Daug'r To Do Born	Jully	10	1726
Ann Daughity Daug'r To Do Born	March	24	1727
Ja's Daughity Daug'r To Do Born (sic)	March	8	1729/30
Aloe Daughity Daug'r To Do Born	Dec'r	2	1741
Mary Dunaway Daug'r To John Born	Oct'r	12	1737
Betty Dunaway Daug'r To Do Born	Aug't	4	1739
Chas Downing Son To John Born	Jully	4	1738
Eliza Downing Daug'r To Do Born	Ap'l	19	1740
Sarah Ann Dunaway Daug'r To Jo'n Born	Jan'y	12	1742
Betty Daughety Daug'r To Ja's Born	March	18	1744
Frances Dunaway Daug'r To Jos'h Born	Oct'r	18	1736
Ja's Dunaway Son To Do Born	March	10	1740
Jo'n Daughety Son To Jo'n Born	Aug't	6	1739
Mary Daughety Daug'r To Do Born	Feb'y	13	1742
Catherine Daughety Daug'r To Do Born	March	23	1745
Eliza Daughety Daug'r To Do Born	Ap'l	8	1736
Sarah Daughety Daug'r To Ja's Born	Oct'r	27	1745
John Dogged Son To Wm Dogged Born	Aug't	21	1734
John Daughety Son To Jas & Mary Born	March	7	1748
Betty Dunaway Daug'r To Joseph & Mary Born	March	24	1744
Rich'd Dunaway Son To Do & Do Born	Nov'r	12	1747
Winifred Daughity Daug'r To John was Born	March	23	1747
Charles Draper Son To William & Katherine was Born	March	22	1749
Sally Draper Daug'r To Do was Born	Aug't	9	1753
Thomas Downing Son To Samuel & Eliza'h was Born	May	23	1744
Samuel & Betty Twins To Do were Born	Feb'y	21st	1747
John Downing Son To Do was Born	May	1st	1755
Hannah Downing Daug'r To John was Born	April	19	174-
Nancy Downing Daug'r To Do was Born	June	20th	174-
Edward Downing Son To Do was Born	April	22	175-
Sarah Downing Daug'r To Do was Born	Feb	18	1753
Betty Danks Daug'r To George & Winifred was Born	July	12th	1745
Rebeckah Danks Daug'r To Do was Born	Nov'm	9	1747
William Danks Son To Do was Born	Dec'r	8th	175-
George Danks Son To Do was Born	April	26th	17--
Nanny Dimsdil Daug'r To Zacharih Hogdon was Born	March	5	- -

page 39, headed "D".

William Dawson Son To John was Born	Decem	20th	1755
-lls Daughity Son To James was Born	Feb'y	27th	1756
Magdalene Duglass Daug'r To John & Susannah Born	Aug'st	13th	1756
Mary Ann Draper Daug'r To William was Born	Dec'r	19th	1756
Grace Ball Downman Daug'r To Travers was Born	Sept'r	26th	1756
Nansy Davis Daug'r To Samuel & Mary was Born	Jan'ry	8th	1757
Betty Dudley Daug'r To Rich'd Born	March	23d	1756
Peter Dimsdell Son To Zachariah Born	Feb'ry	9th	1757
George Dawson Son To John was Born	May	27th	1757
Betty Dawson Daughter to John & Ruth Dawson was Born	March	13th	1758

Thomas Dudly son to Rich'd & Winefred Dudly was born Feb'y   9th 1744/5
Joseph Dudly son to Rich'd & Winefred Dudly was born Aprill   22d 1748
Winefred Dudly Daug'r to Rich'd & Winifred
   Dudly was Born   Jan'ry   15th 1750
William Dudly son to Rich'd & Winifred Dudly
   was Born   Feb'ry   17th 1743/4
Betty Dudley Daughter to John & Maryan Dudley
   was Born   May   2d   1758
Henry Dawson son to William & Magdalene Dawson
   was Born   Aug't   4th 1758
John Dudley son to Rich'd Dudley Jun'r & Sarah
   was born   Octob   24th 1758
Elizabeth Davis Daughter to Sam'l & Mary Davis
   was born   Februery 3   1754
Robert Davis son to Sam'l & Mary Davis was born   April   22d 1759
John Dunaway Bastard of Sarahan Dunaway born   Septem   17th 1759
Winny Dudly Daughter to John & Mary Dudly was
   born   April   24th 1760
Thomas Duglas son to John & Susannah Duglas was born May   5th 1760
John Dawson son to John & Betty Dawson was born   May   21d 1760
Jane Denny Daughter to William & Winnef Denny was born Feb'ry 7th 1755
Winny Denny Daughter to William & Winnif Denny
   was born   March   12th 1757
Mary Denny Daughter to William & Winny Denny
   was born   Febry   5th 1761
Sam'l Davis son to Robert & Judith Davis was born April   13th 1760
Isaac Davis son to Robert & Judith Davis was born Jan'ry   13th 1762
Sarah Dudly Daughter to Rich'd Dudley Ju'r &
   Sarah was born   May   1   1762
John Dudley son to John & Mary Dudley was born   Decem   27   1761
Thomas Davis son to Sam'l & Mary Davis was born   March   8   1762
Francis Davis Son Barbee & Frances Davis was born June   24   1761
Katy Bushrod Drew Bastard Daughter to Joanna Drew
   was born   July   6   1756
James Dudley son to John & Mary Dudley was born   Feb'ry   7   1764
Toulson Daughity son to James & Betty Daughity
   was born   March   5   1763
Samuel Daughity son to James & Elizabeth Daughity
   was   June   16   1766
Mary Ann Dudly Daughter to John & Mary Dudly
   was born   May   20   1766
Hulbay Docksy Daughter to John & Elizabeth
   Docksy was born   Februa   13   1762
Sarah Docksy Daughter to John & Elizabeth
   Docksy was born   March   8   1764

page 40,   headed "D".

William Daughety son to John Daughety & Elizabeth his wife
   was Born   January 6th 1770
Peter Dawson son of William Dawson & Magdillum
   his wife was Born   January 25th 1770
Nancy Dunaway Daughter of Darbey was born   October 21st 1769
Edra Dudley son of Ransom Dudley was born   March   19th 1770
William Doged Son of William & Elisabeth his
   wife was born   May   21   1770

page 40 (continued)

Anne Denny Daughter to William was Born	May	17	1770
Judith Davis Daughter to Robert & Judith his wife was born (Davis)	June	6	1770
Rebeckar Dollins Daughter of John Dollins & Hannah his wife was Born	July	29	1770
Richard Dawson Son of Costelow Doson & Aimme his wife was Born (both dates given)	Febry 1 or 4		1768
William Garner Dasson Son of Costolo Hill Doson & Aimme his wife was born	Janury	20	1771
Mary Drue Daughter to Robert Drue Was Born	March	6	1771
Joseph Dudley the son of John & Mary Dudley was Born	April	26	1771
Mary Dawson Daughter to Costelo hill Dawson & Aimme his wife was born	Sepbr	22	1773
William Dammeron son to William & Nancey his wife was Born	Feb	5	1792
Ailcey Nelums Daughter to Thomas Dugliss & Nancey his wife was Born	Novm	15	1792
Fanney Dawson Daughter to David & Ann his wife was Born	March	22	1793
John Jones Drynan son to Alexander Drynan & Margaret his wife was Born	Novm	5	1795
William Deatley son to John Deatley & Jeney his wife was Born	May	14	1796
Nancey Griffin Dawson Daughter to Thomas Dawson & Hannah his wife was Born	December 25		1797
George Dawson son to George Dawson & Elizabeth his wife was Born	December 27		1793
Jean Self Dawson Daughter to Christopher Dawson & Susannah his wife was Born	September 2		1804

page 41 headed "D".

Richard son of Richard Dawson was born bastard child	Feb	9	176-
Presly son of John Dallias & Elizabeth Dunaway was born	Feb	19	176-
William son of Robert & Eleanar Dickes was born	March	26	176-
James Daughity Son to John Daughity & Elizabeth his wife was born	Novem	13	1767
Richard Dudley son to Richard Dudly Jun'r & Sarah his wife was born	August	13	1766
Ellin Docksie Daughter to John & Eliz'a Docksie was born	Decemb	29	1767
Thomas Dudley Son to John & Maryan Dudley was born	Novemb	11	1768
Elizabeth Doxey Daughter of John Doxey & Elizabeth his wife	November 11th		1769
Elizabeth Diks Daughter of Robert & Helin Dikes was Born	April	1	1771
Churchwil Dunaway Son of Joseph Dunaway Was Born	December 18		1770
Christefier Dawson the Son of John & Elizabeth his wife was Born	Novembr 26		1771
Elizabeth Downing Daughter of Wm & Sarah his wife was Born	Novembr	6	1771
Peter Davis Son of Robert & Judith his wife was Born	April	6	1772

Winne Davis Daughter of John & Elizabeth his wife was Born	March	7th	1772
George Dudley Son of Ransom & Elizabeth his wife was Born	March	26	1772
John Daughety Son of John & Betty his wife was Born	September	4	1772
Onesephrous Damron Son of Mosey & Millicent his Wife was Born	Septmbr	19	1772
Nancey Daughety Daughter of Wm & Elizabeth his wife was Born	March	27	1773
Cloey Dudley Daughter of John & Maryan his wife was Born	March	2	1773
Jessey Denny Seebree the son of John Seebree & Winnean his wife was born	Aprill	4	1774
Molley Dunaway Daughter of Joseph & Judith his wife was born	October	27	1773
Nancey Dawson Daughter of John & Letty his wife Was Born	January	27	1775
John Dugless Son of Edward & Lucy Dugless his wife Was Born	Aug't	18	1774
Jessey Davis Son of Richard was Born	July	30	1773
Elisabeth Davis Daughter of Robert & Judith his wife was born	June	21	1774
Sharlot Dunway the Daughter of Beth Dunaway was born	Decembr	25	1776
Susanner Duglass Daughter of Edward & Lucey his wife was born	February	11	1776
John Dawson son of Costelo hill & Aimme his wife was born	May	11	1776
James & Salley Dawkins Son & Daughter to Moses was born	July	15	1775
James Dudley Son of John & Molley his wife was Born	Novbr	5	1775
Anna Damron Daughter of Jacob & Mary his wife was born	Decembr	1	1775
Ann Doxey Daughter of Charles Lowe & Suffia his wife Born	Agust	18	1775
Sarah Downing Daughter of William & Sarah his wife was Born	June	2	1777
James Grimes son of Ellender Dikes was Born	Sept	22	1776
Salley Davis Daughter of John & Elizabeth his wife was born	July	14	1777
Jean Garner Dawson Daughter of George & Nancey his wife was Born	Sept	24	1777
Jeremiah Duwson son of William & Ellen his wife was Born	Novm	15	1777
Nancey Churchwill Dunaway Daughter of Joseph & Judith his wife was born	Octobr	1	1777
Nancey Downman Daughter of John Downman & Liddey Downman his wife was born	April	5	1778
Sammuel Dunnaway the son of Bettey Dunnaway was born	June	1	1778
Elisha Harcum Daughity son to John & Elizabeth his wife ws born	July	24	1778

Hannah Corban Doged Daughter of William & - -
  his wife   Sept   30   1778
William Self Dawson son to John & Lettey his
  wife ws born   Sept   9   1778
Richard Davis son to Richard & Libbey his wife
  was born   Sept   11   1778
Costalo Hill Dawson son to Costalo Hill & Emry
  his wife was Born   Feb   23   177-

page 42,   headed   "D".

Sukey Dudly Daughter to John & Maryann his wife
  was born   Feb   4   1779
Willoughbby Day son to George & Nancey his wife
  was born   Novm   13   1778
 Salley Corbin Dawson Daughter to George &
  Elizabeth his wife was born   Aug't   10   1779
William Self Dugless son to Edward & Lusey
  his wife was born   March   11   1780
Molley Dosson Daughter to William & Nancey
  his wife was born   May   21   1780
Ailcey Clemmon Dawson Daughter to Wm & Ellin
  was born   May   18   1780
Judith Dugliss Daughter to Edward & Lucey his
  wife ws born   Feb   8   1778
Susannah Dugliss Dawson Daughter to Elizabeth
  Dawson was born   B child   Oct   21   1780
Nancey Davis Daughter to John Davis was Born   May   12   1780
Betsey Smith Dawson Daughter to William &
  Nancey his wife was Born   Sept   5   1781
John Dawson son to George & Elizabeth his wife
  was Born   Jan'y   25   1782
Benjamin Dawson son to David & Ann his wife
  was born   April   8   1782
Rodham Pritchet Dawson son to John & Lettey his
  wife was born   Sept   3   1782
Edward Dugliss son to Edward & Lucey his wife
  ws born   Oct   26   1782
Epaphioditus Dawson son to William & Nelley his
  wife ws born   Jan'y   8   1783
Salley Dawson Daughter to William & - - his wife   Oct   1   1783
Vincent Dawson son to David & Ann his wife was born Jan'y 25   1784
Elizabeth Griffin Dawson Daughter to Elizabeth
  Dawson a bastard child was born   Sept   26   1783
Winney Day Daughter to Winney Day a free Malatto
  was born   Jan'y   11   1784
Judith Day Daughter to Ditto was born   Sept   3   1778
Isaac Day Son to Ditto was born   June   21   1780
John Corbin Damerin Son To William Damerin &
  Nancy his Wife was born   Febr   5   1784
Salley Dawson Daughter to Wm & Nancy his wife
  was born   Decm   10   1784
Vinson Corbin Duglis son to Thomas & Nancey his
  wife was bn   Feb   10   1785

Samuel Dawson son to John & Lettey his wife ws born	Feb	14	1785
Lucey Dugliss Daughter to Edward & Lucey his wife was born	Feb	23	1785
Samuel Dawson son to William & Nelly his wife was born	June	15	1785
Salley McDaniel Daughter to George & Judith his wife was born	Feb	8	1787
Lindsay Trussel Dawson son of George & Elizabeth his wife Born	March	11	1787
Molley Draper Dameron Daughter of William & Nancey his wife Born	Decm	18th	1786
Elizabeth Yearby Dugless Daughter to Edward & Lucey his wife was bn	Apl	1	1787
John Claughton Dawson son to Henry & Molley his wife was Born	Oct	2	1787
Molley Vanlandingham Dawson Daughter to John & Lettey his wife ws bn	April	12	1788
Colisby Duglass son to Thomas & Nancey his wife was born	March	8	1788
Wilson Davis son to Marah Davis a Bastard child	April	30	1789
John Doscey son to John & Nancey his wife was Born	Oct	12	1788
Luke Williams Dameron son to William & Nancey his wife w.b.	March	30	1789
Salley (or Dolley) Dollins Daughter to Rebecah Dollins a bastard child was Born	May	1	1789
John Dawson son to Daniel & Mary his wife ws Born	Sept	12	1789

page 43, headed "D"

Nancey Duglass Daughter to Edward & Lucey his wife was Born	Sept	25	1789
Thomas Fleet Downing son to Thomas Downing & Betsey his wife ws bn	March	30	1789
William Dawson son to Henry & Molley his wife was Born	Oct	12	1790
John Colvin Downing son to Thomas Downing & Bettey his wife was bn	Augt	23	1790
Nancey Dawson Daughter to George & Elizabeth his wife was Born	June	9	1791
Ben Dawson son to John & Molley his wife was Born	Decm	12	1791
Thomas Dugliss son to Edward & Lucey his wife was Born	March	21	1792
John William Dawson son to Thomas Dawson & Hannah his wife was Born	June ,	27	1802
Ewel Ellik Sanders son of William & Darous his Wife was born	february 19		1770
George Edwards son of Jonathen & Winnefriet his wife was Born	March	12	1770
Edmon Evins Son of Mark Eving was Born	April	10	1770
Richard Edwards son to Tho's was Born	January	27	1770
Luke Elliston Daughter to Cuthbert Elliston & Mary his wife was born	April	5	1770
Mary Alexander Daughter of Rawle Elexander & Mary his wife was born	January	25	1771

Frances Edmons the son of Elias Edmons & frances his Wife
   was Born   April   8   1771
Salley Edwards Daughter to George Edwards was Born Septem   2   1770
Winnefrit Edmons Daughter to Robert Edmons & Mary
   More was Born   August   21   1771
Salley Eidson Daughter Creighton & Winneyfret his
   wife was Born   Novm   8   1788
Mary Efford Daughter to Zacheriah & Winney his
   wife was Born   Feb'y   23   1792
Holland Haynie Efford son to George Efford &
   Sharlottey his wife was Born   Jan'y   12   1798
Robert Ewel Elmore son to Thomas Elmore & Maryann
   his wife was Born   October   14   1797
Bettey Nut Everit Daughter to William Everit &
   Winney his wife was Born   Feb   25   1802

page 45, headed "E"

Katharin Edwards Daug'r To Isaac Born   Ot'r   27   1671
Jonathon Edwards son To Do Born   Feb'y   2   1673
Eliza Edwards Daug'r To Do Born   June   14   1674
Mary Edwards Daug'r To Do Born   Oot'r   5   1678
Isaac Edward Son To Do Born   Jully   18   1682
Peter Eaton Son To Jonathan Born   July   31   1702
Sarah Eaton Daug'r To Rich'd Born   Sep'r   14   1685
Jean Eaton Daug'r To Do Born   March   2   1689
Franois Eaton Son To Do Born   March   6   1711
Rich'd Eaton Son To Do Born   Feb'y   27   1694
Hanah Edwards Daug'r To Jonathon Born   Nov'r   25   1703
Isaac Edwards Son To Do Born   Oot'r   13   1709
Catherin Estin was Bap'd   Jan'y   26   1707
Wm Edwards Son To Wm Born   Apl   10   1703
Jo'n Edwards Son To Do Bap'd   June   5   1706
Mary Evans Daug'r To Ann Bap'd   Feb'y   20   1711
Mary & Rich'd Edwards Twins To Wm Born   Beb'y   21   1710
Nicholas Edwards Son To Nicholas Born   Ap'l   17   1698
Mary Edwards Daug'r To Jonathan Bap'd   Sep'r   23   1711
Isaac Edwards Son Te Isaac Bap'd   June   10   1711
John Edwards Son To Nicholas Born   Deo'r   23   1700
Mary Edwards Daug'r To Do Born   Ap'l   3   1704
Wm Edwards Son To Do Born   May   17   1706
Eliz Edwards Daug'r To Do Born   Sep'r   6   1708
Wm Edward son of Wm Born   Feb'y   26   1704
Jo'n Edwards Son To Do Born   Nov'r   10   1706
Eliza & Tho's Edwards Twins To Do Born   Deo'r   25   1709
Ralph Edwards Son To Do Born   Ap'l   10   1713
Jo'n Eaton Son To Jonathan Born   Jan'y   11   1714
Enoch Edwards Son To Wm Born   Jun   20   1715
Frances Edward Son To Do Born   Jun   15   1718
Ann Edwards Daug'r To Do Born   Jan'y   24   1722
Andrew Edwards Son To Do Born   Jully   2   1725
Mary Edwards Daug'r To Charles Born   Ap'l   6   1720
Wm Edwards Son To Do Born   Jan'y   27   1722
Ann Edwards Daug'r To Do Born   Jan'y   4   1726

Elizabeth Eliston Daug'r To Garves Born	Ap'l	22	1727
Wm Edwards Son To Jo'n Born	Dec'r	16	1728
Cuthbert Eliston Son To Garves Born	Nov	25	1730
Winifred Edwards Daug'r Wm Born	Feb'y	16	1728
Sarah Edwards Daug'r To Char's Born	July	8	1729
Ann Edwards Daug'r To Jo'n Born	Dec'r	20	1724
Eliza Edwards Daug'r To Jo'n Born	Jully	9	1729
Mary Edward Daug'r To Wm Born	Jan'y	3	1732
Jo'n Edwards Son To John Born	May	6	1732
Rich'd Edward Son To Cha's Born	Jan'y	23	1734
Briget Edward Daug'r To Wm	Feb'y	7	1735
Eliza Edwards Daug'r To Charles Born	May	10	1736
Isaac Edwards Son To Jo'n Edwards Born	Dec'r	28	1736
Tho's Edwards Son To Enuck Edward Born	Jan'y	1	1736
Mary Edwards Daug'r To William Born	Nov	16	1737
Zachariah Efford Son To Zachariah Born	Feb'y	13	1733

page 46 headed "E"

Catherine Efford Daug'r To Zachareah Born	Feb'y	9	1736
Eliz Efford Daug't To Do was Born	Ap'l	12	1738
Charles Edwards son To Chas Was Born	Nov'r	8	1739
William Edward Son To Wm Born	May	2	1740
Lewas Efford Son To Zach'h Born	Feb'y	28	1740
Sarah Edwards Daug'r To Wm Edwards	May	7	1741
Bette Edwards Daug'r To Ralph Born	Nov	28	1736
Wm Edwards Son To Do Born	June	26	1739
Mary & Ann Edwards Twins To Do Born	Oct	1	1741
Jonathan Edwards Son To John & Elizabeth was Born	March	27	1741
Sarah Edwards Daug'r To Do was Born	Sept	11	1743
Elizabeth Edwards Daug'r To Do was Born	Octob	12	1746
George Edwards Son To Do was Born	May	6	1748
Hannah Edwards Daug'r To Do was Born	June	6	1751
Elizabeth Edwards Daughter To John & Elizabeth Edwards was Born	July	5	1747
Hannah Edwards Daughter To John & Leannah Was Born	Dec	5	1750
Winifred Edwards Daug'r To Do was Born	Dec	15	1753
Pitman Edwards Son To Henry & Letty was Born	Febry	11	1755
Catherine Edwards Daug'r To John & Elisa was Born	May	1	1755
William Edwards Son To Enoch & Hannah was Born	June	23	1744
Betty Edwards Daug'r To Do was Born	May	23	1746
Molly Edwards Daug'r To Do was Born	Jany	1	1749
Thomas Edwards Son To Enoch Was Born	Jan'y	1	1736
Peter Rust Eskridge Son To William & Betty was Born	June	2-	1751
William Eskridge Son To Do was Born	March	10	1754
George Eskridge Son To Samuel was Born	Nov'r	3	1753
Charlotte Foushee Eskridge Daug'r To Do was Born	Aug't	22	1755
Thomas Eskridge Son To Wm & Betty Born	March	9	1757
Elias Edmunds Son To Wm & Ann Born	April	15	1757
William Edwards Son To John & Leannah was Born	Feb'ry	16	1757
Jane Edwards Daughter To John & Leannah was born	April	21	1760
Betty Shapleigh Elliston Daug'r to Cuthbert & Mary Elliston born	Octo	5	1750
John Shapleigh Elliston Son to Cuthb't & Mary Elliston born	April	6	1752

Cuthbert Elliston Son to Cuthb't & Mary
Elliston was born   Marc   5   1754
Hannah Shapleigh Elliston Dau to Cuthb't
& Mary Elliston born   Janry   25   1756
Molly Elliston Dau to Cuthb't & Mary Elliston born   May   16   1758
Enoch Edwards Son to Hannah Edwards was born   July   14   1761

page 47, headed "E".

George Edwards Son to Enoch & Hannah Edwards
was born   Febry   28   1758
Betsy Daughter of Robert & Ann Edwards was born   Jan   1   1767
William son of John & Mary Efford was born   March   17   1767
Katherine Edmonds Daughter to John & Jane
Edmonds was born   Novem   29   1756
Frances Edmond Daughter to John & Jane Edmonds
was born   Novem   1   1760
William Edmond son to John & Jane Edmond was born   Febry   14   1763
Bette Eskridge Daughter of Wm & Bette his Wife
was Born   Novmbr 29   1771
Elizabeth Efford Daughter of John & Mary his
wife was Born   Novmbr   2   1771
Angus Elexander son of Jesse & Mary his wife
was Born   January 7   1773
Robert Elexander Son of Jesse twins Born   January 7   1773
Molley Evans Daughter of Mark Evens Was Born   Augt   16   1772
Lucy Edwards Daughter of Johnnawthun &
Winnifrit his wife was born   Septembr 3   1772
Anne Evans Daughter of John Evans Jun'r &
Doraty his wife was born   August   8   1772
fannie Eskridge Daughter of John & franckey
his wife Was Born   March   23   1773
Frances Edwards Daughter of George Was Born   May   2   1773
lias Edwards son of George & Mary his wife was born   June   27   1773
Ann Eatson Daughter of Joseph & Rebakah his
wife was born   December 27   1773
Richard Swan Edward son of Ellis & Elizabeth
his wife was Born   January   4   1774
William Eskridge Son of William & Bettoy his
wife was Born   February 19   1774
George Efford son of Zacheriah Efford & Patience
his wife was Born   Septmbr 26   1779
Salley Pircefull Daughter of Bette Edwards Born   Septbr   6   1773
Molle Enis Daughter of tho's & Nelley his wife
was Born   April   9   1775
Robert Eskridge son of John & frances his wife
was born   February 3   1775
Winnefritt Eidson Daughter of Joseph & Rebeckah
his wife was Born   Octobr 30   1775
Thomas Efford son of Zachiah & winne Efford his
wife was born   Aprl   20   1776
John Hainnis Efford son of John Efford a
Bastard child was Born   July   6   1775
Bette Efford Daughter of Zacariah & Patiance
his wife was Born   Augt   27   1760

page 47 (continued)

Kattron Efford Daughter of Zacariah & Patience his wife was Born	March	3	1768
Lewis Efford Son of John & Catrine his wife was Born	January	1	1777
George Edwards Son of Georg & Molley his wife was Born	Septbr	20	1775
Salley Evens Daughter of Mark & Leanna his wife was born	August	27	1774
Jessey Hainney Son of Hannah Edwards Was Born	Novembr	20	1774
Judith Shappleigh Elliston Daughter of John S. & Bettey his wife ws born	March	1	1777
Haddeyway Hanie Elxander son of William & Dorcus his wife ws born	July	3	1777
Nancey Efford Daughter of John & Cathrine his wife was born	April	18	1778
Robert Edwards son of George & Molley his wife was born	April	25	1778
Nancey Edwards Daughter of Elles & Elizabeth his wife ws born	April	6	1778
James Blincoe Eidson Son to Joseph & Rebecah his wife was born	April	22	1778
Molley Edwards Saughter to Thomas & L- - his wife was born	July	20	1778
James Evins son to Mark Evins was born	Oct	27	1778
Richard Rice Efford son to Zachariah Efford & Winnefret his wife ws born	Novm	23	1778
John Shapleigh Elliston son to John S. E. & Bettey his wife was born	Decm	20	1778
John Edwards son to Hannah Edwards was born	Apr	27	1779
Catrine Efford Daughter to John & Catrine his wife was born	Jan'y	1	1780

page 48, headed "E".

Samuel Barnes Edson son to Creton & Winnefret his wife was born	Decm	19	1779
Nancey Austin Everit Daughter to William & Daughsey his wife was born	March	30	1780
Charles Bartin Elmore son to William & Mary his wife ws bn	June	10	1780
Sary Eskridge Daughter to George & Nelley his wife was born	Decm	11	1780
Joseph Eidson son to Joseph & Rebeckah his wife was born	June	1	1781
William Eidson son to Creighton & Winneyfret his wife was Born	Jan'y	21	1782
John Everit son to William & Winnifret his wife was born	Feb	10	1783
Bettey Eidson Daughter to Joseph & Rebeckah his wife ws born	Sept	25	1783
Winneyfret Davis Eidson Daughter to Creighton & & Winneyfret his wife was born	Oct	13	1783
Nancy Efford Daughter to Zachariah & Winney his wife ws born	Oct	12	1786
Leanner Edwards Daughter to John & Elizbeth his wife w.b.	July	6	1787

page 48 (continued)

William Conway Everit son to William & Winney his wife was born	Feb	23	1786
William Wilday Elmore son to Elizabeth Elmore a B child was born	May	19	1790
Sarah Everit Daughter to William & Winney his wife ws Born	Feb	10	1792
Fanny Elmore Daughter to John Elmore & Ellinder his wife ws bn	April	4	1795

page 49, headed "F".

Jean Flint Daug'r To Tho's Born	Feb'y	2	1681
Eliz'a Flint Daug'r To Rich'd Flint Born	Oct'r	9	1672
Mary Flint Daug'r To Do Born	May	14	1677
Rich'd Flint Son To Do Born	Feb'y	14	1673
Tho's Flint Son To Do Born	Jan'y	1	1680
Ambros Fielding Son To Edw'd Born	Jan'y	31	1689
Sarah Fielding Daug'r To Do Born	May	12	1695
Rachell Fielding Daug'r To Do Born	Sep'r	26	1697
Tho's Fielding Son To Do Born	Ap'l	22	1689
Meradith Flukar (?) Daug'r To Lawrence Bap'd	June	23	1716
Mary Fogle (?) Daug'r To Do was Bap'd	Jully	1	1720
Catherine Fauntleroy Daug'r To Griffen Born	Jan'y	16	1709
Moore Fauntleroy Son To Do Was Born	Jully	30	1711
Ann Fauntleroy Daug'r To Do Born	Dec'r	29	1713
Wm Fauntleroy Son To Do Born	Aug't	17	1718
Judith Floyd Daug'r To Jo'n Born	Jan'y	7	1712
John Fipps Son To Jo'n Was Born	Feb'y	4	1714
Eliz'a Flaningham Daug'r To Francis Born	Sept'r	9	1700
Mary Flaninghan Daug'r To Do Born	March	9	1702
Ann Flaningham Daug'r To Do Born	Sep'r	28	1705
Frances Flaningham Daug'r To Do Born	Aug'r	9	1707
Benj'm Flaningham Son To Do Born	March	28	1710
Tho's Flaningham Son To Do Born	Feb'y	19	1712
Jane Flaningham Daug'r To Do Born	Oct'r	-	1715
Mary Fushee Daug'r To Jo'n Was Born	Aug't	19	1719
John Flaningham Son To Fra's Born	Jan'y	29	1721
Rob't Foster Son To Wm Born	Oct'r	7	1711
Isaac Foster Son To Do Born	Jully	2	1719
Edmond Foge Son To Laurence Born	Nov	27	1721
Judith Foley Daug'r To Catharin Born	Feb'y	15	1722
John Foster Son To Benj'm Born	Feb'y	21	1729
Samuell Wallas Ferguson son Catherin	Feb'y	14	1723
Ja's Fushe Son To To'n Born (sic)	July	27	1729
Sophia Fushe Daug'r To Do Born	Nov'r	24	1731
Ann Fogg Daug'r To Aaron Fogg	Feb'y	17	1732
Lamkin Foster Son To Edward	Oct'r	19	1723
Mary Ann Foster Daug'r To Do Born	Nov'r	13	1725
Nany Foster Daug'r To De Born	Jully	29	1727
Eve Foster Daug'r To Do Born	Dec	24	1729

page 50, headed "F".

Eliz'a Fushe Daug'r To To'n Born	Nov	9	1733
Sarah Fogg Daug'r To Israell Born	May	4	1739
Levenah Fointain Daug'r To Elliz'a Born	Dec'r	28	1739
John Fling Son To Hannah Born	Nov'r	25	1734
Mary Ann Fointain Daug'r To James Born	Aug't	26	1743
Wm Fointain Son To Do Born	Feb'y	5	1745
Mary Fausit Daug'r To Wm & Sarah Born	Nov'm	30	1749
Agatha Fallin Daug'r To Wm & Eliz'a Born	Dece'r	18	1749
William & Catherine Fauntleroy Senette Twins to Mary Senette Born	May	15	1749
(Note: Introduced here in a later hand is, "was Born the 27 Day 1776")			
Griffin Fauntleroy Son To Bushrode Born m	Sepbr	28	1754
John Foushee Born	Dec'm	21	1754
Joseph Fitzgifferies Son to James & Sarah Ann was Born	Feb'ry	7	1755
Sarah Fauntleroy Daug'r To Griffin & Judy was Born	March	17	1756
Winney France Daug'r To John was Born	March	10	1757
John Flint son to Thomas & Ann Born	May	14	1757
Betty Flint Daughter to Thomas & Ann Flint was born	Decemb	9	1758
Nancy Flint Daug'r To Thomas & Ann Born	Nov	23	1760
Cuddie Flint Son To Thomas & Ann Born	May	26	1763
Katy Hill Folks Daug'r To William & Nanny Folks was Born	July	10	1762
Thomas Flynt Son To John & Chloe Flynt Born	Jan'ry	29	1765
Betty Flint Daughter to John & Chloe Flint was born	Septemb	27	1766
Griffin Forerker son Droget & Do Born	April	30	1766
Elisabeth Fallin Daug'r To Charles & Hannah Fallen his wife was born	March	25	1772
Ann France Daughter of Rhodham & Elizabeth his wife was born	Aprill	8	1773
John Firds Son of Jemimah fords was born	December	25	1773
Winnefrit Fallen Daughter of Charles & Hannah his wife was born	febry	5	1773
John Fallen son to Charles & Hannah his wife was born	Sepbr	5	1773
Nancy Fallen Daughter of Elisha & Sarah his wife was born	January	21	1774
William France son of George & Hannah France was born	Aug't	16	1775
Charlotte Fulchor was Born	Feb'y	15	1777
Mary Fallen Daughter of Charles & Hannah his wife was born	June	6	1775
Judith France Daughter of George & Hannah his wife was born	June	27	1777
Richard Flint son of John Flint was Born	July	18	1777
Nancey France Daughter to John & Sarah his wife was born	Sep't	4	1778
Samuel France son to George & Hannah his wife was born	Dec'm	15	1778
Jean Fallin Daughter to Elisha & Sarah his wife was born	March	3	1779
Nancey Payne Fulks Daughter to William & Lucey his wife ws bn	Nov'm	30	1779
John Foushee Son To James Born July 3 1753			
Frederick Foushee Son To Do Born	Dec	21	1754

page 50 (continued)

Ann Fulcher Daughter to William & Elizabeth his wife was born	Dec'm	5	1779
Elizabeth Futcher Daughter to William & Elizabeth his wife ws bn (sic)	May	21	1781
John France son to John & Sarah his wife was Born	April	14	1782
Stephen Flint son to Samuell & Patty his wife was born (page 51 begins)	March	24	1783
William & Obadiah Fulcher twins sons to William & Elizabeth his wife was born	Oct	4	1782
Elizabeth Griffin Foushee Daughter to Frederick & Ann his wife was born	June	10	1783
Thomas France son to John & Salley his wife was born	Dece'm	20	1784
George France son to James & Saraan his wife was born	March	13	1785
John Fulks son to William & Lucy his wife was born	May	11	1785
Winney Foushee Daughter to Frederick & Ann his wife was born	Jan'r	5	1787
Jeremiah France son to James & - - his wife was born	June	30	1787
Sarah France Daughter to John & Salley his wife was born	Nov'm	8	1787
James Fulcher son to William & Rhoda his wife was Born	Aug't	21	1787
Charles Lovelas Fulks son to William & Lucey his wife was Born	Nov'm	5	1787
Elizabeth Lovelys Fulks Daughter to Ditto & Ditto was Born	April	1	1794

page 52, headed "F".

Edward Fealding Son To Ed'wd Born	June	2	1666
Ann Feilding Daug'r To Do Born	Jan'y	7	1668
Ambroso Feilding Son To Do Born (sic)	May	17	1671
Adam Foster Son To Jo's Born	Aug't	9	1672
Mary Fallin Daug't To Wm Born	Sept	17	1672
Rich'd Feilding Son To Ed'wd Born	March	5	1675

page 53, headed "F".

Salley Fallin Daughter to Dennis and Ellinner his wife was Born	Decembr	26	1769
Harcom fallin son of Elisha Fallin & Sarah his wife was born	April	8th	1770
Richard Fuller son of William & Susaner his wife was born	April	12	1770
David Flint Son of John flint & Clohe his wife was born	May	5	1770
Hannah forda Daughter to Jemima forday Born	December	22	1769
William forday son to Jegemina was Born	December	22	1769
John fisher Son of Willeby fisher Mary kelley was Born	April	7	1762

page 53 (continued)

Sary fallin Daughter of John Fallin & Millison Edwards was Born	March	15	1771
Tignor fallen the Son of Elisha fallin was Born	Feb'r	2	1772
Tho's Fallen Son of Wm fallen & Sary his wife was Born	Novembr	26	1771
Presley France son to James & Sarah his wife was Born	Dec'em	26	1790
William Fulks son to William & Lucey his wife was Born	April	26	1790
James France son to John & Sarah his wife was Born	Jan'r	8	1792
James France son to James & Kessiah his wife was Born	Jan'r	17	1794
Griffin Henry Foushee son to John H. Foushee & Nancy his wife was Born	January	25	1793
John Mcalos France son to John France & Sara his wife was	July	13	1796
Elizabeth Linsa France Daughter to George France & Ann his wife was Born	February	14	1795
Jean France Daughter to John France & Elizabeth was Born	July	5	1807

page 54, headed "F".

William flint Son to John & Clohe flint his wife was Born	February	4	1773
frances fallen Daughter to William & Sary his wife was born	January	3	1775

page 55, headed "G".

Jean Grinsted Daug'r To Jo'n Was Born	May	28	1680
Racholl Grinsted Daug'r To Do Was Born	Decem	1	1683
Ann Grinsted Daug'r To Do Was Born	Aug't	12	1677
Tho's Grinsted Son To Do Was Born	Dec'm	29	1679
John Grinsted Son To Do Was Born	Jan'y	20	1681
Eliz'a Grinsted Daug'r To Do Was Born	Jan'y	18	1689
Eliz'a Grady Daug'r To Walter Born	Dec'r	10	1679
Ann Gradey Daug'r To Do Born	Dec'r	22	1681
Wm Gradey Son To Do Born	March	22	1683
Farnsfield Green Son To Timothy Green Born	May	30	1674
Titus Green Son To Do Born	Nov'r	27	1676
John Gralis Son To Jo'n Born	Aug'r	29	1690
Susana Gwen Daug'r To Christopher Born	Feb'y	9	1695
Mary Greenstoed Daug'r To Wm Born	Ap'l	15	1694
Adam Grinsted Son To Do Born	Oct'r	14	1684
Susana Grinsted Daug'r To Do Born	Jan'y	21	1712
Hannah Grinsted Daug'r To Do Born	June	26	1716
John Grinsted Son To Do Born	March	4	1718
Ignatius Groves Son To George Born	March	5	1698
Eliz'a Gaskins Daug'r To Henry Born	Marc	31	1681
Mary Gaskins Daug'r To Do Born	May	21	1683
Tho's Gaskins Son To Do Born	Sep'r	22	1685
Francos Gaskins Son To Do Born	Aug't	6	1693
Rich'd Gaskins Son To Do Born	Jully	17	1698

page 55 headed   "G".

Tho's Gill Son To Tho's Born	Sep'r	20	1692
Rich'd Gill Son To Do Born	March	10	1699
Sarah Gill Daug'r To Do Born	Ap'l	29	1707
Dinah Gill Daug'r To Do Born (Daug'r To Wm ?)	Jan'y	25	1708
John Gralls Son To John Born	Jully	10	1692
Eliz'a Gater Daug'r To Math'w Born	Ap'l	23	1711
Sarah Gater Daug'r To Do Born	Sept'r	16	1714
Jo'n Gater Son To Do Born	Nov'r	18	1716
Joseph Gater Son To Jo's Born	Jan'y	30	1708
Samuell Gairner Son To Parish Born	Jan'y	9	1710
Mary Ann Gairner Daug'r To Do Born	Jan'y	29	1707
George Gairner Son To Do Born	Jully	29	1704
Parish Gairner Son To Do Born	Jan'y	21	1705
Wm Gairner Son To Do Born	Jan'y	23	1707
Ja's Gell Son To Dav'd Bap'd	Ap'l	27	1712
Susann Gairner Daug'r To Ja's Born	Jan'y	30	1711
Ja's Gairner Son To Do Born	Jully	15	1714
Jo'n Gairner Son To Do Born	Aug't	16	1716
Judith Ginn Daug'r To Ja's Born	Oct'r	29	1713
Mary Ginn Daug'r To Do Born (While this date is actually shown as 1616 it doubtless should be 1716)	Mar	28	1616
Griffethell Gin Daug'r To Tho's Born	Ap	19	1714
Ja's & Mary Ginn Twins To Do Born	Jan'y	12	1715
Jane Gebins Daug'r To Moris Born	De'or	9	1716

page 65, headed "G".

Eliza Grinsteed Daug'r To Tho's Born	Sep't	6	1712
Jo'n Grinsted Son To Pitter Born	Oct'r	11	1712
George Gamewell Son Laurance Born	Oct'r	12	1712
Laurence Gamewell Son To Do Born	Feb'y	29	1714
Sarah Grimsted Daug'r To Eliza Born	Sept	5	1715
Rich'd Gilmet Son To Rich'd Born	March	26	1718
Tho's Ginn Son To Tho's Born	March	14	1718
Ja's Ginn Son To Ja's Born	Aug't	27	1718
Nanny Gairner Daug'r To Ja's Born	Jan'y	27	1718
George Grinsted Son To Wm Born	Feb'y	16	1719
Wm Gairner Son To Jo'n Born	Feb'y	3	1718
Jo'n Ginn Son To Tho's Born	Apl	26	1721
Sarah Gilberd Daug'r To Mary Born	Jan'y	7	1718
John Robinson Gilbert son to Do Born	Ap'l	28	1721
Frances Gairner Daug'r To Ja's Born	Jan'y	18	1721
Isaac Gaskins son to Jo'n Born	Ap'l	2	1722
Daniell Gime Son To Jo'n Born	Oct'r	17	1702
Jane Grensted Daug To Wm Born	Dec'r	29	1722
Eliz Frances Gaskins Daug'r To Hen'y Born	March	15	1724
Eliz Gaskins Daug'r To Jo'n Born	Oct'r	1	1725
Tho's Gilbert Son To Mary Born	Aug't	20	1724
Jo'n Gill Son To Tho's Gill Ju'r Born	Feb'y	10	1726
Tho's Gill Son To Do Born	Aug't	16	1724
George Ginn Son To Tho's Born	Dec'r	13	1729
Mary Gimell Daug'r To Laurence Born	Aug't	24	1729
Jo'n Gimwell Son To Do Born	De'r	23	1730

page 56 (continued)

Isaac Gaskins Son To Fran's Born	Sep'r	19	1730
Elles Gill Son of Tho's Ju'r Born	June	22	1732
Leannah Grensted Daug'r To Wm Born	Aug't	26	1731
Tho's Ginn Son To Tho's Born	March	5	1733
Leanah Gaskins Daug'r To Fra's Born	Jan'y	2	1733
Martha Ann Grensted Daug'r To Wm Born	Feb'y	2	1733
Mary Gater Daug'r To Math'w Born	Nov'r	15	1721
Ann Gater Daug'r To Do Born	Sep'r	1	1725
Jo'n Gemuell Son To George Born	Ap'l	4	1734
Judith Geddes Daug'r To Ja's Geddis Born	Nov'r	12	1734
Jesse Gaskins Son To Fra's Born	Sep'r	1	1737
Sarah Gately Daug'r To Ja's Born	Ap'l	30	1739
Tho's Gaskins Son To Jo'n Born	Aug't	12	1742
Jo'n Gregs Son To Ja's Born	May	25	1742
Joseph Gibson Son to George Born	Ma	21	1744
Samuell Gater Son To Jo'n Born	Dec'r	10	1744

page 57, headed "G".

William Genn Son To Tho's & Ann Born	May	19	1745
Jo'n Gaskins Son To Jo'n & Israell Born	Nov'r	20	1746
Jo'n Gater Son To Jo'n & Grace Born	May	4	1748
Wm Gaskins son to Eliza Born	Dec'r	27	1744
Wm Gill Son To Tho's & Ester Born	Sep't	30	1750
Jesse Gaskins Son To Israell & a Bastard Born	May	19	1752
James Garner son to James & Mary was Born	Sept	6	1748
Winifred Gill Daug'r To Ellis Jun'r was Born	Jan'ry	15	1753
John Gill Son To Do was Born	April	12	1754
John Gaimwell Son To John & Eliz'a was Born	Sep'br	19th	1754
Sarah Gater Daug'r To John & Grace was Born	Dec'r	23	1749
Sarah Gater Daug'r To John & Grace was Born	Dec'r	25	1750
Hannah & Elinor Garners Twins To Samuel & Jean were Born	June	11	1755
Edwin Gaskins Son To John was Born	Feb'ry	9	1755
Mary Ann Gill Daug'r To Thomas was Born	Aug'st	2	1751
Leannah Gill Daug'r To Do was Born	Jan'ry	19	1753
Thomas Gill Son To Do was Born	Dec'r	14	1755
John Graham & Ann Metcalf were Married (prob.1747)	July	20	1741
John Graham Son To Do was Born	Sept	28	1748
William Graham Son To Do was Born	Oct'r	13	1750
Ann Graham Wife To John Died	Nov'r	9	1750
Sarah Gill Daug'r To John was Born	March	5	1757
Ellis Gill Son To Ellis Jun'r was Born	Sep'br	10	1756
Elizabeth Gill Daughter to John & Eliz'a Gill was born	May	19	1759
Jacob Gill Son to Ellis Gill Ju'r & Sarah Gill was born	March	13	1758
Margaret Gill Daughter to John & Elizabeth Gill was born	Feb'ry	10	1760
John Gaskins Son To John & Sarah Gaskins was born	Jan'ry	8	1758
Isaac Gaskins Son to John & Sarah Gaskins was born	June	15	1761
Esther Gill Daughter to Thomas & Esther Gill was born	May	5	1757
Chloe & Nancy Gill Twins Daughters to Thomas & Esther Gill was born	April	28	1760
Winde Gill Son to Wm & Ann Gill was born	Decemb	1	1759

page 57, (continued).

William Gill Son to Wm & Ann Gill was born	Decemb	23	1761
Thomas Gill Son to John & Elizabeth Gill was born	March	15	1763
Betty Gill Daughter to Ellis Gill Ju'r & Leannah his wife was born	June	4	1764
Michael Gilbert Son to William & Susannah Gilbert was born	April	8	1765
John Bailes Gill Son to Thomas & Esther Gill was born	February	4	1762
Daniel Gill Son To Thomas & Esther Gill was born	February	14	1765

page 58, headed "G".

Edwin Gill Son to William & Ann Gill was born	Feb'ry	23	1764
Ann Daughter of Richard & Winny Grinsted was born	Feb	5	1767
Thomas Gill Son to Ellis & Leannah was born	Feb'ry	28	1769
Nancey Grigs the Daughter of Charles & Elizabeth his wife was born	January	3	1772
William Eskridge Garland son of Vincent & Mary his wife was born	August	31	1771
Pegge Grigs Daughter of Mary Grigs was born	Novmbr	8	1771
Sammuel Greensted Son of John & Margot his wife was born	March	27	1779
Sary tune Griffis Daughter of George & Mary his wife was Born	May	6	1772
Mary Greensted Daughter of Richard & Winnifret his wife was Born	Decembr	9	1772
Bettey Gill Daughter of Wm Ju'r & Salley Gill his wife was born	Novmbr	25	1774
Thomas Gill Son of Elliss & Leanner his wife was born	April	28	1774
Rebeckah Greensted Daughter to Richard & Winne his wife was born	Aprill	15	1775
Jeney Greenstreet Daughter of John & Margrat his wife was born	Sep'r	8	1775
Mary Garner the Daughter of Jesse & Bette his wife born	Sept'r	14	1775
Rachel Green the Daughter of Tho's & Ann his wife was born	Decembr	2	1775
William the Son of Ann Gill a bastard child was Born	March	22	1776
Bettey Garner the Daughter of George Smith & Nancey Garner a bastard child was born	February	17	1776
Easter Galaway Daughter of George & Milley his wife was born	March	2	1776
William Garlant Garner Son of Richard & Ann his wife was Born Sonday morning	March	10	1775
Rodham Griffin Son of Ann Gill a Bastard Child was born	March	22	1776
Parrish Garner Son of Wm Parker Garner Was Born	June	23	1776
Lucy Gill Daughter of William & Salley his wife born	May	27	1776
Richard Gill Son of William & Ann his wife was born	Octobr	14	1775

page 58 (continued)

Thomas Gill son of Ellis & Leanner his wife was Born	Sept	19	1777
Winnah Greenstreet Daughter of Rich'd & Winnah his wife ws born	Feb'r	7	1778
Thomas Gill son of William & Salley his wife was Born	March	3	1778
Josiah Galesbory son to Robert & Margret his wife ws born	May	20	1778
Ann Graham Daughter to William & - - was born	-	-	1778
Lucey Garner Daughter to William T Garner & - - ws born	Dec'm	8	1778
Bettey Shadburn Goff Daughter to Benjamin & Winney his wife ws born	Nov'm	20	1778
Shapley Terrey Gill son to Bettey Gill was born	Nov'm	8	1778
Elles Gill son to John & Winnefret his wife was born	June	4	1779
George Garner son to Ann Garner a Bas't child was Born	July	26	1779
Marget Garner Daughter to Jesse & Betty his wife was Born	Feb	25	1780
Martha Grinstead Daughter to Richard & Winney his wife ws bn	Aug't	5	1780
Molley Griffith Daughter to Henry ws Born	Novm	10	1781
Jesse Garner son to Jesse & Betty His wife was born	Dec'r	3	1782
John Grinstead son to Richard & Winney his wife was born	March	19	1783
George Griffis son to George was born	March	22	1783

page 59, headed "G".

Samuel Garner son to James & Susannah his wife was born	Feb	21	1785
Molley Gaskins Daughter to Jesse & Susannah his wife was born	Feb	26	1785
James Claughton Gill son to William Claughton & Salley Gill was born	Dec'm	10	1784
Benjamin Grinstead son to Richard & Winne his wife ws born	April	14	1785
William Everit Garner son to Jesse & Betty his wife was born	April	12	1786
Samuel Humphris Garner son to James & Susannah his wife was born	Nov'm	21	1786
George Brown Son of Charles & Susannah his Wife was Born	March	1	1787
Lawson Williams Garner son to Jesse & Betty his wife was Born	June	30	1789
James Garner son to James & Susannah his wife was Born	Nov'm	11	1789
Nancey Green Daughter to John & Judith his wife was Born	April	10	1790
John Robuck Gibbins son to Thomas & Elizabeth Gibbins his wife was Born	August	28	1791
Salley Garner Daughter to James & Susannah his wife Was Born	Dec'm	28	1793

page 60 headed "G".

James Grinsted Son of John Grinsted & Margit his wife was born	June	8	1769
Spencer Garner Son of Jeremiah Garner & Darcas his wife was born	April	4	1770
Mary Garner Daughter of William Rice & Ann Garner was Born	December	5	1770
Winne Gill Daughter of Ellis & leanner Gill his wife was Born	January	28	1772
Susanna Rausch Griggs Daughter to William & Hannah Griggs his wife was Born	Feb	7	1792
Rebeckah Garner Daughter to James Garner & Susannah his wife was Born	Nov'm	10	1797

page 61 headed "H".

John Heasell Son To Wm Born	Sep'r	29	1684
James Harrel Son To Gilbert Born	May	3	1679
Mary Harrel Daug'r To Do Born	March	25	1680
Gilbert Harrel Son To Do Born	March	25	1682
Sarah Howard Daug'r To Wm Born	Feb'y	25	1672
John Hopper Son To Tho's Born	Aug't	15	1669
Tho's Hopper Son To Do Born	Ap'l	15	1677
Eliz Hopper Daug'r To Do Born	May	17	1679
Stephen Hall Son To To's Born	Oct'r	5	1675
Jo'n Hall Son To Do Born	Sep't	3	1680
Mary Hall Daug'r To Step'n Born	Sep't	21	1704
Tho's Hall Son To Do Born	March	15	1681
Ann Hall Daug'r To Do Born	Jan'r	17	1709
Tho's Hall Son To Do Born	Jan'y	30	1713
Mary Hall Daug'r To Stepen Born	Sep'r	25	1704
Margaret Hall Daug'r To Do Born	Jan'y	13	1706
Catherin Hall Daug'r To Do Born	Oct'r	2	1709
Laurance Hall Son To Do Born	Aug't	12	1711
Stephen Hall Son To Do Born	March	6	1714
Tho's Harding Son To Tho's Born	Sep'r	4	1664
William Harding Son To Do Born	Jully	20	1669
Tho's Harding Son To Tho's Jun'r Born	Feb'y	21	1710
Wm Harding Son To Do Born	Feb'y	15	1690
Cha's Frances Harding Twins To Wm Born	Jully	2	1704
John a Bastard by Phebee	Jully	26	1704
Tho's Harding Son To Wm Born	Feb'y	2	1706
Tho's Hickman Son To Tho's	Jan'y	19	1669
Mary Hackins Daug'r To Jo'n Born	Aug't	13	1677
Jo'n Hackins Son To Do Born	Jully	6	1680
Ephriam Hughlet Son To Jo'n Born	Dec'r	23	1686
Garret Hughlet Son To Do Born	No'v	25	1695
Eliz Hughlet Daug'r To Do Born	Dec'r	21	1697
Wm Hughlet Son To Do Born	Jun	23	1689
Jo'n Hughlet Son To Do Born	Aug't	7	1684
Partin Hughlet Son To Do Born	Nov'r	17	1700
Partin Hudnell Son To Hen'y Born	Dec'r	23	1686
Ann Hudnell Daug'r To Do Born	Mar'h	14	1691
Joseph Hudnell Son To Jo'n Born	Feb'y	4	1675
Jo'n Hudnell Son To Do Born	Ap'l	10	1679
Rich'd Hudnell To Do Born	Nov'r	1	1689

page 62, headed "H".

Deborah Hudnell Daug'r To Jo'n Born	Nov'r	7	1682
Jo'n Hudnell Son To Do Born	Ap'l	10	1679
Ann Hudnell Daug'r To Do Born	March	14	1703
Tho's Hilman Son To Tho's Born	March	20	1689
George Heartley Son To Hen'y Born	Feb'y	14	1680
Bridget Heartley Daug'r To Do Born	Aug'r	8	1691
Eliz'a Haynie Daug'r To Rich'd Born	Dec'r	8	1686
Maximolian Haynie Son To Do Born	Oct'r	31	1688
Elliner Hayne Daug'r To Do Born	Sep't	2	1708
Cha's Hayne Son To Do Born	Jan'y	23	1710
Mary Hayne Daug'r To Jo'n Born	Nov'r	3	1702
Wm Hayne Son To Do Born	Nov'r	5	1704
Winneff'd Hayne Daug'r To Do Born	Ap'l	7	1706
Sarah Hayne Daug'r To Do Born	May	11	1718
Bette Hughlet Daug'r To Ephriam Born	Sep'r	13	1711
Tho's Hughlet Son To Do Born	Oct'r	4	1715
Sarah Hull Daug'r To Rich'd Born	Dec'r	18	1680
Mary Hull Daug'r To Do Born	Dec'r	12	1682
Rich'd Hull Son To Do Born	Ap'l	14	1685
Rich'd Hull Son To Rich'd Jun'r Born	Aug't	4	1709
Sarah Hull Daug'r To Do Born	Nov'r	25	1706
Wm Hull Son To Do Born	Aug't	31	1713
Hen'y Halcomb Son To Wm Born (sic)	Oct'r	12	1680
Wm Halcomb Son To Do Born (sic)	Feb'y	2	1707
Samuell Halcomb Son To Do Born (sic)	Dec'r	31	1703
Eliz'a Halcomb Daug'r To Do Born	Feb'y	2	1707
Mary Harald Daug'r To Walter Born	Aug't	22	1682
Nicholus Harald Son To Do Born	Oct'r	15	1684
Sarah Harald Daug'r To Do Born	Ap'l	17	1687
Nicolus Hack Son To Peter Born	May	28	1687
Hannah Hack Daug'r To Do Born	March	27	1692
Peter Hack Son To Do Born	March	26	1695
Ann Heck Daug'r To Do Born	Jully	18	1696
Spencer Hek Son To Do Born	Feb'y	11	1700
Eliz'a Mary Hack Daug'r To Do Born	Ap'l	2	1703
Rosamond Herwood Daug'r To Tho's Born	Ap'l	2	1693
Tho's Hobson Son To Tho's Born	Aug't	30	1694
Sara Hobson Daug'r To Do Born	Oct	13	1698
Wm Hobson Son To Do Born	Ap'l	28	1700
Jo'n Hobson Son To Do Born	March	4	1701
Eliz Hobson Daug'r To Do Born	Oct'r	14	1698
Lety Sina Hobson Daug'r To Do Born	May	22	1712
Jo'n Hanks Son To George Born	Aug't	7	1694
Ann Hackens Daug'r To Jo'n Born	Sep't	15	1695
Jo'n Hackens Son To Do Born (evidently 1698)	March	27	1798
Nicolis Hughlet Son To Ephriam Born	Apl	18	1716

page 63, headed "H".

Jo'n Haskins son Thomas Was Born	Oct'r	11	1696
Caglin Hunter son To Allen Born	Jan'y	25	1713
Ann Husk Daug'r To Jo'n Born	Oct'r	25	1696
Susanna Husk Daug'r To Do Born	Dec'r	16	1699
Rebecka Husk Daug'r To Do Born	March	20	1702
Jo's Husk Son To Do Born	March	18	1704
Mary Hays Daug'r To Tho's Born	Jully	5	1696
Eliz'a Hays Daug'r To Do Born	Mar	25	1703
Sarah Hays Daug'r To Do Born	Sep'r	29	1706

page 63 (continued)

Jo'n Hall Son To Do Born	Jan'y	12	1706
Wm Hall Son To Do Born	Oct'r	22	1703
Gilber Harrell Son To Mary Born	Jan'y	22	1711
George Haydon Son To George Born	Sep'r	30	1711
Ja's Hadwell Son To Jo'n Born	Sep'r	19	1711
Peter Herdum Son To Eliz'a Born	Oct'r	18	1693
Tho's Harding Son To Wm Born	Oct'r	6	1717
George Hughlet Son To Ephra Born	Nov'r	3	1718
Judith Hughlet Daug'r To Yarrat Born	Sep'r	26	1718
Eliz'a Heartley Daug'r To Jo'n Born	March	18	1719
Mary Hughlet Daug'r To Ephriam Born	March	23	1720
Martha Hall Daug'r To Stephen Born	March	21	1720
Parton Hudnell Son To Parton Born	May	5	1720
Yeanne Hudson Daug'r To Rob't Born	Aug't	25	1720
Jo'n Hughlet Son To yarret Born	Feb'y	27	1719
Jo'n Henry Son To Jo'n Born	Aug't	16	1720
Juddayda Harding Daug'r To Wm Born	Jully	16	1721
Jo'n Herrell Son To John Born	Mar	10	1716
Wm Herrell Son To Do Born	Oct'r	13	1720
Eliz Hickman Daug'r To Tho's Born	Nov'r	25	1719
Winif'd Hall Daug'r To Stephen Born	Jan'y	29	1721
Jo'n Huerdom Son Peter Born	March	31	1722
Ann Hughlet Daug'r Yerret Born	Dec'r	26	1721
Ja's Harrell Son To Ja's Born	No'r	29	1719
Gilbert Harell Son To Do Born	Oct'r	14	1721
Mary Hickman Daug'r To Tho's Born	March	19	1722
To's Hunter Son To Wm Mason B as Born	Oct'r	21	1704
Jo'n Humpres Son To Jo's Born	No'r	8	1702
Shadreck Hadwell Son To Jo'n Born	Aug't	1	1723
Jo'n Hudnell Son To Jo'n Born	Aug't	31	1723
Tho's Harris Son To Wm Born	Sep'r	26	1720
Rob't Harris Son To Do Born	Dec'r	6	1723
Peter Hays Son To Tho's Born	March	16	1725
Uraya Hayne Son To Maxamillian Born	Feb'y	14	1721
Meso'n Hayne Son To Do Born	Oct'r	21	1723
Ezekaaya Hughs Son To Ja's Born	Jan'y	9	1726
Prudence Hays Daug'r To Tho's Born	Jan'y	4	1727
Winif'd Hayne Daug'r To Tho's Born	Feb'y	21	1718

page 64, headed "H".

Mary Hayne Daug'r To Do Was Born	Nov'r	20	1720
Math'w Hayne Son To Do Was Born	Nov	4	1723
Spencer Hayne Son To Do Born	March	9	1728
Winif'd Humprey Daug'r To Jo'n Born	Jan'y	9	1728
Jo's Hunter Son To Jo's Born	Sep'r	10	1728
Jo'n Hayne Son To Wm Born	Jully	22	1727
Maxa'm Hayne Son To Hen'y Born	July	9	1719
Jo'n Hayne Son To Do Born	May	26	1723
Winiff'd Hayne Daug'r To Do Born	Ma	27	1725
Eliz'a Hayne Daug'r To Maxami'n Born	Jully	20	1725
Mary Hicks Daug'r To Tho's Born	May	26	1730
Spencer Hughes Son To Ja's Born	May	23	1730
Nathaniell Hudnell Son To Jo'n Born	Aug't	11	1725
Wm Haynee Son To Wm Born	Oct'r	21	1729

Sarah Hobson Daug'r To Wm Born	May	29	1725
Judith Hobson Daug'r To Do Born	Dec'r	9	1727
Jo'n Hobson son To Do Born	Ap'r	13	1730
Eliza Holcombe Daug'r To Wm Born	May	25	1716
Wm Harcome Son To Do Born	No'r	30	1718
Tho's Harcome Son To Do Born	June	22	1723
Prudene Harcom Daug'r To Do Born	Aug't	11	1725
Hannah Harcom Daug'r To Do Born	Oct'r	30	1728
Winifred Harcom Daug'r To Tho's Born	Nov'r	26	1721
Tho's Harcom Son To Do Born	Nov'r	30	1723
Bette Harcom Daug'r To Do Born	Dec'r	30	1725
Jo'n Harcom Son To Do Born	Ap'l	24	1728
Eliz'a Hays Daugh'r To Tho's Born	June	8	1731
Ja's Harcom Son To Wm Born	Aug't	22	1731
Sarah Hudnell Daug'r To Jo'n Born	Oct'r	21	1731
Ellayjah Humphres Son To Jo's Born	Mar	19	1726
Sarah Humphres Daug'r To Do Born	Jan'y	-	1727
Bette Humphres Daug'r To Do Born	Dec'r	31	1730
Diana Humphres Daug'r To Do Born	Oct'r	6	1731
Rosana Hearald Daug'r To Ja's & Mary Born	Dec'r	24	1731
Hull Chesla Hill Son To Wm	Dec'r	24	1731
Jo's Humphries Son To Jo'n Born	March	16	1732
Tho's Hickman Son To Tho's Born	Ap'l	9	1732
Mary Ann Hobson Daug'r To Wm Born	June	17	1732
Bettee Hughs Daug'r To Ja's Born	Dec'r	8	1732
Jemayma Hayno Dag'r To Tho's Born	Sep'r	4	1730
Jedayde Hayne Daug'r To Do Born	Dec'r	10	1733
Jo'n Harcom Son To Wm Born	Jan'y	18	1733
Elliner Hayne Daug'r To Jo's Born	Oct'r	3	1732

page 65 headed "H".

Hanah Hayne Daug'r To Wm Born	De'r	25	1731
Jo'n Hayne Son To Jo'n Born	Apl	26	1733
Peter Hayne Son To Isaac Born	Dec'r	17	1733
Henry Hayne Son To Hen'y Born	Nov'r	21	1730
Abner Hayne Son To Do Born	Jan'y	1	1734
Senna Hayne Daug'r To Tho's Born	Dec'r	16	1734
Bridget Hayne Daug'r To Do Born	Jan'y	12	1734
Sara Heays Daug'r To Peter Born	Jan'y	25	1735
Jo'n Harding Son To Tho's Born	Ap'l	21	1734
Sara Ann Holcombe Daug'r To Wm	Jan'y	11	1735
Alx'r Hayne Son To Jacob Born	De'r	13	1734
Mary Hill Daug'r To Luck Born	Jully	22	1735
Bettie Hobson Daug'r To Wm Born	Feb'y	8	1736
Francis Hague Son To Jo's Born	Jan'y	15	1736
Tho's & Frances Harding Twins To Tho's Born	Sep't	9	1737
Jo's Hudnell Son To Jo's Born	June	6	1737
Rich'd Hull Son To Rich'd Born	Ap'l	13	1717
Wm Hayne Son To Isaac Born	Sep'r	29	1737
Eliz'a Hill Daug'r To Lucke Born	Aug't	3	1737
Jesie Hayne Son To Benj'n Born	March	2	1738
Joseph Hayne Son To Wm Born	Dec'r	13	1739
Ann Hull Daug'r To Rich'd Hull Born	Jan'y	14	1739/40
Eliz'a Hayne Daug'r To Stephen Born	Dec'r	25	1739
Mary Hays Daug'r To Peter Born	De'r	8	1737
Cha's Hays Son To Do Born	Feb'y	3	1740

page 65 (continued)

Lucretia Hill Daug'r To Looke Born	Mar	26	1740
George Hayes Son To Thos Born	Febry	26	1739
Jo's Hays Son To Jo'n Born	May	19	1740
Jacob Hayne Son To Do Born	Oct'r	30	1740
Frances Hudnell Daug'r To Rich'd	Jan'y	12	1741
Grace Hayne Daug'r To Isaac Born	Nov'r	4	1740
Georg Humfres Son To Jo'n Born	Jully	27	1741
Ja's Hill Son To Luke Born	March	5	1742
Ellis Hudnell Son To Jo's Born	Jan'y	10	1741
Gaskins Hayes Son To Tho's Born	Ap'l	19	1742
Rich'd Hull Son To Rich'd Born	De'r	14	1741
John Hobson Son To Adcock Born	Oct'r	31	1745
William Haynee Son To Stephen	Sep	14	1742

page 66, headed "H".

Aggathey Hanee Daug'r To Isaac Was Born	Dec'r	3	1742
Jo'n Hayne son to Benj'n Born	Jan'y	6	1740
Judith Hayne Daug'r To Tho's Born	June	15	1736
Sara & Thomson Hayne Twins Jo's Born	Jan'y	6	1740
James Hayne Son To Samuell Born	Oct'r	24	1743
Hanah Hayne Daug'r To Rich'd Born	Nov'r	28	1742
Isaac Hayne Son To Isaac Born	Dec'r	28	1735
Rich'd Hayne Son To Ansby Born	Sep'r	29	1729
George Hayne Son To Do Born	Mar	16	1732
Cha's Hayne Son To Do Born	Oct'r	24	1734
Sarah Hayne Daug'r To Do Born	May	11	1737
Wm Hayne Son To Do Born	Nov'r	12	1739
Elliz'a Hayne Daug'r To Do Born	Feb'y	17	1743
Leta Hayne Daug'r To Benj'n Born	Feb'y	15	1744
Hannah Hayes Daug'r To Peter Born	Feb'y	13	1744
Sarah Ann Hays Daug'r To Tho's Born	May	16	1744
Wineff'd Hobson Daug'r To Adcock Born	Feb'y	9	1745
Corbin Hill Son To Luck Born	Oct'r	8	1744
Jo'n Hayne Son To Stephen Born	Dec'r	31	1745
Alce (or Alce) Hudnell Daug'r To Jo'n Born	No'r	7	1745
Betto Hudnell Daug'r To Rich'd Born	Oct'r	18	1745
Luckey Hayne Daug'r To Jacobe Born	March	3	1743
Tho's Hobson Son To Adcock Born	June	11	1746
Jo's Hayne Son To Benj'n Born	Jan'y	14	1746
Jo'n Hudnell Son To Nathan Born	Aug't	10	1746
Eliz'a & Tho's Hall Twins To Rich'd Born	May	1	1745
Rich'd Hayne Son To Isaac Born	Ap'l	19	1746
Winifred Hayne Daug'r To Samuell & Ann Born	Dec'r	24	1746
Hanah Hayne Daug'r To Stephen Born	Feb'y	18	1747
Frances Hogue Son To Jo's Born	March	4	1742
Hana Hague Daug'r To Do Born	Oct'r	3	1744
Jacob Hayne Son To Jacob Born	De'r	22	1746
Sara Hayne Daug'r To Do Born	De'r	15	1737
Lukey Hayne Daug'r To Do Born	March	3	1743
Nansy Hayne Daug'r To Jo'n Born	Sep'r	23	1747
Jo'n Hill Son To Luke Born	No'v	6	1747
Molley Hudnell Daug'r To Nthon	Ap'l	29	1748

page 67, headed "H".

Wm Hobson Son Adcock Born	Sep'r	7	1748
Nansey Hayne Daug'r To Isaac Born	Jan'y	4	1748
Tho's Hayne Son To Spencer Born	Nov'm	12	1748
Peter Hays Son To Peter Born	March	8	1748
Rich'd Hayne Son To Stephen Born	Jan'y	23	1749
Jemayma Harding Daug'r To Tho's Born	May	3	1739
Mary Harding Daug'r To Do Born	Ap'l	6	1741
Samuell Harding Son To Do Born	March	6	1744
Judith Harding Daug'r To Do Born	Jully	18	1745
Hatte Harding Daug'r To Do Born	Ap'l	5	1748
Benj'n Hayne Son To Benj'n Born	Jan'y	22	1748
Milla Hayne Daug'r To Isaac Born	Jan'y	14	1750
Winne Hudnell Daug'r To Jo'n Born	March	15	1750
Shaplegh Hudnell Son To Nathan Born	May	6	1750
Abraham Hayne Son To Benj'n Born	Sept'r	19	1750
Cha's Hayne Son To Stephen Born	Nov'r	4	1750
Nancey Hayne Daug'r To Maximillian	June	16	1750
Tho's Hayne Son To Jo'n Born	Jully	22	1748
Winifred Hayne Daug'r To Jacobe Born	May	25	1750
Molly Hayne Daug'r To Rich'd Born	Nov'r	5	1748
Eliz'a Hayne Daug'r To Do Born	May	21	1750
Calebe Hobson Son To Adcock Born	Jully	13	1751
Betty Hayne Daug'r To Jo'n Born	Oct'r	22	1751
Peter Hardom Son To Jo'n Born	Ja'ny	16	1745
Wm Hardom Son To Do Born	Dec'r	6	1746
Eliz'a Hordom Daug'r To Do Born	Mar	31	1749
Lucey Hayne Daug'r To Rich'd Born	March	9	1752
Hanah Hayne Daug'r To Max'n & Urenia Born	Mar	15	1752
Judathen Hayne Son To Isaac Born	Aug't	31	1752
Nancey Hayne Daug'r To Stephen Born	Sept'r	30	1732
Sarrah Hall Daug'r To Rich'd Born	Sept'r	27	1747
Hannah Hull Daug'r To Do Born	Dec'm	26	1749
Jo'n Hull Son To Do Born	Sep'r	'2	1752
Lawson Hobson Son To Adcock & Joannah his Wife	Dec	31	1753
Martha & Mary Hall Twins To Rich'd & Betty were Born	Nov'r	10th	1754
Sarah Haynie Daug'r To Benj'n & Susannah was Born	June	3	1754
John Haynie Son To Maximilian was Born	July	1	1754
Judith Haynie Daug'r To Henry was Born	April	3	1754
Esther Morris Daug'r To John was Born	April	12	1750

page 68, headed "H".

Betty Hughlett Daug'r To Nicholas was Born	Oct'r	15th	1745
William Hughlett Son To Do was Born	Sept'r	15th	1748
Mary Hughlett Daug'r To Do was Born	April	10th	1750
Ephraim Hughlett Son To Do was Born	April	10th	1752
John Hughlett Son To Do was Born	Dec'r	15th	1753
James Harrison Son To George & Winifred was Born	Octo'r	2d	1754
Lucretia Hudnell Daug'r To Nathan was Born	Nov'r	22d	1754
Elizabeth Hughlett Daug'r To John & Esther was Born	Dec'r	5	1745
William Hughlett Son To Do was Born	Sept	5	1747
Chloe Hughlett Daug'r To Do was Born	Feb'ry	3d	1749
Sarah Hughlott Daug'r To Do was Born	April	26	1751
Esther Hughlett Daughter To Do was Born	March	19	1753
Winifred Hughlett Daug'r To Do was Born	Sept'r	25th	1754

Corbin Hudson Son To Fielding was Born	Sept'r	23d	1754
Thomas Davis Haynie Son To Jacob was Born	Jan'ry	17th	1753
Thomas Hudson Son To Thomas was Born	Feb'ry	18th	1755
William Hilman Son To Thomas Jun'r was Born	May	25th	1755
Hannah Hall Daug'r To John & Hannah was Born	Dec'r	11th	1754
Rodham Hudson Son To Rodham & Elisah was Born	April	16th	1755
Yarret Hughlett Son To Nicholas was Born	April	6th	1755
Elinor Hall Daug'r To John & Ann was Born	Aug'st	10th	1755
John Humphries Son To Joseph & Winifred was Born	Jan'ry	2d	1753
Elias Humphries Son To Do was Born	Oct'r	2d	1755
Elisha Haden Son To Samuel & Mary Ann was Born	Sept'r	28th	1755
William Hammonds Son To Peter & Elizabeth was Born	Oct'r	25th	1742
Sinah Hammons Daug'r To Do was Born	Oct'r	7th	1745
Elisabeth Hammonds Daug'r To Do was Born	May	25th	1749
Peter Hammons Son To Do was Born	June	27th	1752
Mary Hammons Daug'r To Do was Born	Sept'r	3d	1755
Rhoda Haynie Daug'r To Stephen & Ann was Born	Oct'r	23d	1755
Anna Haynie Daug'r To Abraham & Judith was Born	March	30th	1740
Elias Haynie Son To Do was Born	Aug'st	31st	1741
Margaret Haynie Daug'r To Do was Born	July	26th	1743
Dorcas Haynie Daug'r To Do was Born	Jan'ry	31st	1744
Judith Haynie Daug'r To Do was Born	Feb'ry	1st	1746
Dolley Haynie Daug'r To Do was Born	May	13th	1747
Ruth Haynie Daug'r To Do was Born	Dec'r	6th	1751
Molly Haynie Daug'r To John & Mary was Born	Novem'r	1st	1755

page 69, headed "H"

Thomas Hickman Son To Thomas was Born	Dec'r	31st	1755
Winifred Haynie Daug'r To Hezekiah & Hannah was Born	Jan'y	31st	1746
Elisabeth Haynie Daug'r To Do was Born	June	13th	1750
Sarah Haynie Daug'r To Do was Born	Jan'y	12th	1753
Catherine Haynie Daug'r To Do was Born	Aug'st	17th	1755
William Hayes Son To Peter was Born	March	6th	1754
Sarah Crosby Hayes Daug'r To Do was Born	March	1st	1756
Elizabeth Harcum Daug'r To Wm Jun'r was Born	Feb'ry	7th	1756
Hannah Humphries Daug'r To Elijah was Born	July	23d	1750
Judith Humphries Daug'r To Do was Born	April	20th	1752
William Humphries Son To Do was Born	May	19th	1754
Lukee Hammondtree Daug'r To David was Born	March	1st	1756
Lewis Haydon Son To Lewis & Sarah was Born	May	14th	1756
Joseph Hill Son To Spencer & Mary was Born	Nov'r	21st	1752
Nansy Hill Daug'r To Do was Born	Feb'ry	24th	1754
Spencer Hill Son To Do was Born	June	15th	1756
Joseph Haynie Son To Peter & Sinah was Born	March	30th	1756
Sarah Opie Hickman Bastard of Winnefred Born	June	25th	1756
Eliz'a Haynie Daug'r To Henry & Jemimah was Born	Sept'r	2d	1756
Winifred Hudnell Daug'r To John was Born	March	13th	1750
and Died	Oct'r	2d	1756
George Harrison Son To George was Born	Dec'r	10th	1756
John Hill Son To Charles was Born	Oct'r	9th	1756
Hutton Hall Son To John & Hannah was Born	Dec'r	26th	1756
Jacob Haynie Son To Maximilian & Surainah was Born	Dec'r	22d	1756
Yarret Hughlett Son To John & Esther was Born	Sep't	9th	1756

page 69 (continued)

Magdalene Hall Daug'r To Benjamin & Ann was Born   Jan'ry 10th 1757
James Harcum Son To Thomas was Born   March 10th 1757
Sally Harper Daug'r To William & Sarah was Born   Feb'ry 26th 1757
William Hudson Son To Rodham was Born   June 23d 1757
Ann Haynie Daug'r To Henry was Born   Sept'r 11th 1757
Edward Hobson Son To Adcock & Joanna was Born   Aug'st 21 1757
Isaac Haynie Son To Benj'n was Born   Dec'r 15th 1756
Sam'l Haynie Son To Stephen & Ann was Born   Oct'r 6th 1757
Sarah Harper Daug'r To Joshua & Sarah was Born   Feb'ry 26th 1757

page 70, headed "H".

Betty Harcum Daug'r To Thomas & Millicent
Harcum was Born   Decem 9th 1748
Thomas Harcum Son To Thomas & Millicent
Harcum was born   Febru 6th1749/50
Millecent Harcum Daug'r To Do & Do was born   June 29th 1753
Hannah Harcum Daug'r To Do & Do was born   May 25th 1755
James Harcum Son To Do & Do was born   Jan'ry 28th 1757
Sarah Harcum Daug'r To Elisha & Margaret
Harcum was born   Septem 2 1753
Cuthbert Harcum Son To Elisha & Margaret
Harcum was born   April 26 1755
Rodham Harcum Son To Elisha & Margaret
Harcum was born   April 16 1758
Samuel Haynie Son To Spencer & Elizabeth
Haynie was born   Febru 27 1752
John Haynie Son To Spencer & Elizabeth
Haynie was born   Octob 30 1753
Spencer Haynie Son To Spencer & Elizabeth
Haynie was born   March 7 1758
Ann Nutt Harrison Daughter to George &
Winefred Harrison was born   Jan'ry 11 1759
John Hammondtree Son To David & Sarah
Hammondtree was born   Feb'ry 14 1759
William Hill Son To Charles & Sinah Hill
was born   Octob 12 1754
Betty Hill Daughter To Charles & Sinah
Hill was born   Decemb 21 1758
Ann Hughlitt Daughter to John & Esther
Hughlitt was born   July 30 1758
Thomas Hayes Son To Thomas Hayes Jun'r &
Chloe his wife was born   January 9 1760
Maximillion Haynie Son to Abraham & Judith
was born   Decemb 10 1756
William Haynie Son to Jesse & Katherine
was born   Octob'r 29 1759
Maximillian Haynie Son to Maximillian &
Luranah Haynie was born   July 6 1759
Elisha Haynie Son to Henry Haynie Jun'r
& Jemima his wife was born   April 10 1760
William Harcum Son to William & Hannah
Harcum was born   March 20 1755
Lot Harcum Son to William & Hannah Harcum
was born   August 11 1757

page 70 (continued)

Winefred Haroum Daughter to William & Hannah Haroum was born	Feb	14	1760
Huldah Hammonds Daughter to Caleb Hammonds & Eliz'a his wife born	Aug'st	21	1760
Jese Haroum Son to Elisha & Margret Haroum was born Monday morning	April	15	1760
Betty Haynie Daughter to Abner & Winefred Haynie born	Octob	27	1760
William Harrison Son to George & Winefred Harrison was born	Jan'ry	9	1761
Milly Hughlet Daughter to Thomas & Elisabeth Hughlet was born	Jan'ry	17	1746
Judith Hughlet Daughter to Thomas & Elisabeth Hughlet was born	Sep't	1	1748
Lowey Hughlet Daughter to Thomas & Elisabeth Hughlet was born	Feb'ry	9	1751
Winter Hughlet Dau to Thomas & Elisabeth Hughlet was born	Sep't	16th	1754
William Haynie Son to John & Marget Haynie born	Sept	26	1759
Henry Haynie Son to John & Marget Haynie born	March	19	1761
Hannah Haynie Dau: to Ben'jn & Susanna Haynie was born	May	12	1759
Jacob Haynie Son to D'os was born	Novem	17	1760
Samuel Haynie Son to Sam'l & Judith Haynie was born	Octo	28	1756
Richard Haynie Son to Sam'l & Judith Hay was born	Octo	29	1758
Ezekiel Haynie Son to Sam'l & Judith Haynie was born	Septem	29	1760
John Hilmon Son to Thomas & Judith Hilmon was born	April	8	1755
Anna Hilmond Daug'r to Thomas & Judith Hilmond was born	Feb'ry	21	1761
Lurannah Haynie Daug'r to Maximillian & Luranah Haynie was born	Novem	10	1761
Nancy Haynie Daug'r to William & Ruth Haynie was born	Feb'ry	27	1761
Katy Haynie Daug'r To Peter & Sinah Haynie was born	Decem	1	1760
Peggy Harding a bastard Daughter to Francis Harding was born	Decem	15	1759

page 71, headed "H".

Mary Haroum Daughter to Ellis & Judith Haroum was born	Sept	2d	1760
Edwin Hull Son to Richard Hull Gen't & Eliz'a Hull was born	Decem	25th	1756
Mary Hull Daughter to Richard Hull Gen't & Eliz'a Hull was born	March	20th	1759
William Humphris Son to John & Francis Humphris was born	Novem	22d	1760
Ezekiel Hill Son to Charles & Sinah Hill was born	May	14th	1762

Samuel Harrison Son to George & Winifred Harrison was born	Octob'r	28	1762
Sarah Haynie Daughter to Abner & Winnefred Haynie was born	Septem	2d	1762
Champion Hayes Son to Tho's Hayes Jun'r & Chloe Hayes was born	March	26th	1763
John Hughlet Son to John & Esther Hughlet was born	Septem	10	1760
Judith Hughlet Daughter to John & Esther Hughlett was born	March	22	1762
Stephen Haynie Son to John & Margaret Haynie was born (June 26 1763)	June	26	1763
Sarah Haynie Daughter to Isaac Haynie Jun'r & Martha was born	Feb'ry	21	1763
Martin Luther Haynie Son to Samuel & Judith Haynie was born	Jan'ry	14	1763
Henry Haynie Son to Henry & Jemima Haynie was born	Jan'ry	10	1764
Mary Hill Daughter to Spencer & Mary Hill was born	Jan'ry	11	1758
Winny Hill Daughter to Spencer & Mary Hill was born	March	23	1760
Martha Hill Daughter to Spencer & Mary Hill was born	Septem	26	1763
Griffin Merida Humphris Son to John & Frances Humphris was born	Jan'ry	6	1763
Hezekiah Haynie Son to Maximillion & Lurannah Haynie was born	April	7	1764
George Haynie Son to Abner & Winefred Haynie was born	March	28	1764
Judith Harcum Daughter to Ellis & Judith Harcum was born	June	1	1763
Sinah Hill Daughter to Charles & Sinah Hill was born	April	1	1764
Vincent Harrison Son to George & Winefret Harrison was born	January	19	1765
Billy Haynie Son to William & Ruth Haynie was born	January	29	1765
John Hayes Son to George & Sarah Hayes was born	Jan'ry	9	1765
Peter Harrison Son to Samuel & Elizabeth Harrison was born	March	19	1765
Sarah Million Hammondtree Daughter to David & Sarah Hammondtree born	July	3	1765
Winefred Humphris Daughter to Joseph Humphris Ju'r & Winefred his wife born	July	4	1762
Nancy Humphris Daughter to Joseph Humphris Ju'r & Winefred his wife born	March	31	1764
David Haynie Son to Jacob & Sarah Haynie was born	August	23	1763
Molly Haynie Daughter to John & Margret Haynie was born	January	7	1766
Ezekiel Hill Son to Charles & Sinah Hill was born	Februa	22	1766

page 71 (continued)

Elisha Harcum Son to William & Hannah Harcum
was born .... May 1 1762
Betsy Harcum Daughter to William & Hannah
Harcum was born .... April 15 1765
Judith Hilmond Daughter to Thomas & Judith
Hilmond was born .... Novem 29 1763
Alice Hilmond Daughter to Thomas & Judith
Hilmond was born .... March 15 1766
Ezchiel Hayes Son to Thomas & Chloe Hayes
was born .... June 5 1765
Helen Daughter of William & Hannah Harcum
was born .... Dec'r 3 1766
Presly son of Henry & Jemima Haynie was born .... Dec'r 6 1766
Betty Daughter of Isaac & Martha Haynie was born .... Jan'r 14 1767
Agie Daughter of William & Ruth Haynie was born ..... Feb'r 15 1767
Henry son of Benjamin & Susannah Haynie was born .... March 3d 1766
Hezekiah son of Benjamin & Susannah Haynie was born   March 3d 1763
Jemima Daughter of John Corbin & Jemima Hudson
was born .... Feb 28 1767

page 72, headed "H".

Sally Daughter of John & Hannah Hall born .... March 30 1767
Sally Daughter of Henry & Betty Hartford was born ... - - -
Susannah Hill Daughter to Spencer & Mary Hill
was born .... June 29 1766
Alexander Haynie Son to Maximillion & Luranah
Haynie was born .... October 9 1767
Betsy Hilmond Daughter to Thomas & Judith
Hilmond was born .... June 13 1760
Stephen Haynie Son to George & Marget Haynie
was born .... Novem 22 1768
Judith Hill Daughter to Spencer & Mary was born ..... february 3 1770
Nance Hainnies Daughter of Peter & Sinah his
wife was born .... Octobr 7 1771
Abishai Jones the son of Winnefrit Hudson A
Bastard was Born .... feb'r 20 1772
Elizabeth Hudson Daughter of John Corbin Hudson
& Jemima his wife was Born .... December 19 1758
Salley Hudson Daughter to Do was Born .... Novembr 24 1761
Robert Hudson Son To Do was Born .... May 7 1764
Winne Rogers Hainnie Daughter of Tho's Hainnie
& Jean his wife was Born .... March 8 1772
Elizabeth Hudson Daughter to Robuck & Winnefrit
his wife was Born .... January 12 1765
William Hudson Son to Do was Born .... March 26 1768
Judith Hall the Daughter of John & Judith hall
his wife was Born .... Novembr 17 1772
John Corbin Hudson Son of Do & Mime Hudson his
wife was Born   (sic) .... February 16 1773
Thomas Hall Son of James & Mary his Wife was Born   December 28 1772
Ann Hale Daughter of John & Ruth his wife was Born   December 27 1772
William Hawkins Son of John Hawkins was Born .... October 12 1772
Nancy Headley Daughter of William & jean his wife
was Born .... May 14 1773

page 72 (continued)

Bettey Hainnie Daughter of Tho's & Hannah his
  wife was Born   March   9   1773
Abner Hainnie Son of John & Margitt his wife
  was Born   April 21   1773
Rodham Hainnie Son of John & Margett his wife
  was Born   April 21   1773
Pegge Harris Daughter of William of Westmorland
  County was Born   April 15   1773
Richard Hull Son of John Hull was Born   May   22   1773
Bettey Hanie Daughter of Richard Was Born   April 29   1773
John Hughs Son of John & Mary his wife Was Born May   6   1773
Elizabeth Hudnell Daughter of Tho's & Lucy
  his wife Was Born   February 26   1773
Nancy Harcom Daughter of Tho's & Sary his
  wife Was Born   february 25   1773
Thomas Hudson Son of Robuck & Winefret his
  wife was Born   March   22   1773
Richard Harford Son of Hannery & Elizabeth
  his wife was born   March   20   1773
William Haynie Son of George & katy his wife
  was born   novemb 20   1773
Ellen hall the Daughter of Ruth hall was Born May   22   1773
Judith humphris Daughter of George & Judith
  his wife, was born   Docemb 26   1773
Rachel headley Daughter of henory & Temprance born August 23   1773
Sary Haynie Daughter of Richard & Jeane his
  wife born   December 25   1773
Joseph Hudnell Son of Joseph & Mary his wife Born April   8   1774
Salley hall Daughter of John & Ann his wife was Born Novembr 11   1773
James Hesterson son to William & Elizabeth his
  wife was born   January 4   1774
Bette Hayes Daughter tho's Hayes & Choloe his
  wife was born   November 29   1768
George hayes Son of Do Was Born   Feb'ry 9   1771
James hayes Son of Do Born   Septmbr 14   1773
Elizabeth Kemnor hayes Daughter to Peter & Jean
  his wife born   June   29   1774
Nancey Hall Daughter of Salley Was Born   July   25   1773
John hill Son of Eskell & Molle his wife was born Novembr 8   1773
John Hunter Son of James Was Born   Septombor 23 1767

page 73, headed "H".

Thornton Hainice Son to Maxemillian & Luraniah
  his wife was born   July   5   1773
Randell Headley son of William & Jeanny his
  wife was born   Novmbr 11   1774
Jeanney Hale (or Hall) Daughter to John & Ruth
  his wife was born   April   2   1775
Alse Shiurell (?) hill Daughter to Lucy was Born April   1   1775
George Harcom Son of winnefrit was Born   march   4   1774
John Hornsby Son of John & Ann his wife was Born June   8   1774
Nancy Hall Daughter of John & Ann his wife was Born March 15   1775
John Hainey Son to herekiah hainney was Born   July   6   1775
Nacey Sorrill Daughter to Bettey Hill was Born   Decembr 11   1774

Lealon Hambleton Son to Big Belled Molle Born in	June	23	1775

(Note: The frankness of the Northumberland records may
or may not be perfectly satisfactory to the persons
whose ancestors prospered in this county.   B.F.)

Jean Harkley the Daughter of John & Jeane his wife born	february	6	1775
Lewis Hatton the Son of Peter & Molley hatten his wife born	Feb'ry	7	1775
Devenport hainey son of tho's & hannah hainey his wife was born	December	7	1774
Richard hainey son of George & Katey his wife was born	July	17	1775
Nancy hall Daughter of John & Judah his wife was Born	Aprill	8	1775
John Williams Haynie son of Richard Haynie & Molley Hainice was born	Sep'r	5	1775
James Hainie Son of John Hanie was Born	July	29	1775
Samuel Hudson son of John Corbin & Jemima his wife was Born	Dec'r	8	1775
Presley Hall the son of Stephen Hall & Elizabeth his wife was born	Dec'r	2	1775
Thomas Hornsbay son of John & ann his wife was born	April	10	1776
Winne Hudson Daughter of Judith a bastard child Born	June	8	1776
Elizabeth Hall Daughter of Stephen & Ann his wife was born	April	26	1776
Rhodham Hudson son of Salley Gill was Born	Aprill	27	1777
George Hall son of Benjamin & Frances his wife was born	february	5	1777
John Hall Son of John & Ann his wife was Born	March	2	1777
Magdillen Huse Daughter to John & Mary his wife was Born	Novmbr	8	1776
Benjamin halo son of John & Ruth his wife was Born	July	3	1776
Eppe headley the son of hennery & temperrance his wife was born	May	26	1776
William Ellis Harcom Son of Ellis & Judith his wife was born	July	6	1775
Samuell Hainney Son of William & Lucy his wife was Born	October	27	1774
Elisha paine Beekley son of Luckreshe Hammondtree and William Hammrick was Born	April	28	1775
Thomas Hainney Son of Thos & Hannah his wife was Born	May	25	1776
Katharine Harcom Daughter of Tho's & Sarah his wife was born	Aprill	15	1775
Salley Humphris Daughter of John & - was Born	July	29	1775
Janney Harcom Daughter of Cudbuth & Ellinor his wife was Born	Aprill	10	1775
Lee Peter Harcum son of Cudburth & Ellin his wife was Born	March	24	1777
Nancey Hayney Daughter of John & Winney his wife was Born	April	9	1777
Ann Rust Harrison Daughter of Jesse & Bettey his wife Born	Nov'm	30	1777
Patty Williams Harcum Daughter of William & Patty his wife was born	Feb	11	1777

page 73 (continued)

Charles Harfard a bastard child of Mary Harfard was Born	August	27	1777
Elizabeth Backer Harris Daughter of George & Lucey Harris his wife was Born	Sep't	22	1777
Thomas James Harcum Son of Thomas & Sarah his wife was born	Sep't	22	1777
Jemima Haynie Daughter of John & Judith his wife was Born	Feb	9	1778
Fanney Hall Daughter of Salley Hall was Born	Feb	15	1778
Bettey & Salley Hall twins Daughters of Ruth Hall was Born	October	14	1777

page 74, headed "H".

Rodham Hudson Son of Robuck & Winnefrit his wife was born	Sept'm	22	1768
Salley Hudson Daughter to Ditto was Born	Feb'r	1	1778
Charles Hanie Son of Thomas Hanie & Hannah his wife was born	Jan'r	30	1778
George Washington Harcum son to William & Hannah his wife ws born	March	1	1778
George Steel Hartley son of John & Jane Hartley Second: Abner Haynie son to John & Margett his wife was born	May	21	1778
	Febry	20	1776
Robert Gilmore Hudson son to Winnefret Hudson was born	Febru	22	1778
Joseph Hague son to Joseph Hague was born	June	11	1778
Nancey Haynie Daughter to Maximillion & Winnefret his wife was born	August	21	1778
Peter Francis Hayes Son to Peter ws born	July	24	1778
Jeremiah Hall son to John & Judah his wife was born	August	30	1778
Molley Corbin Hudson Daughter to John & Jemima his wife ws born	August	13	1778
James Harding son to William & Milley his wife was born	Nov'm	18	1775
William Harding Son to Ditto was Born	Jan'r	7	1778
Thomas Harding Son to Ditto was born	Jan'r	7	1778
Phil Brown Hail son to Benjamin & Francis his wife was born	Sep'r	20	1778
William Haynie son to William & Lucy his wife was born	Oct	16	1778
Sarah Ball Haynie Daughter to Charles & Elizabeth his wife ws bn	Dec'm	16	1778
Walter Haynie son to Charles & Hannah his wife was born	Dec'm	12	1778
Bettey Hughlett Daughter to John & Judith his wife was born	Dec'm	7	1778
Nancey Headley Daughter to Henry & Temparance his wife was born	Dec'm	14	1778
Joaney Hill Haynie Daughter to Richard & Jean his wife was born	January	27	1779
Ann Haynie Daughter to William & Salley his wife was Born	Nov'm	27	1778
Mary Russ Hill Daughter to Joseph & Ammoney his wife was born	Feb	17	1779

page 74 (continued)

William Humphris son to Elias & Leucey his wife was Born	Feb	23	1779
John Haynie son to Samuel & Sarah his wife was born	June	15	1779
Salley Headley Daughter to Luke & Mary his wife was born	Nov'm	22	1779
Aileey Boanham Hudson Daughter to Jeremiah & Nancey his wife ws bn	Dec'm	24	1779
Susannah Thomas Harris Daughter to Maryan Harris a bastard child was born	Jan'r	28	1780
Mary Hardwick Daughter to John & Susannah his wife was born	Nov'm	8	1779
Salley Haynie Daughter to John & Winnefret his wife was born	March	8	1780
John Dugles Headley son to William & Jean his wife ws born	July	26	1780
Henry Puo son to Ditto & Ditto twins was born	July	26	1780
Jane Haynie Daughter to Richard & Mary his wife was born	Nov'm	21	1780
Thomas Hudson son to Raughley & Hannah his wife was Born	April	24	1781
Henry Self Headley son to Henry & Temperance his wife was born	May	27	1781
Elizabeth Hardwick Daughter to John & Susanah his wife was born	Jan'y	11	1781
Elizabeth Headley Daughter to James & Winnah his wife was Born	Oct	14	1781
Thomas Trussel Hudson son to John C. Hudson & Jemima his wife ws Born	Aug't	30	178-
William Harford son to Mary Harford a bastard Child was born	Jan'r	29	178-

page 75, headed "H".

John Blinooe Harrison son to Jesse Harrison & Bettey his wife was born	Nov'm	13	1779
Ailsey Harrison Daughter to Ditto & Ditto was born	Oct	10	1781
Isaac Haynie son to Jacob & Robeckah his wife was born	March	4	1782
Joseph Hardwick son to John & Susannah his wife was born	April	17	1782
Pegga Headley Daughter to William & Jean his wife was born	Aug't	2	1782
Rebeckah Headley Daughter to Luke & Mary his wife w's b	June	5	1782
Nancey Hughes Daughter to John & Mary his wife was born	June	15	1782
Martha Hall Daughter to John & Ann his wife was born	Oct	10	1782
William Hill son to Spencer & -- his wife was born	Nov'm	23	1782
Bettey Booth Haynie Daughter to Richard & -- his wife was born	Nov'm	18	1782
George Robook Hudson son to Robook & Winnefret his wif was born	April	26	1783
Ann & John Hail twins Daughter & son to John & Ruth his wife ws b	Aug't	2	1779

James Self Hail son to Ditto & Ditto was born	Aug't	31	1783
Jean Headley Daughter Henrey & Temperance his wife was b	Sept	9	1783
Hannah Brown Hogan was B Daughter to Thomas Hogan & Ann his wife was born	Apl	20	1784
Winneyfred Headley Daughter To James Headly was Born	April	16	1784
Nancey Shapply Hudson Daughter to John C & Jamima his wife ws born	Sept	13	1784
Ailecey Headley Daughter to William & Janey his Wife was born	Feb'r	28	1785
Fanney Hill Daughter to Spencer & Mary his wife was born	Dec'm	11	1784
Elizabeth Harrison Daughter to George & Caty his wife ws b	Dec'm	29	1784
William Hughs son to John & Molley his wife was Born	Jan'y	2	1785
Jean Hardwick Daughter to John & Susannah his wife was Born	March	16	1785
Winnefret Robuck Hudson Daughter to Robuck Hudson & Winnefret his wife ws b	April	3	1785
Joshua Tarpley Harrison son to Peter Harrison & Lucey his wife was born	March	4	1785
Molley Haynie Daughter to Richard & Molley his wife was Born	March	15	1785
Judith Barrett Hughlett Daughter to John & Judith his wife was Born	Feb	10	1783
Mary Cotrell Hughlett Daughter to Ditto & Ditto his wif was Born	Aug't	13	1785
James Headley son to James & - - his wife was born	Nov'm	13	1786
Moses Hail son to John & Ruth his wife was born	April	11	1786
Jeremiah Headley son to William & Jean his wife was Born	May	1	1787
Ailcey Hogan Daughter to Thomas & Ann his wife was Born	Apr	7	1786
Presley Hudson son to John C Hudson & Jemima his wife was Born	Decm	10	1787
Elizabeth Hall Daughter to Daniel & Sarahann his wife ws br	Augt	15	1785
Winneyfret Hall Daughter to Ditto & Ditto was born	Dec'm	4	1787
Molley Harrison Daughter to Peter & Lucey his wife was Born	Jan'r	22	1789
Thomas Hail son to John & Ruth his wife was Born	Feb	24	1789
John West Beacham son to John W Beacham & Ann his wife was Born	Feb	4	1789
Salley Headley Daughter to Henry & Temperance his wife ws B	Aug't	20	1786
Molley Headley Daughter to Ditto & Ditto was Born	May	1	1789
George Vincant Cox Hudson son to Robert Hudson & Nancoy his wife ws Br	Sopt	21	1789
Jane Headley Daughter to William & Jean his wife ws Born	Sept	6	1789

Lewis Hopkins son to Joseph & Milley his wife was Born   Sept   25   1789
Thomas Headley son to Luke & Mary his wife was Born   October   1   1789
Richard Henry Hogan son to Thomas & Ann his wife was born   January   16   1790
Salley Hughs Daughter to John & Molley his wife was Born   Feb   8   1790
Harriet Coelman Hall Daughter to Sarah Hall was Born   July   17   1790
George Henry Harrass son to Hugh Harrass & Salley his
   wife was B   Nov'm   20   1789
Peter Holland Hall son to Thomas F Hall & Salley his
   wife was Born   March   10   1794
Fanney Hall Headley Daughter to William Headley & Jane
   his wife was Born   Sept   1   1794
Isaac Bray Hogan son to Nancey Hogan a Bastard child
   was Born   Decemb   15   1786

    page 77, headed "H".

Charlot Hainne Daughter of Richard & Jean his wife was Born February 16 1770
Thomas Huse son of John huse and Mary his wife was Born   March   24   1770
Lucy Hainney Daughter to Stephen & Elizabeth his wife
   was born   february 28   1769
Sammuel Harrison Son to Sammuel & Elizabeth His wife Born   April   4   1770
Mille Hudson Daughter of John Corbin Hudson & Jemima
   his wife was born   May   3   1770
Rhodham Hall Son to Stephen & Elizabeth his wife was Born   June   28th   1770
Thos Hall son of John Hall Juner & Ann his wife was Born   May   7   1769
Mary Hall Daughter of John Hall & Judah his wife was Born   August   9   1770
Rhodham Hudson son of Robuck & Winnefrit his wife was Born   Sept'br   20   1770
Griffin son of George Hainney and Katty his wife was born   Novembr   10   1770
Hannah Hall Daughter of John & Ann Hall was born the   November 10 1770
Elizabeth Harcom Daughter of Jos (To's ?) Harcom was Born   August   22   1770
William Hall son of John Hall & Judith Hall his wife
   was Born   Novembr   21   1770
    (Note: In the foregoing entry the words "Hall his wife"are
    underscored. While the first part of the entry is in the same
    handwriting, these three words were added at a later date-or
    I decidedly miss my guess. The ink is different, and the
    position of the writer's arm was different in making the
    two parts of the entry. Then there may have been two men
    named John Hall living at this time in Northumberland Co.
    If there was only one John Hall his position must have been
    a little difficult to explain to either one or both of the
    mothers.   B.F.)

Juda Wildey Harcum Daughter of Ellis harcum & Juday
   his wife was Born   Octobr   27   1770
Judah Haynis Daughter of Maximilian Hanice & Luranah
   his wife was born   January   2   1771
Joseph Humfris Son of John Humphris & Frances his
   wife was Born   Novembr   26   1770
John Humphris son of Do was Born   Aprill   1st   1765
Elizabeth Humphris Daughter of Do Was Born   March   9   1768
John Humphris the son of George Humphris & Judith
   his wife was Born   Octobr   21   1771
Winne Hainnice Daughter to John Hainnice & Margit
   his wife was Born   March   5   1771

page 77 (continued)

Name	Month	Day	Year
Leroy Hudson son of thos & Mary Hudson his wife was Born	June	4	1753
Jeremiah Hudson son of Do was Born	Decembr	10	1759
Susanner Hudson Daughter of Do Was Born	March	30	1762
Rhodham Hudson son of Do was born	March	21	1765
John Hudson Son of Do was Born	October	8	1767
Lott Hudson Son of Fielding & Mary Hudson his wife was Born	April	11	1757
Kissiah Hudson Daughter to Do Was Born	May	12	1768
Frances Hunt Daughter of Charles Hunt was Born	August	30	1770
James Hornsbe the son of John Hornsbe & Ann Hornsbe his wife was Born	August	31	1770
Cud Birth Hainnice son of Thos & Juanis (?)	May	20	1771
Bettey Haroum Daughter of Winnefret Haroum was Born	March	14	1771
Salley Hordum Daughter to John & Winnefrit Hordom was Born	April	29	1771
Jordan Hanis son of Martha Hanis was Born	June	28	1771
Molley Hudson Daughter of Tho's & Mary Hudson his wife was Born	Sept	25	1771
Ann hornsbe Daughter of John & Ann his wife was Born	February	18	1772
Isaac Hanice Son of Richard & Jean Hanice his wife was Born	January	27	1772
Hannah haroom Daughter of Joseph haroom was Born	Janry	5	1772
Hannah Wilday Haroom Daughter Wm & Hannah his wife was Born	October	29	1771
Tho's Hall the Son of Tho's & Elizabeth his wife was Born	Novembr	11th	1771
Wm Hudnell Son of Tho's & Elizabeth hudnell was Born	March	23	1766
John Hudnell Son of Do was Born	June	29	1768
Mary Hudnell Daughter of Do was Born	August	29	1771
Stephen hainnice Son of Wm Haynice & Lucy his wife was Born	Octobr	3	1771
Thomas Hillman son of thos & Judah his wife was Born	January	3	1772
Jenne Hall Daughter to John & Ann hall his wife was Born	May	4	1772
James Hall Son of Stephen & Elizabeth his wife was Born	April	10	1773

page 78, headed "H".

Name	Month	Day	Year
Bette Hudson Daughter to Tho's & Mary his wife was Born	May	26	1774
Jean Whroe Daughter to Judith Hudson a B child was born	Sept	13	1774
Prysilla Hall Daughter to Daniel & Saraan his wife ws b	Sept	28	1790
John Harrys son to William & Molley his wife was Born	Novm	18	1791
Molly Lamkin Hogan Daughter to Thomas Hogan & Nancey his wife was Born	March	17	1792
Betsey & Nancey Harrys twins Daughters to William & Molley his wife was Born	Oct	3	1793
Isaac Haynie son to Samuel & Sara his wife was Born	March	5	1791
William Hill son to Ann Hill a Bastard child was Born	March	26	1791
Roston Harison son to Willoughby & Susannah his wife was Born	May	8	1794
James Williams Heirs son to James Heirs & Rebeccah his wife ws Born	March	21	1796
Nancey Headloy Daughter to James & Winney his wife was Born	January	5	1796
William Hoadley son to Henry Headley & Temperence his wife ws Born	August	21	1795
John Hailo son to Benjamin & Pegga his wife was Born	July	15	1796
Isaac Bray son to Isaac Bray & Nancey Hogan a Bastard child ws Born	Dec'm	15	1786
Harriot W Harrison Daughter to Eizah Harrison & Salloy his wife ws Bn	April	27	1797

page 78 (continued)

Nancey Harison Daughter to Willoughby & Susannah his wife was Born	September	20	1796
George Opey Headley son to Luke Headley & Mary W Headley his wife was Born	Nov'm	10	1792
Samuel Headley son to William & Jane Headley his wife was Born	September	18	1798
William Hill son to Ann Hill a Bastard child was Born	March	26	1791
Nancey Russel Harrison Daughter to Elisha & Salley Harrison his wife was born	March	19	1800
Landman Headley son to William Headley & Nancey his wife was Born	Sept	17	1806
Randal P Headley son to William & Nancy his wife Was Born	Jany	3	1809

page 79, headed "R".

Jane Rodgers Daug'r To Rich'd Born	Apl	12	1686
Jo'n Rodgers son To Do Born	Dec	18	1676
Wm Rodgers Son To Do Born	Feby	12	1679
Ann Reynals Daug'r To Jas Born (Prob. 1671)	Feby	25	1771
Ann Rice Daug'r To Rich'd Born	Jan'y	9	1686
Frances Routt Daug'r To Rich'd Born	June	14	1686
Ann Routt Daug'r To Do Born	Aug	17	1675
Mary Rout Daug'r To Do Born	Feby	26	1689
George Rout Son To Do Born	Augt	26	1692
Jo'n Rout Son To Thos Born	Octr	10	1679
Susana Rout Daug'r To Do Born	Dec'r	15	1681
Catherina Rout Daug'r To Do Born	June	20	1684
Tho's Rout Son To Do Born	Sepr	30	1686
Chas Rout Son To Do Born	Dec'r	18	1688
Wm Rout Son To Do Born	Jany	30	1689
Eliza Rout Daug'r To Do Born	Octr	20	1694
Hanah Rider Daug'r To Hen'y Born	Mar	27	1684
Mary Ryder Daug'r To Do Born	Jully	27	1686
Sarah Ryder Daug'r To Do Born	Jany	21	1681
Thos Rydor Son To Do Born	May	22	1684
Hen'y Rydor Son To Do Born	Jully	29	1692
Jonna (or Joana) Rider Daug'r To Do Born	Oct	27	1695
Jo'n Rider Son To Do Born	Nov'r	6	1698
Rich'd Robeson Son To Jo'n Born	Jany	18	1670
Jo'n Robeson Son To Do Born	Jany	23	1672
Anthoy Robeson Son To Do Born	Feby	24	1676
Thos Robeson Son To Do Born	Decr	26	1678
Nicho's Robeson Son To Do Born	Sep'r	6	1681
Samuell Robeson Son To Do Born	June	18	1682
Eliza Robeson Daug'r To Do Born	May	17	1685
Joseph Robeson Son To Do Born	Jany	8	1686
Benj'n Robeson Son To Do Born	Decr	26	1688
Matthew Robeson Son To Do Born	Decr	5	1693
Wm Robeson Son To Do Born	Novr	17	1697
Edward Reed Son To Jo'n Born	July	14	1670
Wm Reed Son To Do Born	Novr	23	1677
Ann Reason Daug'r To Jo'n Born	Oct	15	1670
Jo'n Reason Son To Do Born	Apl	2	1672
Wm Reason Son To Do Born	Octr	2	1680
Rachell Rason Daugr To Do Born	Octr	2	1683

page 79 (continued)

Elias Rout Son To Wm Born   May   31   1694

page 80, headed "R".

Elinor Robeson Daug'r To Steven Born	May	7	1692
Susana Robeson Daug'r To Do Born	Nov	11	1679
Henry Robeson Son To Do Born	Feby	14	1681
Jane Robeson Daug'r To Rich'd Born	Nov'r	27	1698
Jo'n Reason Son To Jo'n Born	May	14	1700
Rich'd Reed Son To Wm Born	May	4	1701
Rich'd Robinson Son Rich'd Born	Decr	5	1716
Sarah Robinson Daug'r To Thos Born	Decr	29	1717
Allex'r Rydor Son To Hen'y Born	Sep'r	4	1717
Edward Reed Son To Wm Born	Mar	25	1703
Jo'n Robinson Son To Rich'd Born	Feb'y	26	1700
Winef'd Robinson Daug'r To Do Born	Sep'r	24	1708
Winef'd Robinson Daug'r To To's Born	May	29	1704
Aron Robinson Son To Antho'y Born	Jully	6	1705
Grace Robinson Daug'r To Nicho's Born	Sep'r	29	1704
Wm Robinson Son To Do Born	May	11	1707
Winef'd Robeson Daug'r To Rich'd Born	Octr	24	1708
Martha Robinson Daug'r To Antho'y Born	Apl	5	1710
Mary Robinson Daug'r To Do Born	June	9	1712
Luke Row-d (4th letter illegible) Son To Rob't Born	Oct'r	11	1719
Thos Rives Son To George Born	Oct'r	17	1719
Sarah Ann Rydor Daug'r To Hen'y Born	Jully	17	1719
Hannah Rydor Daug'r To Do Born	Sept'r	16	1721
Marthew Rives Daug'r To Jo'n Born	Octr	8	1720
Eliza Rives Daugr To Do Born	Mar	23	1722
Frances Robinson Daug'r To Jos Born	Dec'r	6	1715
Joseph Robinson To Do Born (sic)	Apl	8	1720
Charles Reason Son To Jo'n Born	Sep'r	12	1719
Grace Reade Daug'r To Wm Born	No'r	23	1704
Jo'n Reed Son To Do Born	Jan'y	22	1710
Judith Rodgers Daug'r To Ja's Born	May	6	1707
Ja's Robinson Son To Tho's Born	Dec'r	15	1709
Thos Robinson Son To Do Born	Aug't	22	1712
Jo'n Robinson Son To Benj'n Born	Sep'r	19	1712
Rich'd & Wadington Robinson Twins To Rich	Sept	25	1713
Grace Reede Daug'r To Wm Born	Dec'r	10	1715
Allex'r Rodgers Son Allex'r Born	Nov	14	1713
Winef'd Rodgers Daug'r To Do Born	Nov	14	1715
Hannah Rives Daug'r To Tho's Born	Dec	5	1714
Rosana Rose Daug'r To Benj'n Born	Octr	23	1714

page 81, headed "R".

Benj'n Rives Son To George Born	Jany	4	1721
Saml Robinson son Nicho's Born	June	-	1712
Nicho's Robinson Son Do Born	June	-	1715
Wm Robinson Son To Benj'n Born	Aug	29	1718
Benj Robinson Son To Do Born	Oct'r	17	1721
Susana Robinson Daugr To To's Born	Apl	24	1723

page 81 (continued)

Mary Roland Daug'r To Robt Born	Aug't	30	1721
Robt Roland Son To Do Born	June	13	1723
Rich'd Rives Son To Jo'n Born	Mar	18	1734
Betty Rodger Daug'r To Jo'n Born	June	16	1725
George Roland Son To Robt Born	March	15	1725
Winef'd Raydor Daugr To Hen'y Born	Sep'r	17	1724
Elisha Robinson Son To Winef Born	Sepr	1	1725
Jo'n Robinson Son To Joseph Born	June	16	1726
Ann Rives DaugR To Jo'n Born	June	10	1726
Sarah Rives Daugr To Jo'n Born	Mar	16	1729
Lucretia Robinson Daugr Jo's Born	Decr	15	1729
Tho's Rives Son To Tho's Born	Sepr	16	1730
Ann Rice Daugr To Jo'n Born	Decr	14	1731
Natha'l Roe (This name may possibly be Ros) Son To Nath'l Born	July	20	1733
Eliza Rodgers Daugr To Edw'd Born	July	2	1735
Judith Reed Daugr To Rich'd Born	Jany	31	1735
Jo'n Rodgers Son To Edw'd Born	Jan'y	10	1738
Wm Rice Son To Jo'n Born	July	31	1736
Sarah Reed Daugr To Rich'd Born	Nov'r	25	1738
George Rodgers Son Edward Born	Sepr	15	1740
Tho's Robinson Son To's Born	May	22	1733
Mary Robinson Daugr To Do Born	Apl	18	1739
Bety Reed Daugr To Rich'd Born	May	12	1741
Winif'd Rayan Daugr To Edward Born	Aug	12	1742
Hanah Rodgers Daugr To Edw'd Born	Mar	1	1743
Nich0's Ringe Molato Son To Mary	Nov	13	1741
Winef'd Robinson Daug'r To Jos'h Born	May	27	1743
Judith Reed Daugr To Rich'd Born	June	13	1744
Wm Robinson son To Jo'n Born	Sep'r	9	1744
Sarah Ann Rodgers Daugr To Edwd	Mar	11	1745
Judith Rayan Daugr To Edw	Dec'r	23	1744

page 82,   headed "R".

Hanah Range Daugr To Mary Born A Mullatto	March	9	1744
Wm Rayan Son To Edw'd Born	June	25	1746
Nansey Reed Daugr To Rich'd Born	Octr	9	1746
Grace Reed Daugr To Do Born (sic)	Octr	13	1732
Charity Robinson Daugr To Jo'n Born	Sep'r	29	1746
Winif'd Rodgers Daug'r To Edw'd Born	Apl	21	1747
Luckey Robinson Daugr To Jo's Born	March	28	1746
Fra's Rodgers Son To Noah Born	Decr	18	1743
Hanah Rodgers Daugr To Do Born	Apl	23	1744
Edward Rodgers Son To Edw'd Born	Oct'r	22	1748
Jo'n Robinson Son To Jo's Born	Nov'r	17	1748
Sarah Riley Daug'r To Daniell Born	Sop	17	1735
Jobe Riley sone To Do Born	Aug't	17	1738
Ellis Riley Son To Do Born	Oct	10	1742
Juny Riley Daugr To Do Born	Sepr	18	1744
Sinah Riley Daugr To Do Born	March	28	1746
Jo'n Robinson son to Jo'n Born	Dec'r	10	1749
Sarah Rice Daugr To Rich Born	Decr	2	1739
Charolos Rice a Twine sone To Do Born	Jany	14	1742

Issac Rice Son To Jo'n Born	Apl	21	1743
Wm Rice Son To Do Born	July	31	1736
Wine Rice Daugr To Do Born	Febry	9	1739
Bety Rice Daugr To Do	Jully	4	1748
Sarah Ann Rice Daugr To Do Born	Aug't	1	1743
Jo'n Rice Son To Do Born	March	23	1741
Lucretia Rayon Daugr To Edw'd Born	Ja'y	3	1750
Ta's (may be Ja's) Rayan Son To Do Born	Dec'r	28	1751
John Rooker Son To Jennings & Betty was Born	March	12th	1755
William Roebuck Son To Rawleigh was Born	June	10th	1755
Joseph Robinson Son To Joseph & Mary was Born	July	8th	1753
Mary Haynie Robinson Daugr To Do Born	April	29th	1755
Eliza Roberson Daugr To Wm was Born	July	30th	1756
Rawleigh Roebuck Son To Rawleigh Born	Janry	30	1757
George Roebuck Son To Rawleigh & Hannah Robuck was born	Aug't	5	1759
Helen Rogers Daughter to John & Lucretia Rogers was born	January	25	1760

page 83 headed "R"

Judith Rice Daughter to Issac and Sarah Rice born	Septem	26	1763
Winny Rice Daughter Daughter to Issac and Sarah Rice was born	April	21	1766
Joseph Rice son to Issac and Sarah Rice was born	July	22	1768
Molly Rice Daughter to Issac & Sary Rice was born	Novembr	5	1771
An Infant of Winne Rainger Baptized the name of the child was not set Down	Aprill	14	1772
William Roggers Son of John Roggers was Born	August	29	1772
Richard Rice Son of William Peudley (?) Rice & Hannah his wife was born	Janu'ry	25	1773
Nancy Haugus Robbusson Daughter of William & Sinah his wife was born	Decemb	10	1772
John Rice Son of Issack & Sary his Wife was Born	februaryl2		1773
James Rainger Son of Nickless & Ann his wife Born	Novmbr	28	1772
Issack Richerson son of Issac & Margit his wife was born	Novmbr	23	1773
James Rainger & Hannah Son & Daughter to winne was Born	Novmbr	22	1773
George Rice Son of John Rice & Hannah Rice his wife was Born	Septmbr	2	1774
Elizabeth Rice Daughter of William & Ruth his wife was Born	July	7	1774
John Robinson son to William & Sinah was Born	Dec'r	31	1774
Richard Rice Son to Charles & Sary his wife was born	March	23	1776
Nancy Rice Daughter of William & hannah his wife was Born	Aprill	10	1775
Ezekill Robosson was Born	Feby	9	1777
Jeane Rout Daughter of Richard & Caty his wife was Born	Sepbr	16	1776
William Reay Son of John & Luckrie his wife was Born	Novmbr	15	1773
Edward Roggers Son of George & Sary his wife Born	May	22	1775
Bettey Rice Daughter of Issac & Sary his wife Born	Augst	28	1775
Richard Rice son of Richard & Judith his wife Born	April	28	1777

page 83 (continued)

Hannah Robinson Daughter of William & Sinah his wife was Born	July	21	1777
Lucey Rautt Daughter of George & Winnefret his wife was Born	April	27	1777
John Rion son of Lukey Rion A Bast'd child was Born	April	28	1777
Isaac Richeson son of Isaac & Margret his wife was Born	Dec'm	26	1777
Sammuel Rice son of William Pendley Rice & Hanner his wife ws born	March	6	1778
Ann Reason Daughter of John & Maryan his wife was born	Jan'r	5	1777
Hannah Trussel Self Daughter of Matthiss Self & Nancey his wife ws born	April	5	1778
William Rice the son of Isaac & Sarah his wife was Born	Sep't	19	1778
Betsey Stonum Robinson Daughter to James & Judith his wife ws born	Sep't	22	1778
Bettey Rice Daughter to Richard & Judith his wife was Born	Nov'm	28	1778
Elezebeth Rogers Daughter to John & Lucretia his wife was born	Dec'm	24	1778
Nicholas Robinson son to James & Judith his wife was born	March	11	1771
William Martin Robinson son to Do & Do was born	Dec'r	18	1772
Thomas Pope Robinson son to Do & Do was born	March	2	1774
James Robinson Son To Do & Do was Born	Aug't	18	1776
Mollay Rautt Daughter to Richard & Catey his wife was born	Jan'ry	21	1779
Mary Ray Daughter to John & Lucreshe his wife was born	Ma'r	4	1779
William Rice son to William & Ruth his wife was Born	Jan'r	6	1780
John Rice son to Charles & Sarah his wife was born	May	11	1780
John Anderson Russel son to Thomas & Salley his wife was born	June	15	1780
Judith Rice Daughter to Richard & Judith his wife was born	Sept	16	1780
William Rice son to Wm Pendla Rice & Hannah his wife was born	June	16	1781

page 84, headed "R".

Winney Sydnor Routt Daughter to George & Winney Routt his wife was Born	Oct	24	1781
William Routt son to Richard & Catharine his wife was Born	June	30	1781
Salley Rice Daughter to Richard & Judith his wife was Born	April	25	1782
Lucey Rice Daughter to William & Ruth his wife was born	Jan'r	23	1783
John Haynie Robertson son to Joseph & Sarah his wife was born	Feb	23	1783
Leannah Chilton Rice Daughter to William T Rice & Hannah his wife was born	Aug't	1	1783
Katharine Rautt Daughter to Richard & Katharine his wife was born	Sep't	9	1783

page 84 (continued)

Winnefret Rice Daughter to Charles & Selley his wife was born   Oct   8 1783
Joseph C Robertson son to Joseph & Sarah his wife was born   April   4 1785
Salley Rice Daughter to John & Hannah his wife was born   .   March   14 1785
John Darby Roberts Son to Henry D Roberts & Leannah his
    wife was Born   Aug't   31 1785
Willoughby Churchwell Robertson to Joseph & Salley his
    wife was born   Jan'r   23 1787
Richard Dimor Routt son to George Routt & Betty his wife
    was Born   Jan'r   27 1787
Fanney Rich Daughter to Bettey Rich a Molatto ws born   March   25 1787
William Rice son to Charles & Salley his wife was Born   Jan'r   4 1788
Fanney Sydnor Rautt daughter to Rich'd Routt & Betty his
    wife was born   Oct'r   6 1786
Mary Barcroft Robertson Daughter to Joseph & Salley
    his wife was Born   Aptil   22 1789
Peggay Nutt Routt Daughter to George Routt & Betty his
    wife was Born   Feb   20 1790
Ailcey Routt daughter Richard Routt & Bettey his wife was born March   27 1790
Salley Beacham Robertson Daughter to Joseph & Sarah his
    wife ws bn   Dec'm   23 1790
Catey Rice Daughter to Charles & Sarah his wife was Born   Nov'm   6 1791
Betsey Rice Daughter to William Penley Rice & Catey his
    wife was born   June   29 1791
Hannah & James Rice twins Daughter & son to Ditto & Ditto
    was Born   Sep't   6 1792
Caty Rice Daughter to William P Rice & Caty his wife was Born Nov'm   14 1794
Beckey W Robertson Daughter to Joseph Robertson & Judith
    his wife was Born   October   25 1797
Hiram B Robertson son to Ditto & Ditto was Born   October   3 1799
John Sydnor Rout son to Richard Routt & Bettey his wife
    was Born   April 11 1800

page 85   headed   "S".

Theophalus Satcheveril Son T. Timothay Born	Oct'r	20	1709
Hanah Sims Daughter To Tho's Born	Jan'y	8	1709
Sam'l Sims Son To Do Born	March	2	1706
Cathrin Sims Daughter To Do Born	Dec'r	29	1703
Jo'n Scott Son To Jo'n Born	June	24	1703
Jo'n Spray Son To John Born	Jully	25	1703
Joshua Spray Son To Do Born	Nov'r	23	1705
Ann Smith Daughter To Tho's Born	Dec'r	1	1691
Tho's Smith Son To Do Born	Sep'r	5	1697
Mergery Smith Daug'r To Do Born	June	13	1699
Woodrge Smith Son To Do Born	Feb'y	18	1701
Eliza Smith Daug'r To Do Born	May	6	1703
Jo'n Smith Son To Do Born	Dec'r	23	1707
Mary Sullivant Daug'r To Timothy Born	June	14	1706
Jo'n Saingel Son To Edw'd Born	Dec'r	1	1704
Mary Saingel Daug'r To Do Born	July	1	1706
Edw'd Saingel Son To Do Born	Aug't	24	1708
Jane Ann Swift Daugr To Jo'n Born	Feb'y	20	1710
Jo'n & Ann Shaddock Twins to Aibee Bap'd	Feb'y	19	1712
Betty Smith Daug'r To Jo'n Born	Ap	1	1712
Rich'd Shurley Son To Rich'd Born	July	9	1712
Ja's Shurley Son To Jo'n Born	Feb'y	8	1712

page 85 (continued)

Jo'n Sullivant son to Timothy	Ap'l	8	1710
Jo'n Standley Son TO Jo'n Born	Oct'r	28	1711
Ann Shurley Saug'r To Jo'n Born (1706)	July	31	1706
Jo'n Shurley Son To Do Born	Sep'r	24	1708
Grace Shurley Daug'r To Do Born	Feb'y	17	1710
Sarah Sebree Daug'r To Ja's Born	Sep'r	9	1702
Ja's Sebree Son To Do Born	Aug't	1	1704
Winif'd Sebree Daug'r To Do Born	Marc	6	1707
Wm Sebree Son To Do Born	Sep'r	1	1709
Ann Sebree Daug'r To Do Born	Ap'l	17	1712
Tho's Shurley Son To Rich'd Born	Feb'y	1	1701
Ann Shurley Daug'r To Do Born	March	31	1703
Rich'd Shurley Son To Do Born	Jan'y	20	1705
Ann Spence Daug'r To Dav'd Born	Ap'l	5	1702
Eliza Shapley Daug'r To Thos Born	Ap'l	19	1702
Tho's Shurley Son To Tho's Born	Oct'r	22	1666
Rich'd Shurley Son To Do Born	Aug't	6	1669
Phebus Shurley Daug'r To Do Born	Ap'l	14	1673

page 86, headed "S".

Mary Shurley Daug'r To Tho's Born	June	8	1676
John Simes Son to Walter Born	March	26	1679
Mary Stedham Daug'r To Hugh Born	Sep'r	12	1664
Eliz'a Stedham Daug'r To Do Born	Sep'r	3	1666
Presilar Stedham Daug'r To Do Born	Feb'y	20	1664
Rachel Stedham Daug'r To Do Born	Ap'l	29	1671
Jo'n Sandfourd Son To Tho's Born	Oct'r	13	1680
John Spane Son To Cuthbert Born	Feb'y	26	1686
Rich'd Sane Son To Do Born (sic)	June	15	1684
Rich'd Smith Son To Rich'd Born	March	19	1676
Jo'n Smith Son To Do Born	Oct'r	18	1690
Ann Smith Daug'r To Do Born	Oct'r	7	1692
Rob't Sadler Son To Tho's Born	March	5	1691
Tho's Smith Son To Rich'd Born	June	7	1692
Wm Simpson Son To Wm Born	July	1	1693
Samu'l Smith Son To Sam'l Born	June	12	1692
Jo'n Shapley Son To Phillap Born	Jan'y	23	1687
Hanah Shapley Daug'r To Do Born	Oct'r	2	1690
Judith Shapley Daug'r To Do Born	Sep'r	13	1692
Sarah Shapley Daug'r To Do Born	Jully	14	1695
Wm Sanders Son To Jo'n Born	Jan'y	28	1699
Eliz'a Spray Daug'r To Jo'n Born	June	16	1699
Jobe Sims Son To Tho's Born	Oct'r	20	1700
Margaret Suten Daug'r To Wm Born	May	18	1701
Rich'd Scott Son To Jo'n Born	Dec'r	23	1692
Ann Scott Daug'r To Do Born	Jully	27	1701
Jo'n Scott Son To Do Born	June	24	1703
Eliz Shapley Daug'r To Tho's Born	Ap'l	19	1702
Eliz'a Selfe Daug'r To Stiven Born	Feb'y	23	1679
Wm Short Son To Wm Born	June	6	1700
Josian Satcheverel To Timothy Born	Oct'r	6	1705
Timothy Satcheveril Son To Do Born	March	23	1707
Jo'n Spense Son To Dav'd Born	March	21	1707
Wm Short Son To Patrick Born	Mar	6	1708
Jo'n Smith Son To Jo'n Born	Oct'r	30	1709
Edward Sander Son To Wm Born	Oct'r	11	1705

page 86 (continued)

Joseas Satcheveril Son Timothy Born	Nov'r	25	1705
Mary Smith Daug'r To Do Brayant (sic)	Oct'r	24	1708
Hanah Smith Daug'r To Do Bern	Dec'r	27	1717
Winif'd Smith Daug'r To Do Born	Aug't	17	1720
John Smith Son To Jo'n Born	Mar	7	1707

page 87, headed "S".

Betty Smith Daug'r To Jo'n Born	March	9	1712
Judith Smith Daug'r To Do Born	Ap'l	7	1718
Ann Smith Daug'r To Do Born	July	30	1719
Tabaythe Shurett Daug'r To Abr'm Born	-	-	1721
Eliz Smith Daug'r To Brayant Born	Jan'y	2	1717
Rich'd Sebree Son To Rich'd Bern	Oct'r	27	1721
Ja's Straughan Son To Dav'd Born	May	28	1712
Mary Straughan Daug'r To Do Born	Feb'y	17	1704
Winif'd Straughan Daug'r To Do Born	Feb'y	22	1706
Dav'd Straughan Son To Do Born	Feb'y	26	1708
Jo'n Straughn Son To Do Born	May	12	1710
Tho's Straughan Son To Do Born	May	12	1712
Margret Straughan Daug'r To Do Born	March	22	1715
Ann Straughan Daug'r To Do Born	Nov'r	8	1719
Rich'd Straughan Son To Do Born	Oct'r	22	1722
Dan'l Shurley Son To Jo'n Born	Mar	24	1717
Ergilian Shurley Son To Do Born	Ap'l	17	1721
Newman Shurley Son To Do Born	Feb'y	11	1719
Mary Shurley Daug'r To Do Born	Aug't	1	1722
Tho's Stuckee (?) Son To Rich Born	Aug't	14	1722
Betsy Sanders Daug'r To Zacarias Bern	Sep	17	1717
Judith Smith Daug'r To Samu'l Born	Feb'y	28	1724
Jane Smith Daug'r To Do Born	Aug't	-	1722
Eliz'a Swifte Daug'r To Jo'n Born	Sep'r	16	1728
Judith Sanders Daug'r To Jane Born	Jan'y	8	1729
Wm Smith Son To Jo'n Born	Mar	8	1727
Tho's Sims Son To Tho's Born	Sep'r	3	1723
Jobe Sims Son To Do Born	Dec'r	15	1727
Israel Simpson Son To Isrraell Born	Jan'y	14	1730
Samuel Smith Son To Jo'n Born	June	25	1730
Winif'd Simes Daug'r To Tho's Born	Mar	7	1730
Grace Smith Daug'r To Samuel Born	Dec'r	3	1729
Sarah Smith Daug'r To Do Born	Dec'r	5	1725
Ja's Smith Son To Luck Born	Sep'r	27	1731
Ruth Smyth Daug'r To Sam'l Born	July	15	1732
Ann Smith Daug'r To Jo'n Born	July	8	1734
Jude Smith Daug'r To Luck Born	Feb'y	26	1734
Jo'n Savage Son To Dav'd Born	Ap'l	28	1733
Wm Suillevant Son To Jo'n Born	Aug't	3	1734
Wm Swift Son To Jo'n Born	Sep'r	13	1734
Winif'd Smith Daug'r To Wooldrige Born	Aug't	12	1733

page 88 headed "S".

Bety Smith Daug'r To Wooldredge Born	Jan'y	9	1735
Spencer Spradley a molato Born	Jan'y	9	1735
Grace Savige Daug'r To Dav'd Born	March	22	1736
Margaret Smith Daug'r To Jo'n Born	July	27	1736
Jo'n Smith Son To Do Born	Jan'y	4	1739
Tho's Serell Son To Judith a Molato Ws bn	Oct'r	15	1738
George Shepard Son To Hinmor Born	Feb'y	13	1741
Hannah Swillivant Daug'r To Jo'n Born	Aug	14	1739
Ja's Simes Son To Tho's Born	Nov	30	1735
Jerimiah Sims Son To Do Born	Feb'y	8	1738
Septehan (?) Swift Daug'r To Jo'n Born	Dec'r	25	1737
Susana Swift Daug'r To Do Born	Feb'y	8	1742
Mary Sulevant Daug'r To Jo'n Born	Dec'r	26	1737
Peggie Sulevant Daug'r To Do Born	Aug't	9	1742
Tho's Smith Son To Jo'n Born	Aug't	2	1742
Judith Shepard Daug'r To Henmor Born	Aug't	23	1743
Winif'd Smute Daug'r To Edw'd Born	July	18	1724
Ann Smute Daug'r To Do Born	Oct'r	13	1726
Tho's Smute Son To Do Born	July	9	1729
Sarah Ann Smute Daug'r To Do Born	June	4	1732
James Spray Son To Ann Born	Sep'r	1	1738
Judith Scofild Daug'r To Hen'y Born	Dec'r	25	1743
Eliz'a Simes Daug'r To Ja's Born	Jan'y	27	1740
Sarah Simes Daug'r To Do Born	Jan'y	18	1743
Alce Smith Daug'r To Jo'n Born	Ap'l	14	1745
Wm Shepard Son To Hen'y Born	March	13	1746
Judith Smith Daug'r To Jo'n Smith	Nov'r	12	1737
Ann Smith Daug'r To Do Born	Feb'y	8	1734
Tho's Scofield Son To Hen'y Born	Aug't	2	1744
Betsy Scofield Daug'r To Do Born	Oct'r	19	1746
John Swellivant Son To Jo'n Born	Aug't	21	1747
Rich'd Spane Son To Cuthbert Born	Jan'y	19	1741
Tho's Streyton Bastard Sone To Sarah Born	Nov'm	20	1746
Cloye Swift Daug'r To Jo'n Born	June	15	1748
Bety Swelevant Daug'r To Jo'n Born	Nov'r	10	1749
Eliz'a Smith Daug'r To Jo'n Born	Ap'l	24	1748
Bety Smith Daug'r To Antho'y Born	May	3	1748
Jo'n Shirley Son To Daniell Born	Aug't	16	1741
Ja's Shirley Son To Do Born	Aug't	22	1745
Rich'd Sharley Son To Do Born	Jully	12	1748

page 89. headed "S".

Judith Shirley Daug'r To Daniel Born	Sep'r	6	1751
Wm Sims Son To Ja's Born	Aug't	1	1747
Ja's Simes Son To Do Born	Sep'r	30	1751
Jo'n Shepard Son To Henmor Born	Dec'r	20	1751
Judy Sullivan Daug'r To John Born	Jan'ry	25	1754
Charles Snaut Son To Thomas Born	Sept	5	1753
Susannah Selfe Daug'r To William & Jean was Born	Nov'r	10	1754
Thomas Shepard Son To Henmor was born	Dec'r	25	1754
John Swift Son To William Born	March	16	1754
John Short Son To Benedict & Ann was Born	April	4	1755
Elisabeth & Susannah Stanleys Twins To Thomas & Susannah were born	Sep'r	27	1755

James Sullivant Son To John & Jean was Born   Dec'r   24   1755
George Smith Son To Wooldridge & Betty was Born   Dec'r   14   1755
Argeland Sharley Son To Argeland & Elisabeth was Born Feb'ry 20   1756
Lucy Self Daug'r To William & Taby was Born   Dec'r   9   1755
William Sebry Son To James was Born   July   30   1739
Richard Sebry Son To Do was Born   Dec'r   26   1741
John Sebry Son To Do was Born   May   10   1743
Corbin Straughan Son To Rich'd & Joan was Born   Aug'st   4   1756
Samuel Sebree Son To Wm & Mary was Born   June   8   1756
Nancy Sims Daug'r To James was Born   Nov'r   19   1756
Nancy Smith Daug'r To Thomas was Born   Sep'r   11   1756
John Self Son To James was Born   Nov'r   20   1755
Winifred Shirley Daug'r To John & Eliz'a was Born   July   31   1742
Thomas Self Son To Wm & Tabie was Born   March   20   1757
Wm Self Son To Wm & Jean was Born   June   3   1757
Jesse Sullivan Son To John & Jane was Born   Nov'r   24   1757
Daniel Shurley Son To Daniel & Martha was Born   May   1   1754
Jane Shurley Daug'r To Do & Do born   Jan'ry   4   1758
William Stoneman Son To George & Ann Stoneman born   Feb'ry   17   1758
Winefred Schofield Daug'r To Henry & Betty
   Schofield born   Februry 7th 1749
Sarah Schofield Daug'r To Do & Do was born   March   22d 1752/3
William Schofield Son To Do & Do was born   Novem   9th 1754
Ellis Schofield Son To Do & Do was born   March   22d 1757
Rebekah Standly Daug'r To Thomas & Susannah
   standley was born   August   17   1758
Thomas Self Son To Thomas & Sarah Self was Born   October   9   1758

page 90, headed "S".
Samuel Lamkin Straughan Sen to Richard Straughan
   was born   February 6   1759
Thomas Self Son to James & Peggy Self was born   June   2   1759
Nancy Schofield Daug'r to Henry & Betty
   Schofield was born   August   30   1759
William Smith son to John & Jane Smith was born   February 27   1760
Elizabeth Suillavant Daug'r to William & Judith
   Suillivant born   Sepy'r   6   1760
John Smither Son to Moses & Judith Smither was born   August   13   1760
Winny Swift Daug'r to William & Lucretia Swift
   was born   Novem   19   1757
Rhoda Swift Daug'r to William & Lucretia Swift was born March 19 1760
Ellis Sims son to James & Ann Sims was born   October   5   1753
John Sims Son to James & Ann Sims was born   January 26   1759
Katy Sims Daughter to James & Ann Sims was born   Novem   7   1760
Thezia Self Daughter to William & Tabitha Self
   was born   Feb'ry   24   1761
Robert Schefield Son to Henry & Betty Schofield
   was born   Decem   11   1761
Moses Self son to James & Margaret Self was born   January 17   1762
John Smither son to George & Sarah Smither was born   Novemb   23   1761
Susannah Self Daughter to James & Margaret Self
   was born   Feb'ry   25   1764
Elizabeth Stephens Daughter to William & Sarah
   Stephens born   January 20   1764
Elizabeth Smith Daughter to Richard & Deborah
   Smith was born   June   10   1764

page 90 (continued)

Henry Schofield son to Henry & Betty Schofield was born	Feb'ry	23	1764
George Smither son to George & Sarah Smither was born	August	23	1764
Ann Smither Daughter to George & Sarah Smither was born	May	31	1766
Rhoda Sims Daughter to James & Anne Sims was born	October	11	1765
Salley Self Daughter to William & Tabby Self was born	Novemb	2	1766
Elisha Harcum Schofield Son to Henry & Betty Schofield was born	Feb'ry	1	1767
John son of Richard & Deborah Smith was born	Decembr	24	1766
Hannah Sanders Daughter to John & Ann Saunders was born	May	25	1767
Sarah Smither Daughter to Geo Smithers & Sarah Smither was born	April	13	1769
Hannah Daughter of Jas & Leazur Self was born	dec'r	23	1766
Elizabeth Batheen Self Daughter to James & Margit Self was Born	february	16	1778
John Self son to Wm & Tabe his wife was Born	March	4	1759
Mishel Self Daughter of Do was born	June	19	1764
Nance Daughter of Do was born	June	8	1769
Judah Ellexander Daughter of John & Judah his wife Born	Novmbr	4	1771
Shapley Ellexander Son Wm & Dorcos his wife was Born	October	7	1771
Cty Sebrey Daughter of Wm Sebree & Jean his wife was Born (sic)	March	1	1772
Gabril Smither Son of George & Sary his wife was Born	March	14	1772
George Middleton Son of Judith Shurley Was Born	february	24	1772
Mary Shrap Daughter of Aron & Mary his Wife was Born	Novmbr	15	1771
William Sanders Son of John Sanders & Rhodey his wife was born	March	8	1772
Alse Self Daughter of William & tabbe his wife was Born	March	20	1772
Peter Seebrey Son of Thos & Ann Sebre his wife was Born	April	13	1772
Elizabeth Smith Daughter of John & Saryan Smith his wife ws bn	April	23	1772
Fleet Smith Son of Spencer & Elizabeth Smith his wife was Born	May	28	1772

page 91, headed "S".

Judith Shappleigh Elleston Daughter to John & Bettey his wife Born	March	1	1777
Hannah Ritts Smither Daughter to George & Sarah his wife was Born	April	28	1777
Nancey Sebre Daughter to James & Bettey his wife was Born	Sep'r	7	1777
Elizabeth Sinclair Daughter of John & Mary his wife was Born	Aug't	22	1777
Samuel Self Son of Abraham & Susanner his wife was Born	October	8	1777
Mary Swift Daughter of William & Sarah his wife was Born	Sep't	12	1777
Appleby Sorrel Son to James & Elezebeth his wife was born	April	29	1778
Elezebeth Schofield Daughter to Salley Schofield a bastd was born	March	31	1779
George Skinner son to Charles & Pegga his wife was born	Jan'ry	7	1780
Jeremiah Shurley son to Peter & Ann his wife was born	Feb	11	1780
Sethey Shurley Daughter to Joy Shurley a bastard child was born	Nov'm	18	1779
George Walker Sebree son to William & Jean his wife was Born	Nov'm	18	1779
Sarah Sinclair Daughter to John & Margerett his wife was Born	March	9	1780
William Lane Self son to Matthias & Nancey his wife was Born	March	17	1780

page 91 (continued)

Herodias Short Daughter to John & Martha his wife was born Jan'r 30 1781
Molley Harris Self Daughter to John & Sarah his wife was born Feb 12 1781
Sharlotte Gordon Daughter to George Gordon & Elizabeth
    Saunders A B C   Feb 16 1773
Shapley France Son to Saraan Smith a Bastard Child born   May 12 1781
Hannah Trussel Self Daughter to Matthias & Nancey his wife
    ws born   April 5 1778
Corbin Straughn Son to David & Salley his wife was born   June 9 1781
John Shearley Son to Joseph & Mary his wife was born   Sep't 20 1781
John Posey Self Son to Matthias & Nancey his wife was born Dec'm 30 1781
John Corbin Straughn Son to Samuel L Straughn & Phebe
    his wife was Born   Oct 21 1781
Ailsey Banks Self Daughter to Thomas & Keziah his wife ws bn Feb 22 1782
Nancey Shurley Daughter to Peter & - his wife was born   March 3 1782
Mary Skinner Daughter to Charles & Pegga his wife ws bn   June 12 1782
Winnefret Stephens Daughter to Smith & Molley his
    wife was born   Oct 28 1781
Thomas Self Son to John & Sarah his wife was Born   Feb 28 1783
Holland Stephens Son to John & Mary his wife was Born   July 24 1783
William Stephens Son to Smith & Mary his wife was bn   Aug't 4 1783
Samuel Lamkin Straughn Son to Samuel & Phebele h wife ws bn July 30 1783
Nancey Straughn Daughter to David & Salley his wife ws bn Aug't 8 1783
Pegga Skinner Daughter to Charles & Pegga his wife ws bn   Oct 20 1783
Thomas Chinn Self Son to Matthias & Nancey his wife ws born Nov'm 20 1783
James Blince Self Son to Thomas Self & Keziah his wife ws bn May 25 1784
Salley Sutten Daughter to Isaac & Nancey his wife ws born Oct 18 1778
Frances an Shurley Daughter to Peter & - his wife was born March 24 1785
Elizabeth Smith Daughter to Stephen & Sarah his wife was born Sep't 15 1784
Molley Sims Daughter to Ellis Sims & Winney his wife was born Aug't 25 1785
Samuel Davis Swilleman son to Elizabeth Swilleman was born Dec'm 22 1786
Thomas Steward Short son to John & Martha his wife was born Nov'm 9 1785

page 92, headed "S".

James Skinner Daughter (sic) to Charles & Marget his
    wife ws born   April 4 1786
Peter Smith Self son to Moses & Ann his wife was Born   Feb 1 1787
Bennie Cole Self Daughter to Matthias & Nancey his
    wife was born   Oct 6 1786
Sammuel Allason Self Son to Jeremiah & Hannah his wife Born Nov'm 11 1786
Samuel Smith Stephen son to John & Mary his wif ws Born   Sept 17 1787
Pegga Battan Self Daughter to Thomas & Keziah his wife was
    born   June 9 1787
Mary Smith Daughter to James & Elezebeth his wife ws Born Jan'r 12 1788
Fanney Hanson Self Daughter to Matthias & Nancey his wife June 15 1788
Betsey Shearley Daughter to Jeseph & Molley his wife
    was Born   Feb 15 1789
Elias Stephen son to Smith Stephen & Molley his wife
    was Born   Nov'm 9 1787
James Mealey Stephens son to Ditto & Ditto was Born   April 8 1789
Samuel Smither son to Launce L. Smither & Nancey hs wf ws Born Sep't 5 1789
Thomas Bearcrofft Self son to Thomas Self & Keziah his
    wife was Born   Jan'r 2 1790
Samuel tha son of Cattron Seabrey (a bastard child) was born June 9 1790

page 92 (continued)

William Diver Warran Short son to Winney Short A B C was born	Dec'r	17	1789
Benney Ramey Stuckey Daughter to Job Stuckey & Mary his wife ws bn	Oct	16	1790
Genney Shirley Daughter to Joseph & Molley his wife ws Born	Sept	14	1790
Charles Skinner son to Charles & Pegga his wife ws Bn	Jan'r	2	1791
Ann Smith Daughter to James & Elizabeth his wife ws bn	Dec'm	13	1790
James Lewis Straughn son to Samuel L. Straughn & Phebe his wife was Born	Nov'm	6	1785
Richard Straughn son to Ditto & Ditto his wife ws bn	May	28	1787
Jean Lewis Straughn Daughter to Ditto & Ditto his wife was born	Feb	6	1791
John Shearley son to George & Sarahann his wife was Born	April	15	1793
Thomas Nuton Smith son to Peter Smith & Sara his wife was Born	Dec'm	24	1795
William Brisco Stephens son to James Stephens & Jean his wife was Born	December	22	1798

page 93, headed "S is carried forward"

Dolley Schofield Daughter of Thomas & Sary Scofiele his wife was born	May	10	1772
Sary Smith Daughter to Richard & Deborah Smith his wife was born	May	28	1772
James Blinco Self Son of James Self & Margit his wife was Born	January	5	1773
A child of John Suillevant Born	March	14	1773
William Sotton Son of John & Mary his wife was Born	October	15	1772
Winnefrit Sims Daughter of Jobe & Susannah was born	March	17	1773
Nancey Garding Sanders Daughter of Elizabeth Sanders was Born	february	16	1773
Richard Seebree Son of James & Winnefrit was Born	October	17	1758
Thomas Seebree Son of Elizabeth Seebree was Born	November	10	1762
Bette Daughter to Do Was Born	February	6	1764
James Seebree Son of Do & Do was Born (sic)	October	13	1765
William Seebree Son to Do & Do was Born	May	5	1768
Rhoda Seebree Daughter to Do & Do	Janry	12	1774

(Note: The above entries look as though somebody did not write down everything they knew.   B.F.)

Elizabeth Seebree Daughter of William & Jean his wife was born	April	28	1774
William Swift son of William & Sarah his wife Born	July	21	1773
Sammuel Smith Son of thos & Sary Smith his wife was Born	Septmbr	10	1773
Lewhah Sorrell Daughter of Dafney Sorrell was born	July	1	1773
John Sanders son of John & Rhoday his wife was Born	Novembr	4	1773
Nancey Smith Daughter of Thos Smith & Caty his wife was Born	October	1	1773
John Stuckke Son of James & Elizabeth his wife was Born	Novembr	29	1773
Philip Swift Son of William & Lucresha his wife was Born	Decembr	31	1762
George Swift Son of William & Lucresha his wife was Born	February	2	1768
Rachel Garner Daughter of Elizabeth Self	December	27	1755
George Sanford Hambelton the son of Elibeth Sanford was Born	April	18	1773
Betsey Smither Daughter of George & Sary his wife was Born	December	30	1774
Elizabeth Stepoe was Born	Aprill	7	1774
John Shurley Son of Argeland & Elizabeth his wife was Born	August	18	1774
fanney Smith Daughter of Lewis & Mary his wife was Born	March	18	1775
Nancy Suillevint Daughter of John Swillivent was Born	March	12	1775
Nancy Swift Daughter of William & Sarah his wife was Born	March	21	1775
Charles Grayham Son of Salley Schofield was Born	Decembr	31	1775
William Quille Sinclair Son of John & Margaret his wife was Born	Octo	10	1775

Job Stuckey Son of Job & Elizabeth his wife was Born   January 6 1776
Elizabeth Hill Daughter of Matthias & Nancey Self was Born   February 11 1775
Richard Straughn Son of David & Salley his wife was Born   July   9 1776
Ann Cole Self Daughter of Matthias & Ann Self his wife was Born Augst 24 1776
Cantance Self Son of Abraham & Susanner his wife was born   Agust   17 1776
Salley Schofield Daughter of Thomas & Sarah his wife was born July   3 1775
Joseph Smith Son of Thomas & Cattreen his wife was Born   March   21 1775
William Smith Son of Wm & Mary his wife was Born   Decmbr 28 1775
Nancey Striddels Daughter of Elizabeth was born   Aprill 26 1775
Ann Sims Daughter of Job & Leanner his wife was Born   Aprill 24 1775
Hannah Shapley Daughter of Bettey Shapley was Born   May   7 1775
Judith Silivant Daughter of John Silivant was Born   March   20 1777
Cloee Straton Daughter of John & Elizabeth his wife was Born June   6 1777
George Simmons Son of James & Darkey his wife was Born   January 13 1777
Hannah Shearley Daughter of Argagland Shearley a Bsd child
   was Born   Augt   3 1777

Page 94 headed "T"

                Peter Turner Son To John Bap'd   Ap'l   5 1702
                Tho's Turner Son To Tho's Bap'd   Feb'y   9 1700
                Edward Turner Son To Jo'n Bap'd   May   14 1693
                William Tignor Son To Wm Bap'd   June   11 1693
                Wm Templer Son To Wm Bap'd   July   23 1693
                Edw'd Taycor Son To Edw'd Bap'd   June   20 1693
                Eliz'a Tho's Daug'r To Jo'n Born   Dec'r   17 1693
                Tho's Thomas son to Do Born   Feb'y   23 1691
                Wm Thrope son To Eliz'a Bap'd   Ap'l   29 1705
                Mary Thrope Daug'r To Wm Bap'd   Nov'r   9 1705
                Eliz'a Tignon Daug'r To Philope Bap'd   Ap'l   11 1708
                Garvas Tho's son to Jo'n Born   Jan'y   6 1709
                George Trussell son To Jo'n Born   Nov'r   21 1710
                Jo'n Tolson son To Wm Born   May   27 1712
                Rich'd Thomson son To Rich'd Born   July   2 1712
                Rich'd Tulles son To Jo'n Born   Jan'y   1 1701
                Sarah Tulles Daug'r To Do Born   July   7 1704
                Jo'n Tulles Son To Do Born   May   11 1709
                Susana Tules Daug'r To Do Born   Dec'r   18 1707
                Rodham Tules Sone To Do Born   May   24 1712
                Winif'd Tules Daug'r To Do Born   Jully   15 1709
                Jane Tules Daug'r To Do Born   Feb'y   9 1714
                Rich'd Thomson son To Ja's Born   Ap'l   18 1704
                Ann Thomson Daug'r To Do Born   Marc   14 1707
                Mark Thomson Son To Do Born   Feb'y   5 1710
                Ja's Thomson Son To Do Born   Dec'r   12 1714
                Wm Tignor Son To Philop Born   Feb'y   22 1714
                Jo'n Thomas Son To Jo'n Born   Ap'l   16 1715
                Hannah Thomson Daug'r To Rich'd Born   Aug't   3 1715
                Mathew Trussell Son To Jo'n Born   Oct'r   19 1715
                Rich'd Tules son To Cloud Born   Mar   29 1667
                Susana Tules Daug'r To Do Born   Feb'y   6 1672
                Jo'n Tules Son To Do Born   June   12 1682
                Ann Timens Daug'r To Tho's Born   Oct'r   29 1681
                Tho's Timens Son To Do Born   Sept'r 29 1684
                Rich'd Thomson son To Rich'd Born   -   - 1674
                Ja's Thomson Son To Do Born   Oct'r   29 1671

Charles Wade Son of the Hon'rble Presley & Charlotte
  Thornton was born   June   1 1764
John Tayloe Son of the Hon'rble Presley & Charlotte
  Thornton was born   Feb'r   19 1766
Elizabeth Daughter of John & - (wife's name omitted)
  Taylor was born   Feb'r   18 176-
Dennis Son to James & Winnifred Tignor was born   Jan   31 1767
John Williams son of Aaron Williams & Sarah Toulson
  was born   Nov'r   16 1767
Lucretia Tempelman Daughter of James & Hannah his
  wife was born   Feb'y   12 1772
Elizabeth Tolson Daughter of Partrick Toleson was Born   August   31 1772
Elizabeth Trop Daughter of William & Mary his wife
  was born   Septmbr 20 1772
Margit Spilman Traysee Daughter of John & Margit
  was Born   December 8 1772
Hanice Townsin Son of Hanice Townsin was Born   Aprill   22 1773
Richard Toulson Son of tho's was Born   Aprill   4 1773
Pattey Ticer Daughter of Judeth Ticer was born   March   15 1774
Gideon Ticer Son of William & Margit his wife
  was born   December12 1773
Robert Thomas Son of Robert & Sarah his wife
  was born   May   16 1774
James Toulson son of Sary Toulson was born   July   15 1775
William Trop Son of Wm & Mary his wife was Born   February18 1774
Samuel & Issack Thomas twins Sons to Robert Thomas
  was born   December29 1771
George Thomas son of John & Mary his wife was Born   January 27 1775
Sura Thomas Daughter to James & Hannah his wife
  was Born   May   31 1775
William Todd Son of Cornelus & hannah his wife
  was Born   february23 1775
Elizabeth thomas Daughter to John & Bettey his wife
  was Born   Septembr16 1775
Edward townsin Son of Hanney & Elizabeth his wife
  was born   September4 1775
John Todd Son of Cornolius was Born   Feb'ry   14 1777
Gilburd hambelton Ticor Son of William & Margit his
  wife Born   June   1 1776
Elizabeth Trop Daughter to Aron was Born   December10 1774
Bettey Toulson Daughter of John & Mary his wife
  was born   September10 1775
Sary Toulson Daughter of Partrick & Elinder his wife
  was Born   Novem'br 20 1775
John Thomas son of John & Mary his wife was born   Septembr 6 1777
James Thomas son of Thomas Thomas & Darkey his wife
  was Born   March   16 1778
Winder Toulson son of John & Molley his wife was barn   Jan'y   16 1778
Milloy Thomas Daughter of Siner was born   Decembr 14 1777
William Throp son of Winnefrot was born   March   26 1778
John Townsend son to Haynie & Bottey his wife was born   May   26 1778
Winnefrot Tigner Daughter to James & Salloy was born   July   13 1778
James Thrift Son to Nathanael was Born   Feb   27 1779
Henry Tod son to Cornelus & Hannah his wife was born   Sept   13 1779
Winney Thomas Daughter to John & Mary his wife was Born   Sept   4 1780
Thomas Doscey Trasee son to John & Susannah his wife
  was born   Oct   9 1780

page 95 (continued)

Thomas Jones Thomas son to Tho's Thomas & Dorca his wife ws born	Nov'm	2	1781
John Todd son to Cornelious Todd & Hannah his wife was Born	Feb	14	1782
Susanna Trig Trasee Daughter to John Trasee & Susanna was born	March	7	1783
William H. Tillery son to James O. Tillery & Elizabeth his wife	April	3	1783
Pattey Thomas Daughter to John & Mary his wife was born	Oct	15	1783

page 96, headed "T"

John Thrift son to John & Mary his wife was born	Dec'm	7	1783
Peter Todd son to Cornelias Todd & Hannah his wife was Born	April	19	1784
Elizabeth Hamilton Thomas Daughter to Thomas Thomas & Dorkey his wife was Born	Decem	25	1783
Salley Thomas Daughter to David Thomas & Mary his Wife was Born	April	22	1784
Sanford Trasee son to John & Susannah his wife ws bn	Sept	14	1784
Jesse Thrift son to Nathaniel & Elizabeth his wife was born	Jan'r	19	1785
Peter Dewkins Thomas son to Peter & Judith his wife ws born	Jan'r	1	1786
William Thomas son to James & Ann Simmons a bast'd was born	Apriell	11	1786
Pattey Rabey Tealis Daughter to Rhodam & Hannah his wife ws born	Sept	29	1786
Thomas Doxey Trasee son to John Trasee & Susannah his wife ws bn	July	7	1787
Epaphroditus Tillery son Fortunatus & Susannah his wife ws born	Augst	23	1790
John Washington Tillery son to Samuel Tillery & Ailsey his wife was Born	Feb'r	21	1807

page 97, headed "Hudson".

Molly Haynie Daug'r to John & Mary Died	Nov'r	26	1755
Eliz'a Haynie Daug'r to Henry Died	Nov'r	25	1756
Sarah Harper Daug'r to Joshua Died	March	11	1757
Sarah Harper Wife to William Died	March	11	1757
Mary Hickman Died	March	8	1757
John Hobson son to Adcock & Joanna Died	March	18	1757
Abraham Haynie son to' John & Sarah Haynie Died	November	19	1759
Fielding Hudson Died	September	16	1774
Molley Hudson wife to Thos Hudson Died a little after midnight Apriel 2 1776

page 98, headed "T".

Sarah Taylor Daug'r To Wm Born	Nov'r	26	1688
Phobey Taylor Daug'r To Wm Born	May	18	1691
Wm Taylor Son To Do Born	Feb'y	23	1693
Jo'n Turner Son To Jo'n Born	Dec'r	2	1671
Mary Tigner Daug'r To Wm Born	Sep'r	6	1666
Mobel Tigner Daug'r To Do Born	Dec'r	28	1670
Philope Tigner Son To Do Born	Feb'y	26	1674
Eliz'a Tignor Daug'r To Do Born	Nov'r	14	1685
Wm Tignor Son To Do Born	June	11	1693
Honry Templay Son To Wm Born	June	3	1680
Jo'n Thomson Son To John Born	Mar	10	1684
Mary Tepley Daug'r To Thomas Born	May	18	1692

page 98 (continued)

Benj'n Tolson Son To Benj'n Born	July	23	1693
Peter Turner Son To Jo'n Born	Ap'l	5	1702
Sarah Thornton Daug'r To Tho's Born	May	23	1699
Fielding Turner Son To Jo'n Born	June	10	1706
Mary Turner Daug'r To Do Born	Jan'y	22	1708
Eliz'a Tolson Daug'r To Tho's Born	March	18	1705
Susanah Tolson Daug'r To Do Born	Aug't	10	1707
Sarah Thomson Daug'r To Rich'd	Mar	31	1721
Jo'n Tayeor Son To Edward Born	Aug't	15	1721
Medcalfe Thomson Son To Ja's Born	Sep'r	24	1722
Jo'n Thorpe Son To Rob't Born	March	4	1705
Moses Thrope Son To Do Born	Ap'l	5	1708
Aaron Thrope Son To Do Born	Oct'r	2	1709
Rob't Throp Son To Do Born	Jan'y	14	1712
Hanah Thope Daug'r To Do Born	Dec'r	16	1714
Ann Talbert Daug'r To Edward	July	4	1719
Winif'd Talbert Daug'r To Do Born	Aug't	30	1722
Mary Ann Turner Daug'r To Jo'n Born	Sep'r	17	1719
Samuell Tayeor Son To Edw'd	May	8	1726
Eliz'a Thomas Daug'r To Tho's	Oct'r	20	1716
Rich'd Thomas Son To Do Born	Sep'r	25	1719
Mary Tho's Daug'r To Do Born	Sep'r	20	1725
Tho's Tignor Son To Ja's Born	Jully	1	1728
Bety Butler Tolson Daug'r To Tho's Born	Dec'r	1	1721
Judith Tolson Daug'r To Do Born	Oct'r	9	1729

page 99 headed "T".

John Tolson Son To Ben'jn Born	Sep'r	22	1724
Benj'n & George Tolson Twins To Do Born	Dec'r	22	1726
Spencer Tolson Son To Do Born	Oct'r	31	1730
George Tolson Son To Jo'n Born	Oct'r	21	1718
Sarah Tolson Daug'r To Do Born	Jully	27	1721
Benj'n Tolson Son To Do Born	March	6	1723
Jo'n Tolson Son To Jo'n Born	Aug't	5	1727
Judith Tolson Daug'r To Do Born	Jan'y	1	1729
Eliz'a Tolson Daug'r To Tho's Born	Sep'r	1	1721
Susanah Tolson Daug'r To Do Born	Jan'y	2	1724
Tho's Tolson Son To Do Born	July	3	1726
Eiuch (?) Tolson Daug'r To Do Born	Dec'r	22	1722
Mary Tolson Daug'r To Do Born	Sep'r	4	1712
Judith Tolson Daug'r To Do Born	Jan'y	5	1717
Sarah Tignor Daug'r Philope Born	Oct'r	1	1722
Ja's Tignor Son To Do Born	Ap'l	15	1724
Philope Tignor Son To Do Born	Oct'r	26	1726
Luckey Tignor Daug'r To Do Born	Oct	30	1735
Lucreash Tigner Daug'r To Do Born	March	5	1730
Wm Tignor Son To Ja's Born	May	18	1731
Jereboam Tho's Son To Tho's Born	March	14	1732
Rich'd Tleles (?) Son To Rich'd Born	March	30	1730
Moses Trape Son To Jo'n Born	Feb'y	27	1731
Sarah Ann Tho's Daug'r To Peter Born	Feb'y	25	1729
Dav'd Teles Son To Jo'n Bern	Jully	26	1731
George Turner Son To John Born	June	3	1731
Winif'd Thomas Daug'r To Peter Born	May	17	1732
Jo'n Tolson Son To Tho's Born	Sept'r	8	1732
Mary Tolson Daug'r To Do Born	Dec'r	7	1732
Ja's Tigner Son To Ja's Born	Feb'y	28	1733
Tho's & Ann Tolson Twins to Jo'n Born	Feb'y	4	1733

Denis Tigner Son To Philope Born	Mar	1	1733
Wiloughbey Thomson Son To Rich'd	July	3	1729
Samuell Thomson Son To Do Born	Ap'l	11	1731
Mary Ann Thomson Daug'r To Do Born	Sep'r	23	1733
Ann Toles Daug'r To Rich'd Born	June	11	1728

page 100, headed "T".

Mary Ann Tignor Daug'r To Ja's Born	Jan'y	8	1736
Phillidia Tho's Daug'r To Ann Born	May	18	1736
Betty Tolson Daug'r To Jo'n Born	Sep'r	3	173-
Wm Tolson Son To Benj'n Born	Jan'y	28	1737
Eliz'a Tignor Daug'r To Wm Born	May	26	1737
Nany Elvett Tour Daug'r To Rich'd Born	Oct'r	27	1738
Eliz'a Tignor Daug'r To Ja's Born	Nov'r	6	1738
Winif'd Tolson Daug'r To John Jun'r Born	March	21	1734
Eliz'a Tolson Daug'r To Do Born	Aug	27	1736
Wm Tolson Son To Do Born	Oct'r	19	1737
Jo'n Tolson Son To Do Born	May	17	1739
Phillidia Thomas Daug'r To John Born	May	21	1738
Thamiar Tho's Daug'r To Do Born	Feb'y	24	1739
Wm Tignor Son To Wm Born	Ap'l	5	1739
Tabb Taycor Son To Edward Born	Dec'r	3	1741
Morgin Tho's Daug'r To Jo'n Born	Aug't	12	1742
Aaron Thrope Son To Aaron Born	Sep'r	13	1756
Sarah Taycer Was Born	June	25	1741
Sainer Tycer Was Born	March	24	1744
Judith Taycer Daug'r To Edward Born	March	19	1744
Hanah Tolson Daug'r To George Born	Aug't	17	1742
Jesse Tolson Son To Do Born	March	16	1744
Haynie Townsend Son To Wm Born	Dec'r	22	1745
Rowley Tho's Sone To Eliz'a Born	Oct'r	30	174-
Jo'n Thrope Son Aaron Bern	Mar	23	174-
Wm Thrope Son Do Born	March	15	1746
Sainah Townsend Daug'r To Wm Born	Feb'y	23	1748
Amy Thomas Daug'r To Eliz'a Born	Jan'y	19	1748
Jo'n Taycar Son To Edward Born	Jan'y	2	1746
Edw'd Taycar Son To Do Born	May	24	1748
Leannah Thomas Daug'r To Rich'd Born	May	11	1747
Peter Tho's Son To James Born	Sep'r	18	1747
Jas Tho's Son To Do Born	Ap'l	28	1749
Ann Towsend Daug'r To Wm Born	Oct'r	24	1749
Emannuel Walker Taycar Son Jane Born	Feb'y	4	1747
Jo'n Tho Son To Ja's Born	Mar	18	1751
Elinor Thomas Daug'r To Rich'd	Feb'y	19	1752
Wine Thomas Daug'r To Peter Born	Feb'y	15	1753
Moses Thrope Son To Moses Born	Mar	22	175-
Tolson Tignor Son To Ja's Born	June	2	1741
Rich'd Tiles Son To Rich'd Born	Mar	31	1730
Eliz'a & Sarah Ann Tiles Twins to Rich'd	Dec'r	6	1731
Wm Tiles Son To Do Born	Aug't	18	1734
Sarah Troth Daug'r To Rich'd	Sep'r	2	1734
Ann & Mary Ann Tolson Daug'r To Benj'n	Nov'r	3	173-

page 101 headed "T".

Mary Ticar Daug'r To Edward & Eliz'a his wife Born	Nov'r	21	1753
Betty Tignor Daug'r Philip & Aloe was Born	July	29	1748
Nancy Tignor Daug'r To Do was Born	Sept'r	5	1750

page 101 (continued)

Dennis Tignor Son To Do was Born	Nov'r	13	1752
Thomas Tignor Son To Do was Born	Nov'r	26	1754
Philip Tignor Son To James & Winefred was Born	Oct'r	5	1748
James Tignor Son To Do was Born	Feb'y 18		1750
Sarah Tignor Daug'r To Do was Born	July	27	1752
Winifred Tignor Daug'r To Do was Born	Dec'r	17	1754
Sarah Taylor Daug'r Thomas & Eliz'a was Born	March	1	1752
William Toone Son To Mark & Elisa'h was Born	April	8	1755
John Toulson Son To John & Nelly was Born	Dec'r	16	1756
Betty Throp Daughter to Moses & Eleanor Throp was born	March	29	1756
Ewell Townsend Son To Joshua Townsend & Mary his wife was born	Septmbr	12	1757
Sarahann Taylor Daughter to John & Judith Taylor was born	Septmbr	3	1751
Maryan Taylor Daughter to John & Judith Taylor was born	February	7	1753
Moses Taylor son to John & Judith Taylor was born	April	19	1754
John Taylor Son To John & Judith Taylor was born	January	29	1757
Judith Taylor Daughter to John & Judith Taylor was born	January	21	1759
Nancy Throp Daughter to Moses & Eleanor Throp was born	October	15	1758
Lucky Tignor Daughter to James & Winifred Tignor was born	Septem	9	1757
Martha Tignor Daughter to James & Winifred Tignor was born	May	27	1760
Thomasin Taylor Daughter to John & Judith Taylor was born	April	14	1761
Molley Tignor Daughter to Wm & Hannah Tignor was born	Septem	11	1761
Robert Throp son to Aaron Throp Ju'r & Mary was born	March	28	1759
Samuel Templeman son to James & Hannah Templeman	Decem	27	1761
William Tignor son to Phillip & Marget Tignor was born	Septem	6	1758
Phillip Tignor Son to Do was born	Decemb	4	1760
Peggy Tignor Daug'r To Do was born	October	29	1762
Martha Tignor Daughter to James & Winifred Tignor born	May	17	1760
(Note: The above entry is cancelled in the original B.F.)			
George Tignor son to James & Winifred Tignor was born	April	9	1762
Isaac Tignor son to James & Winifred Tignor was born	Aug't	6	1764
John Townsend son to William & Betty Townsend was born	March	26	1752
Griffin Townsend son to William & Betty Townsend was born	March	26	1758
Elizabeth Templeman Daughter to James & Hannah Templeman	Septem	8	1764
Hannah Throp Daughter to Aaron Throp Jun'r & Mary his wife was born	Septemb	18	1763
John Throp Son to Aaron Throp Jun'r & Mary his wife was born	April	19	1765
Elizabeth Daughter of Coll Presley & Elizabeth Thornton was born	March	2	1748/9
Peter Presly son of Coll Presly Thornton & Elizabeth was born	August	16	1750
Winifred Daughter of Coll Presley & Elizabeth Thornton was born	Dec'r	3	1751
Presley son of the Hon'rble Presly & Charlotte Thornton was born	March	2	1760
Charlotte Daughter of Do & Do was born	March	9	1762

page 102.

William Lewis Died	Sept'r	22	1755
William Lewis Glazier Died	Dec'r	7	1755

page 103   headed "H".

Lucretia Hudnall daug'r to Nathan Died	Feb'ry	27	1755
Peter Hayes Died	June	19	1756
William Haroum Junr Departed this life	June	16	1757
William Hughlett son to John & Esther Hughlett Died	May	30	1759
Abraham Haynie son to John & Sarah Died	Novem	19	1759
David Hammontree son to David & Sarah Hammontree Died	Novem	12	1764

page 104, headed "St Stepens N Parish"

Jo'n Norman Son Jo'n Born	Nov'r	7	1708
Filding Nash Son To Keesih Born	May	24	1706
Charity Nowland Daug'r To Rioh'd Born	Sep'r	29	1699
Jo'n Nelms Son To Jo'n Born	June	20	1711
Sarah Nelms Daug'r To Do Born	March	4	1713
Samuell Nelms Son To Rich'd Born	March	9	1712
Rich'd Nelms Son To Do Born	Nov'r	4	1714
Wm Nelms Son To Do Born	March	12	1714
Nane Nelms Daug'r To Do Born	March	23	1717
Mary Nelms Daug'r To Wm Born	Sep'r	27	1710
Hanah Nelms Daugh'r To Do Born	Feb'y	2	1712
Wm Nelms Son To Do Born	Jully	27	1715
Jo'n Niel Son To Rod'm Born	Jan'y	13	1716
Mary Newton Daug'r To Christopher Born	March	3	1687
Rioh'd Nutt Son To Rioh'd Born	Jan'y	17	1694
Ann Newton Daug'r To Christo'r Born	May	6	1697
Abner Niel Son To Daniell Born	May	5	1696
Nathan Niel Son To Do Born	Mar	3	1699
Eliz Nelms Daug'r To Char's Born	Oct'r	19	1692
Cha's Nelms Son To Do Bern	Jun	27	1694
Ann Nelms Daug'r To Do Born	Nov'r	8	1696
Wm Nelms Son To Do Born	Ap'l	23	1699
Eliz Nelms Daug'r To Wm Born	Dec'r	22	1702
Samuell Nellms Son To Do Born	June	19	1699
Christopher Niel Son To Chr Born	June	23	1671
Daniell Niel Son To Do Born	Jully	26	1673
Mathew Niele Son To Do Born	Feb'y	6	1677
Rioh'd Niell Son To Do Born	Aug't	28	1682
Rodham Niel Son To Do Born	Oct	8	1685
Patience Newton Daug'r To Christo'r Born	Aug't	6	1693
Tho's Newton Son To Do Born	Nov'r	17	1690
Eliz'a Newton Daug'r To Do Born	Ap'l	23	1699
Christo'r Newton Son To Do Born	Oct'r	14	1701
Daniell Son To Daniell Niel Born	May	29	1677
Luoretia Niel Daug'r To Do Born	Sep'r	6	1680
Wm Niel Son To Do Born	July	1	1682
Hannah Niel Daug'r To Do Born	July	12	1684
Winif'd Nelms Daug'r To Wm Born	Aug't	11	1705
Moses Nelms Son To Rioh'd Born	Mar	30	1704
Wm Nelms Son To Jo'n Born	May	11	1704

page 105, headed "N".

Luoretia Nelms Daug'r To Rioh'd Born	Feb'y	16	1705
Winif'd Nelms Daug'r To Do Born	Sep'r	5	1719
Luoretia Nelms Daug'r To Do Born	Sep'r	16	1723
Winif'd Niell Daug'r To Abnar Born	Nov'r	16	1720
Eliz Norman Daug'r To Jo'n Born	Jan'y	10	1718
Tho's Norman Son To Do Born	March	20	1721
Jane Norman Daug'r To Do Born	Feb'y	6	1724
Wm Niel Son To Abner Was Born	Sep'r	21	1724
Judith Nelms Daug'r To Cha's Born	Jully	24	1717
Ann Nelms Daug'r To Do Born	Oct'r	31	1719
Cha's Nelms Son To Do Born	Jan'y	31	1721
Hannah Nelms Daug'r To Do Born	Jully	12	1724
Ailoe Nelms Daug'r To Do Born	June	5	1726
Daniell Niel Son To Abner Born	Jan'y	25	1727
Abee Nelms Son To Cha's Born	May	12	1728
Abner Niel Son To Abner Born	Feb'y	2	1729
Jo'n Nelms Son To Joshua Born	Ap'l	26	1730

page 105 (continued)

Danill Norman Son To Wm Born	Jan'y	-	1728
Presly Nelms Son To Cha's Born	Oct'r	5	1730
Rodham Niel Son To Peter Born	March	30	1727
Lucke Niel Daug'r To Abner Born	May	3	1731
Wm Norman Son To Jo'n Born	Feb'y	10	1726
Cathron Norman Daug'r To Do Born	Jan'y	1	1729
Rich Nutt Son To Fernaford Born	Ap'l	23	1725
Jo'n Nutt Son To Do Born	Feb'y	12	1728
Maulder Nutt Son To Do Born	Sep'r	19	1729
Fernaford Nutt Son To Do Born	Sep'r	14	1731
Wm Nutt Son To Do Born	Dec'r	6	1733
Eliz Nelms Daug'r To Joshua Born	July	16	1734
Jo'n Norman Son To Jo'n Born	March	11	1736
Joshua Nelms Son To Joshua Born	March	24	1732
Sarah Nelms Daug'r To Do Born	Aug't	27	1736
Christo'r Niel Son To Abner Born	Ap'l	8	1737
Fernafold Nutt Son To Fernaf'd Born	Sep'r	28	1736
Jo'n Niel Son To Abner Born	Feb'y	28	1739
Peter Niel Son To Do Born	Dec'r	5	1740
Nene Nutt Daug'r To Fernaf'd Born	Aug't	20	1740
Letie Nelms Daug'r To Joshua Born	Nov'r	14	1738
Edmon Northen Nelms Son Do Born	March	6	1741
Rodham Niel Son To Abner Born	Jan'y	24	1743

page 106, headed "N".

Sarah Ann Nutt Daug'r To Fernafold Born	May	1	1743
Mary Niel Daug'r To Abner Born	May	27	1745
Danell Niel Son To Dan'l Born	June	3	1727
Judith Niel Daug'r Shapleigh Born	Oct'r	4	1742
Hannah Niel Daug'r To Do Born	June	5	1746
Jeremah Nelms Son Joshua Born	Sep't	6	1743
Wm Nelms Son To Do Born	Oct'r	25	1746
Nansey Nelms Daug'r To Do Born	Oct'r	20	1748
Christopher Niel Son To Daniell Born	Sep'r	25	1749
Daniell Niel Son To Do Born	Jan'y	14	1751
John Nutt Son To Farnifold & Mary was Born	Feb'ry	16	1749
Thomas Nutt Son To Do was Born	Jan'ry	25	1753
Winy Norman Daug'r To Daniel & Judith was Born	Feb'ry	22	1754
Charles Nelms Son To Eben & Rhoda was Born	Sept'r	11	1752
Luca Nelms Daug'r To Do was Born	Feb'ry	7	1755
Ann Nelms Daug'r To Presly was Born	Oct'r	3	1756
William Nash Son To John & Mary Nash Born	May	24	1758
Katy Nutt Daug'r To Rich'd & Alice Nutt was born	April	9	1759
Katy Norman Daug'r To Tho's & Eliz'a Norman was born	Octob	31	1758
Winny Nutt Daughter to Rich'd & Alice Nutt was born	June	8	1760
John Nash Son to John & Mary Nash was born	May	10	1761
Dicky Nutt son to Richard & Alice Nutt was born	Jan'ry	9	1762
Betty Nash Daughter to John & Mary Nash was born	June	25	1764
Cudbirth son to Daniel & Judith Norman was born	March	6	1767
frances Newsom Daughter of Robert & Nancey Newsom his wife was born	May	12	1772
Salley Kennor Niel Daughter of John Neale & Marthaan was born	November	29	1772
James Nutt Son of Richard & Alce was Born	May	9	1773
Charles Nelums Son of Charles & Bettey his wife was Born	November	4	1773
Nancev Night Daughter to George & - was Born	June	24	1773
William Nelums Son of Aron Nelums was Born	June	24	1774

page 106 (continued)
Salley Benneham Daughter to Robert Nusom & Nancey his wife
    was born   January 16 1775
Mary Neale the Daughter of John & Martha his wife was Born Decembr 6 1776
Mary Griffin Neale Daughter of Richard & Jeane his wife
    was Born   March 11 1776
William Neale Son of John & Marthaann his wife was born May   10 1764
Jeane Neale Daughter of John & Marthaann his wife was born Aprill 29 1769
John Neale Son of John & Martha his wife was Born   Aprill - 1777
Nancy Davis Daughter of Richard was Born   March 17 1776
Ann Nelms Daughter of William & Grace his wife was Born June   1 1777
Ann Norris Daughter of William & Mary his wife was Born August 14 1777
James Nightingill Son of Matthew & Ann his wife was Born April 7 1778

page 107, headed "N".
James Neale Son to John & Martha his wife was Born Sep't 24 1778
Winnefret Nash Daughter to George & Lucey his wife was Born October 27 1779
Thomas Neale Son to John & Martha his wife was Born April 9 1780
Mary Satchell Neale Daughter to Presly Neale & Susannah
    his wife was Born   July 26 1781
William Newsom Son to Milley Newsom a bastard child was Born Dec'm 4 1781
Matthew Neale Son to Presly & Susannah his wife was Born Jan'y 13 1783
Sarah Presley Neale Daughter to William & - his wife Augt 1 1784
Elizabeth Nash Daughter to John & Ammoney his wife was born March 18 1786

page 108, headed "J".
John Jones son to William & Sarah his wife was born May 19 1779
Chreton Jones son to John Jones & - (wife's name omitted)
    was born   Nov'mbr 13 1780
Willis Jones son to John Jones & Hannah his wife was born Feb 22 1781
Salley Jones Daughter to William & Sarah his wife was born Oct 12 1781
Polley Jackson Daughter to Thaddeus & Elizabeth his wife
    was born   Oct 16 1782
Fanney Jones Daughter to John & Marget his wife was born April 13 1783
Milley Jones Daughter to John & Hannah his wife was born July 1 1783
Thomas Jones Son to John & Marget his wife was born Dec'm 13 1786
Isaac Bray Son to Isaac Bray & Nancy Hogan a Bastard Child
    was Born   Dec'm 15 1786
Thomas Jackson son to Daniel & Sarah his wife was born March 30 1790
Lewsinda Lidford Jones Daughter to Willis Jones & Peggæ
    his wife was born   October 7 1804

page 109, headed "K"
Rodham Kenner Son To Rich'd Born   March 22 1671
Rich'd Kenner Son To Do Born   March 3 1673
Jo'n Kenner Son To Do Born   Dec'r 27 1677
Frances Kenner Son To Do Born   Dec'r 18 1681
Eliz'a Kenner Daug'r To Do Born   March 19 1682
Hannah Kenner Daug'r To Do Born   March 13 1684
George Knott Son To George Born   Sep'r 14 1668
Wm Knott Son To Do Born   Nov'r 15 1673
Jo'n Knott Son To Do Born   Nov'r 15 1671
Jane Knott Daug'r To Do Born   March 1 1681
Wm Keen Son To Wm Born   Sep'r 11 1665
Eliz'n Keen Daug'r To Do Born   May 16 1669
Jo'n Keen Son To Do Born   Aug't 12 1671
Hannah Keen Daug'r To Do Born   Feb'y 4 1676

Sarah Keen Daug'r To Do Born	Oct'r	7	1678
Tho's Kingwell Son To Nicholus Born	March	7	1686
Sarah Kingwell Daug'r To Do Born	Feb'y	8	1689
Eliz'a Kesterson Daug'r To George Born	Jan'y	21	1694
Tho's Kesterson Son To Do Born	Ap'l	26	1696
George Kesterson Son To Do Born	May	8	1701
Wm Kesterson Son To Do Born	May	18	1701

(The above entry dates only go to prove that the Register
must be taken with a pinch of salt occasionally.)

Ann Kesterson Daug'r To Do Born	March	25	1705
Mary Key Daug'r To Rich'd Born	Jan'y	12	1695
John Kilpatrick Son Edward Born	May	21	1697
Meredith Kilpatrick Daug'r To Do Born	May	21	1699
James Kilpatrick Son To Do Born	Jan'y	11	1703
Ann Kilpatrick Daug'r To Do Born	March	29	1704
Winifred Kesterson Daug'r To George Born	Ap'l	8	1708
Sarah Kesterson Daug'r To Do Born	Dec'r	12	1706
Judith Kesterson Daug'r To Do Born	Jan'y	30	1708
George Kesterson Son To Do Born	March	17	1710
Sarah Kesterson Daug'r To Do Born	Oct'r	30	1706
Ephraim Knight Son To Lenard Born	Oct'r	13	1706
John Kettle Son To Mary Born	Sep'r	30	1711
Hannah Kenner Daug'r To Rodham Born	Aug't	30	1695
Rodham Kenner Son To Rich'd Born	Jan'y	2	1717
Rich'd Kenner Son To Do Born	Ap'l	6	1722
Hon'y Knott Son To Wm Jun'r Born	Nov'r	15	1719
Mary Knott Daug'r To Do Born	Oct'r	15	1718
Humphres Knott Son To Do Born	May	2	1720
Rodham Kenner Son To Fra's Born	Sep'r	28	1707
Eliz'a Kenner Daug'r To Ditto Born	Feb'y	16	1709
Houson Kennor Son To Ditto Born	May	10	1712
Joycoan Knott Daug'r To Wm Born	Feb'y	26	1720
John Kesterson Son To George Born	Nov'r	26	1712

page 110   headed "St. Stepons Parish K   "

Hanna Reta Kesterson Daug'r To George Born	July	31	1719
William Kesterson Son To Wm Born	Sep'r	22	1722
Elinor Keen Daug'r To Jo'n Born	Sep'r	29	1710
Eliz'a Keen Daug'r To Do Born	March	26	1715
Edmond Kelly Son To Hugh Born	Feb'y	29	1726
Winif'd Kesterson Daug'r To George Born	Oct'r	20	1730
Breuoton Kenner Son To Wind'r Born	Feb'y	8	1730
Rich'd Kenner Son To Do Born	Feb'y	29	1733
Ann Kennedy Daug'r To Rich'd Born	Nov'r	2	1735
Winder Kennor Son To Wind'r Born	Aug't	16	1735
Eliz Kennedy Daug'r To Rich'd Born	Feb'y	13	1737
George Kennedy Son To Do Born	Ap'l	24	1739
Sarah Kennedy Daug'r To Do Born	Oct'r	9	1741
George Kesterson Son To George Born	March	10	1732
Wm Kesterson Son To Do Born	Aug't	4	1737
Eliz'a Kesterson Daug'r To Do Born	Feb'y	11	1739
John Kesterson Son To Jo'n Born	Decemb'r	4	1742
Hannah Kesterson Daug'r To Do Born	July	20	1742
Mary Kennedy Daug'r To Rich'd Born	Ap'l	12	1744
Wm Kesterson Son To John Born	Feb'y	12	1735
Ann Kesterson Daug'r to Do Born	Sep'r	15	1744

Winif'd Keeve Daug'r To Beverley Born   Feb'y   20   1743
Jo'n Keeve Son To Do Born   Jully   8   1745
Judith Kesterson Daug'r To George & Eliz'a   June   6   1745
Sarah Kesterson Daug'r To Do & Do Born   March   24   1748
Wm Keeve Son To Beverley & Eliz'a Born   March   15   1748
Jo'n Kennedy Son To Jo'n & Katherin Born   Sep'r   16   1741
Sarah Kennedy Daug'r To Do & Do Born   Aug't   20   1743
George Waughop Kennedy Son To Do Born   Jan'y   28   1747
N icholis Kennedy Son To Rich'd & Eliz'a Born   Ap'l   10   1747
Tho's Keeve Son To Beverley & Eliz'a Webb Born   March   19   1750
Eliz'a Keeve Daug'r To Now'n & Sarah Born   March   4   1750
George Knight Don To Benj'n & Winif'd Born   Dec'r   10   1749
Rich'd Keeve Son To Beverley & Eliz Born   Sep'r   13   1753
Wm Kee ne Son To Newton & Sarah his Wife Born   Dec'r   4   1753
Judeth Kelley Daug'r To Moses & Margaret was Born   March   1   1754
William Knott Son To Richard & Betty was Born   Aug'st   5   1755
Thomas Keene Son To Newton & Sarah was Born   March   5   1756
William Kennedy Son To Richard & Elesabeth was Born   June   21   1751
Sarah Keene Daug'r To Newton & Sarah Keene was Born   October   28   1751
Elisabeth Keeve Daug'r To Beverley was Born   May   17   1756
Maggy Kurtley Daug'r To George & Agnes was Born   Febry   13   1757
Malcolm Kennon Martin Kennon Bastard Son to Sarah Martin
     was three months & eight days old on   March   13   1757

page 111, headed "Northumborland County K".

Elisabeth Knott Daug'r To James & Nelly was Born   Dec'r   22   1757
John Keene Son To Newton Keene Gen't & Sarah his
     wife was Born   May   18   1758
Peter Keeve Son To Beverley & Eliz Webb Keeve was born
     on Saturday abt 4 in morn   December   16   1758
James Knott Son to William & Magdalene Knott was born   February   14   1759
Betty Reason Kelly Daughter to Mary Kelly was born   Novemb   18   1759
Sally Kesterson Daughter to Wm & Ann Kesterson was born   April   18   1758
Rhoda Kesterson Daughter to Wm & Ann Kesterson ws born   October   17   1759
Winefrid Kesterson Daughter to Wm Kesterson Jun'r &
     Eliz was born   April   23   1758
Hannah Kesterson Daughter to Wm Kesterson Jun'r &
     Eliz was born   March   23   1760
Nancy Kesterson Daughter to Geo Kesterson Jun'r &
     Mary Do was born   May   29   1761
Sarah Keeve Daughter to Beverley & Eliz'a Webb Keeve
     was born   April   20   1762
Elizabeth Knott Daughter to James & Eleanar Knott was born Decemb 22   1757
Jane Knott Daughter to James & Eleanar Knott was born   August   10   1760
Eleanor Knott Daughter to James & Eleanor Knott was born August   10   1763
Chloe Kesterson Daughter to George & Mary Kesterson
     was born   January   27   1763
Molly Keeve Daughter to Beverley & Eliz'a Webb Keeve
     was born   April   10   1765
Unice Kesterson Daughter to William & Elizabeth
     Kesterson was born   June   4   1762
George Kesterson Son to William & Elizabeth Kesterson
     was born   August   29   1765
Beverly Keeve Son to Patrick was born   (sic)   April   25   1705
John Smith a bastard son of Sarah Kesterson was born   Fob   27   1767
Thomas Kesterson Son to William & Eliz'a Kesterson
     was born   May   17   1768

page 111 (continued)

Wm Kesterson Son of Wm & Elizabeth his wife was born	September	25	1771
Saley Kennedy Daughter of George was Born	february	13	1773
Peter Brickley Kirkum Son of tho's & Winnefrit his wife was born	Aprill	11	1773
James Kircom son of Tho's & Winnefrit Kircom was born the	Oct'r	4	1774
Fanne McKarter the daughter of Richard & Mary his wife was born	September	7	1775
Elizabeth Kennon Daughter of John & Sarah his wife was born	February	26	1776
Winefritt Knight Daughter of George was Born	October	30	1775
Ann Kiroum Daughter of Thomas & winnefred his wife was born	July	26	1777
James Kiroum son of James & Elizabeth his wife was born	June	20	1777
Peter Beverley Keeve son of Thomas & Salley his wife was born	October	11	1777
Nancey Kesterson Daughter to William & Elizabeth his wife ws bn	June	1	1778
William Graham Kenhen son to James & Peggey his wife was born	October	8	1780
Nansey Taylor King Daughter to Henry King & Elizabeth his wife ws bn	Jan'r	18	1781
Peter Kirkham Son to Thomas & Winnifred his wife was born	Feb	22	1781
Elizabeth Lewis Knott Daughter to James C & Mary his wife was born	Aug't	19	1782
Thomas King son to Henry & Elizabeth his wife was born	May	13	1783
William Knott son to Richard & Marget his wife was born	July	31	1783
Jeane Knott Daughter to George & Polley his wife was born	Nov'm	25	1784
Elizabeth Corbin Knott Daughter to George & Martha his wife ws bn	Sep't	2	1787
William Parker Kenner son to William & Ann his wife was born	Feb	2	1788
Elizabeth Brickey Kirkham Daughter to Thomas & Winney his wife was Born	May	18	1789

page 112, headed "St Stephens Parish K"

Bettey McAdam Keene Daughter to Thomas Keene & wife was bn	Feb	2	1786
Baptized	April	30	
Joseph McAdam Keene Son to Ditto & Ditto was born	Augt	9	1788
Baptized	Sep'r the	5	
Ann Keene daughter to Ditto & Ditto was born	Oct'r	5	1789
Janitta Keene daughter to Ditto & Ditto was born	Ap'r	19	1791
John Newton,Tho's,Gaskins,Edward,Keene,son to Do & Do was born (sic)	Sep't	3	1796

page 113, headed "K".

William Keene son of William & Ann Keene was Born	December	10	1695
Hannah Keene Daughter of Do was Born	June	28	1699
Elizabeth Keene Daughter of Do was Born	May	2	1701
William Keene Son of William & Elizabeth Keene bn died	Octo	4	1700
Elizabeth Keene Daughter of Wm & Elizabeth Keene was Born	September	23	1722
Newton Keene Son of Do Born	September	6	1725
William Keene Son of William & Anne Keene Died	November	3	1725
Cap'n Nuton Keens Childrens Ages			
Elizabeth Keene Daughter of Nuton & Sarah Keene was Born	March	4	1749/50
Sary Keene Daughter of Do was Born	October	28	1751
William Keene Son of Do was Born	December	4	1753
Tho's Keene Son of Do was Born	March	5	1756
John Keene Son of Do was Born	May	18	1758
Ann Keene Daughter of Do was Born	June	2	1760
Mary Keene Daughter of Do was Born	April	30	1763

page 113 (continued)

John Keene Son of Do was Born	February	15	1764
Hannah Keene Daughter of Do was Born	April	6	1766
Nuton Keene Son of Do was Born	March	9	1768
Catherine Keene Daughter of Do was Born	April	13	1770
John Keene Son of above Nuton Keene Died	November	10	1759
Catherine Keene Daughter as above Died	September	25	1770
Aggey King Daughter of John & Catherinia his wife was Born	September	4	1783
Sary Kircom Daughter to James & Elizabeth his wife was born	December	4	1774
James Kirtley Son of John & Cloey his wife was Born	January	8	1775
Ann Straughan Daughter of Rachel King was Born	Apriel	1	1775
William King Son of Hennery & Bettey was born	February	1	1777
Sammuel Kesterson Son of William was Born	October	31	1775
Thomas Kennor Son of William & Bettey was Born	Agust	15	1775
John Kelley son of Spencer & Elender his wife was Born	Feb'r	16	1777
William Bonum Kenner son of William & Bettey his wife was Born	Septemb	4	1777
Hannah Kookman daughter of Rice & Hannah his wife ws bn	Feb'r	9	1778
Richard Knott son to Richard Born	May	9	1778
Tomzey Kelley Daughter to Mary Kelley Born	Dec'm	10	1778
John King son to Henry & Elizabeth his wife was born	Dec'm	3	1778
Anna Cookman Daughter to Rice & Hannah his wife was born	April	20	1781
Jean King Daughter to William & Elizabeth his wife was born	Augt	10	1783
Sarah Gaskins Edwards Keen Daughter to Thomas Keen & wife was born	March	6	1784
Elizabeth King Daughter Henry & Elizabeth his wife ws Born	March	10	1787
Thomas Keene son to Hannah Keene a bastard child was Born	April	10	1788

page 114, headed "St Stephens L Parish".

Susana Laurance Daug'r To Jo'n Born	May	7	1678
Henry Leasure Son To Bartho'w Born	Jun	6	1667
Bartho'w Lesure Son To Do Born	Feb'y	2	1671
Rebeckah Leasure Daug'r To Do Born	Aug't	2	1673
George Leasure Son To Do Born	Ap'l	26	1678
Eliz'a Leasure Daug'r To Do Born	March	4	1680
Tho's Leasure Son To Do Born	Dec'r	19	1682
John Lewas Son To Jo'n Born	Sep'r	30	1683
Wm Lewas Son To Do Born	Jan'y	6	1685
James Lane Son To James Born	Jan'y	17	1686
Tho's Lane Son To Do Born	March	16	1688
Jo'n Lattrell Son To James Born	Nov'r	10	1691
Christian Longe Daug'r To Josias Born	Dec'r	2	1683
Josian Long Daug'r To Do Born	Jan'y	27	1685
Josias Long Son To Do Born	June	10	1687
Eliz Long Daug'r To Do Born	Aug't	10	1689
Jane Legg Daug'r To John Born	Jully	16	1685
Rachel Lancaster Daug'r To John Born	Jully	21	1695
Jo'n Lancaster Son To Do Born	Nov'r	26	1698
Sarah Lancaster Daug'r To Do Born (Hanah)	March	25	1700
Grace Lancaster Daug'r To Do Born	Augt	24	1701
Ann Lancaster Daug'r To Do Born	Sep'r	1	1706
Aaron Lancaster Son To Do Born	Feb'y	15	1708
Ann Lancaster Daug'r To Richard Born	June	18	1699
Rich'd Lancaster Son To Do Born	May	12	1706
Jo'n Lancaster Son To Do Born	Ap'l	16	1710
Nich'o Lancaster Son To Nicholas Born	March	18	1683
Jo'n Lancaster Son To Do Born	Jully	9	1710
Nicho Lancaster Son To Do Born	Jan'y	17	1714
Joseph Lancaster Son To Do Born	Oct'r	12	1716

page 114 (continued)

Hanah Langsdell Daug'r To Jo'n Born	Jully	22	1702
Rich'd Langsdell Son To Do Born	Oct'r	3	1714
Betty Langsdell Daug'r To Do Born	Oct'r	7	1712
Allex'r Lunsford Son To Wm Born	May	23	1697
Eliz'a Lawson Daug'r To Jo'n Born	Ap'l	30	1707
Eliz'a Love Daug'r To Allex'r Born	Nov'r	25	1705
Susana Luttrell Daug'r To Jo'n Born	Aug't	12	1713
James Luttrell Son To Do Born	May	6	1715
Jo'n Luttrell Son To Do Born	Jully	16	1717
Rich'd Luttrell Son To Do Born	Jully	22	1719
Barbery Lane Daug'r To Mary Born	Feb'y	4	1711
Mary Lewas Daug'r To Ja's Born	Feb'y	13	1717
Ja's Lewas Son To Do Born	Jan'y	8	1719
Hanah Lewas Daug'r To Do Born	Octobr	21	1721
Betty Lealand Daug'r To John Born	Sepbr	3	1714
Ann Lealand Daug'r To Do Born	Nov'r	27	1716
Jo'n Lealand Son To Do Born	Feb'y	20	1718
Ailce Lealand Daug'r To Do Born	Octobr	2	1721
Hannah Lucas Daug'r To Tho's Born	Nov'r	4	1719

page 115, headed "St Stephens Parish L ".

Lewas Lamkin Son To Ja's Born	March	19	1719
Ja's Lamkin Son To Do Born	Oct'r	2·7	1722
Mary Lowas Daug'r To Lewas Ab Lewas Born (sic)	Jan'y	28	1720

    (Note: This is doubtless an attempt to use the prefix
    "ap" from Wales, meaning junior.   B,F.)

Tho's Lewas Son To Tho's Born	Feb'y	8	1721
Wm Longsdell Son To Jo'n Born	Feb'y	9	1721
Mary Lyles Daug'r To Eliner Born	May	19	1707
Ann Lewas Daug'r To Wm Born	Dec'm	16	1717
Judith Lewas Daug'r To Do Born	Sep'r	24	1719
Betty Lewas Daug'r To Do Born	Ap'l	2	1722
Sarah Laurence Daug'r To Edw'd Born	May	26	1723
Samuell Luttrell Son To Jo'n Born	Sep'r	26	1721
Sarah Lealand Daug'r To John Born	Oct'r	10	1724
Winifred Lancaster Daug'r To Nicho's Born	June	8	1724
John Lason Son To Rob't a Mulatto Born	Dec'r	10	1722
Elisha Lancaster Son To Nicho's Born	March	11	1727
Peter Lealand Son To Jo'n Born	Jan'y	4	1729
Ruth Luttrell Daug'r To Jo'n & Ann Born	June	23	1729
Ann Luttrell Daug'r To Do Born	Dec'r	23	1729
Jo'n Lancaster Son To Jo'n & Eliz'a Born	Feb'y	18	1730
Rich'd Lealand Son To Jo'n Born	Aug't	31	1732
Jeremiah Lamkin Son To Ja'·? Born	Sep'r	9	1732
Winif'd Larance Daug'r To Edward Born	Dec'r	3	1733
Hanah Lamkin Daug'r To James Born	Dec'r	21	1734
Nichol's Lamkin Son To Joseph Born	Aug't	31	1736
Rich'd Lamkin Son To Jo'n Born	Aug't	31	1736
Sarah Leach Daug'r To Jo'n Born	June	26	1738
George Lancaster Son To Jo'n Born	Ap'l	7	1739
Winifret Lancaster Daug'r To Do Born	Sep'r	3	1734
Joseph Lancaster Son To Do Born	Oct'r	10	1742
Jo'n Lancaster Son To Do Born	Ap'l	10	1744
Samuell Lucas Son To Tho's Born	Feb'y	26	1745
Jo'n Leach Son To Jo'n Leach Born	Ap'l	5	1741
Judith Layland Daug'r To Jo'n & Jane Born	Sep'r	24	1742
Jo'n Layland Son To Do & Do Born	Aug't	1	1744
Tho's Lucas Son To Tho's & Sarah Born	May	21	1748

Wm Leach Son To Jo'n & Joannah Born	Jully	10	1748
Eliz'a Layland Daug'r To Jo'n & Sarrah Born	Aug't	24	1749
Betty Hanes Lucas Daug'r To Tho's & Sarah Born	Aug't	2	1750
Peter Layland Son To Jo'n & Sarah Born	Feb'y	3	1751
Jeremiah Lamkin Son To James & Winifred Born	Aug't	9	1743
Richard Lamkin Son To Do B orn	Octob'r	5	1745
Samson Lamkin Son To Do Born	March	22	1749
Hannah Lamkin Daug'r To Do Born	July	28	1751
Betty Brown Lamkin Daug'r To Do Born	Jan'y	11	1754
Eliz'a Lecompte Born	May	22	1749
Mary Lecompte Born	June	4	1750
Thomas Lecompte Born	March	16	1753
Sarah Lecompte Born	March	16	1753
A Son Born to George Lampkin Named Peter	Oct'r	26	1754
James Lewis Son To John was Born	Oct'r	9	1757

page 116, headed "Northumberland L County"

Richard Longsdale Son to Richard & Elizabeth was born	March	12	1739
Mary Longsdale Daug'r To Do Born	April	27	1742
Betty Longsdale Daug'r To Do Born	April	9	1746
William Longsdale Son To Do Born	Decemb	25	1750
Leannah Longsdale Daug'r To Benjamin & Sarah was Born	Nov'r	2	1748
Benjamin Longsdale Son To Do Born	June	11	1750
John Longsdale Son To Do Born	Aug't	29	1752
Winifred Longsdale Daug'r To Richard & Elis'h was Born	March	21	1755
John Lawless Son To Dennis Born	May	12	1755
Sarah Lucas Daug'r To Thomas & Sarah was Born	Jan'ry	7	1754
John Lewis Son To John & Ann was Born	Nov'r	17	1755
Lewis Ablewis Lamkin Son To Lewis was Born	Jan'ry	24	1756
Nansy Lewis Daug'r To Ann was Born	Oct'r	1	1755
Thomas Leach Son To John & Joanna was Born	Feb'ry	29	1756
James Lamkin Son To James & Winifred was Born	April	20	1756
Priscilla Lewis Daug'r To James was Born	Feb'ry	6	1757
Sally Lamkin Daug'r To George Born	April	22	1757
George Lucas Son To Thomas was Born	March	10	1757
Janny Lamkin Daug'r To James & Winefrid Lamkin was born	March	21	1758
Griffin Lewis Lamkin Son To Peter & Winefred Lamkin was born	August	28	1758
John Lowry Son To William & Betty Lowry was born	August	20	1758
William Lucas Son to Thomas & Sarah Lucas was born	May	28	1759
Cleophas Lamkin Son to James & Winofred Lamkin was born	February	22	1760
Peter Lewis Son to John & Ann Lewis was Born	Novemb	14	1759
Joseph Lancaster Son to Wm & Helen Lancaster was born	Feb'ry	7	1761
George Lamkin Son to Peter Lamkin & Winofred his wife was born	Decemb	5	1760
Mary Lansdell Daughter to William & Sarah Lansdell was born	June	8	1746
Ellison Lowry Daughter to William & Betty Lowry was born	April	23	1761
Susannah Lewis Daugh to John & Ann Lewis was born	Novem	20	1761

Phoby Lewis Daughter to James & Priscilla Lewis
was born   Octob'r   4 1763
Poter Lamkin Son to Poter & Winefred Lamkin was born Novemb 13 1763
Sarah Daughter of John & Nancy Lewis was born   January 27 1767
Peggy Boll Lancaster Daughter to Helen Lancaster
was born   October   8 1765
John Cuthbert Lancaster Son to Helen Lancaster
was born   February 19 1767
Sarah Layland Daughter to John & Sarah Layland
was born   March   5 1766
Janny Swan Layland Daughter to John & Millicent
Layland was born   Novem   3 1767
Winnefrit Lewis Daughter of Mary M. Lewis a basterd
was Born   January   27 1772
John Leland Son of Peter & Betty his wife was Born October 28 1772
Mary Magdellin Leeder the Daughter of Samuell
was Born   Septembr 22 1772
Sanford Low Son of Charles & Saffiah his wife
was Born   Septembr 15 1772
John Lewis Lathrum Son of Wm & Wilmuth a basterd
was born   May   20 1773

page 117.   headed "L"
John Landmon Son of Mary Landmon Was Born   January   27 1773
Catron Louis Daughter of Sammuel & Sarah His Wife
Was Born   February 27 1773
Robert Lawson was Born   March   16 1773
Sarah Lewis Claughton Daughter of Richard & Prisoilla
his wife was born   Aug't   26 1775
Susanner Lewis Daughter of Jeremiah & Magdillon his
wife was born   Decemb   8 1775
Nancey Latrom Daughter of William & Wilmuth his wife
was Born   Decemb   27 1775
James Lamkin Son of James & Ann his wife was Born Decemb   4 1775
Sarah Littrell Daughter of Moses & Patience his wife
was Born   March   8 1776
Thomas Lucas Son of Samuell & Sary his Wife was Born April 21 1774
Elezebeth Lansdell Daughter to John & Jeminia his
Wife was born   May   8 1777
William Littrell Son To Moses & Patience his Wife
ws born   July   4 1778
Sarah Lathrum Daughter To William Lathrum ws born Sept 28 1778
Sarah Sharp Lewis Daughter to William & Ann his wife
was born   April   20 1779
Salley Lewis Daughter to Jeremiah & Magathon his
wife was born   March   12 1780
John Littrell Son To Moses & Patience his wife
was born   October   14 1780
Charles Nelms Lewis Son to James Lewis & Ailsey his
wife was born   June   26 1773
Elezebeth Lewis Daughter to Ditto & Ditto was born Feb'r 14 1775
Bridget Loveless Lewis Daughter to Ditto & Ditto
was born   March   5 1777
Ailsey Lewis Daughter to Ditto & Ditto was born Sept   4 1779
Griffin Jones Lathram Son to William Lathrom was Born Dec'm 26 1781

page 117, (continued)

William Lewis Son to Hannah Lewis a bastard child was born	Feb	6	1782
Leroy Luttrel Sun to Moses & Patience his Wife was born	March	12	1783
John Lewis Son to Griffin & Molley his wife ws bn	Aug't,	16	1783
John Trussel Lewis Son to William Lewis & Ann his wife ws bn	May	5	1784
Winnefred Lewis Daughter to Willoughby & Winnefred his wife ws bn	Sept'r	3	1784
Prissillor Lewis Daughter To Jeremiah & Mary his wife was born	May	9	1785
John Self Lewis Son To Charles Lewis & Betty his wife was born	May	1	1785
George Lewis Son To Do & Do born	February	20	1780
Jean Lewis Lamkin Daughter To Ann Lamkin Bast'd ws born	Nov'm	15	1785
Samuel Hadon Lathram Son to William & Wilmuth his wife was born	Nov'm	12	1786
James McCadams Lewis son to William & - (wife's name omitted) his wife was born	Oct	15	1786
William Lewis Son to Griffin & Molley his wife was Born	Oct	16	1786
Thomas Leder Son to Edward & Ann his wife was Born	May	20	1787
Betty Littrell Daughter to Moses & Patience his wife was born	July	1	1787
Thomas Self Leader son to Richard Ledor & Salley his wife ws bn	December	17	1787
John Littrell Son to John & Milley his wife was born	Feb'y	26	1788
Fanne Parker Lewis & Jean Self Mitchell Lewis, Twins & Daughters to Jeremiah Lewis & Mary his wife was born	April	8	1788

page 118, headed "L".

Jenne Lewis Daughter of Sary Lewis was Born	May	3	1772
John Griffin Lewis Son of William & Ann his wife was Born	Sep'br	23	1773
Mary Ann Littell Daughter of Moses & Patience his wife was born	Octo'br	7	1773
Samuel Lewis Son of John was Born	October	25	1774
Nancey Lucas Daughter of Sammuel & Sary his wife was born	June	26	1776
Vinson Lewis a bastard shild of Elizabeth Lewis was born	July	9	1777
Susannah Lavender Daughter of John Lavender was Born	April	10	1778
Jean Lamkin Daughter of Peter Lamkin was Born	April	6	1778
Winifred Lansdel Daughter to - (name omitted) was Born	Oct	21	1778
Haynie Layland son to peter & Bettey his wife was born	June	18	1779
William Lewis Son to Willoughby & Winny his wife ws bn	April	11	1779
John Lewis Son to Ditto & Ditto was born	March	18	1781
Nancey Lewis Daughter to John Lewis & - (wife's name omitted) wife was born	Mar	9	1782

page 118 (continued)

Nansey Trusell Lamkin Daughter to Nancey Lamkin a Bas'd ws bn April   4 1782
John Dugliss Lewis Son to Jeremiah & Magdalene his wife ws born Oct   8 1782
Fanney Lewis Daughter to Willoughby & Winney his wife ws bn   Nevm   24 1782
Thomas Leader son to Richard & Salley his wife ws born   Dec'm   17 1786
Thomas Littrell son to John & Milley his wife was Born   Jan'r   20 1786
Lindsy Lewis son to William & Ann his wife was Born about
    4 o'clock in the morning   Sept   12 1787

page 119, headed "L".

Richard Rust Lee Washington Lewis son to William Lewis
   & Mary his wife was Born   Sep'r   4 1788
Samuel Lewis son to Griffin & Molley his wife was Born   Dec'm   14 1788
Griffin Lamkin son to George & Rebecah his wife was Born   June   27 1788
Willoughby Lewis son to Willoughby & Winney his wife was Born Sep'r   27 1789
William Littrell son to John & Milley his wife was Born   March   25 1790
Betsy Garner Leader daughter to Rich'd Leader & Jean
   his wife was born   October 10 1790
Daniel Beacham Lewis & Alce Randal Lewis twins son &
    daughter to Jeremiah Lewis & Molley his wife was Born   March   9 1791
Alfred Randal Lewis son to Alcey Lewis a Bastard child was Born November 15
                                         1791

Nancy cuttance Lamkin Daughter to Mary Lamkin a Bastard
   child was Born   March   12 1794

page 120, headed "K".

Richard Kenneda Son to George & Elizabeth his wife was born   february 13 1770
Sary Kannon Daughter of John & Sary his wife was Born   July   6 1770
Ann King Daughter of John King & Katharina his wife was Born October   1 1770
George Cookman the son of Rice Cookman & hannah his wife
   was Born   December 9 1771
Ginne kelle daughter of Moses & Mary his wife was born   Aug't   8 1766
Meriah Keysor Daughter to James & Salley Keyser his wife was born Sept 15 179-
Vincent Brown Kirkham son to Thomas Kirkham & Betsey his
   wife was Born   April   17 1796
William Keyser son to James & Salley Keyser was Born   Dec'm   28 179-
John Kirtley son to James Kirtley & Mary his wife was Born   Feb   5 1798
Moloy King Daughter to Harry King & Betsey his wife was Born   Feb   10 1799
Jean Lamkin Kirtley Daughter to Ja mes Kirtley & Molley his
   wife was Born   March   23 1801
John Washington Kezer son to Claisce Kezer was Born   August   18 1807

page 121, headed "L"

William Leach Son of John Leach & Lucreshe his wife was Born April   25 1769
Nancy Coleter Long Daughter of Baker Long & Mary his wife
   was Born   October 22 1769
William Lathrum Son of William & Wilmuth Lewis a basterd as
   she Says was born   May   30 1770
Lewis Lamkin Son of James & Ann Lamkin his wife was Born   May   2 1771
Mary Lamkin Daughter to James & Ann Lamkin his wife was Born February 18 1773
John Leader son to Richard & Jane his wife was Born   April   29 1792
Susey Lewis Daughter to Willoughby & Winney his wife was Born Aug't   13 1792
Richard Leader s on to Richard & Jeaney Leader his wife
   was Born   May   8 1796
Randal Lewis son to Willibay Lewis & Winney his wife was Born Sept   28 1796
Thomas Lewis son t o Willoughby & Winney his wife was Born   November 4 1801
Vollin Garland Lewis son to Jeremiah Lewis & Mary his wife
   was Born   Jan'r   11 1801

Frederic W. Lewis son to John & Alice Lewis his wife was Born   July 26 1808

page 122, headed "M"

Ruth Masey Daug'r To Henry Born	June	12	1682
Mary Masey Daug'r To Do Born	Aug	20	1684
Wm Masey Son To Do Born	Feb'y	28	1688
John Matthew Son To Tho's Born	March	23	1677
Ann Matthew Daug'r To Do Born	Feb'y	27	1679
Tho's Matthew Son To Do Born	Jan'y	23	1680
Wm Matthew Son To Do Born	Feb'y	21	1682
Jo'n Mosley Son To Wm Born	Ap'l	10	1670
Phillip Medcalfe Son To Hen'y Born	Sep'r	17	1679
Rich'd Melton Son To Michell Born	Aug't	14	1682
Ann Melton Daug'r To Do Born	Feb'y	18	1677
Jo'n Macknot Son To Jo'n Born	Aug't	27	1687
Rich'd Morton Son To Jo'n Born	Feb'y	14	1694
Mary Mocalar Daug'r To Jo'n Born	Feb'y	27	1692
Wm Mash Son To Arthur Born	Sep'r	2	1693
John Mash Son To Do	May	10	1696
Sarah Middleton Daug'r To Sollomon Born	Mar	18	1694
Tho's Moon Son To Jo'n Born	Sep'r	18	1686
Mary Moon Daug'r To Do Born	May	18	1688
Francis Moon Son To Do Born	Jully	11	1693
Wm Moon Son To Do Born	March	3	1703
Mary Mulran Daug'r To Allex'r Born	March	5	1671
Rob't Milian Son To Jo'n Born	May	8	1695
Elinor Miricah Daug'r To Nich'o Born	June	4	1699
Ann Miricah Daug'r To Do Born	Oct'r	19	1707
Charity Miricah Daug'r To Do Born	Feb'y	3	1705
Micah Milton Son To Michoall Born	Feb'y	6	1699
Elinor Melton Daug'r To Do Bap'd	Oct'r	19	1707
Jo'n Millian Son to Jo'n Jun'r Bap'd	Feb'y	22	1702
Grace Millian Daug'r to Do Born	Ap'l	19	1706
Eliz'a Millian Daug'r To Do Born	Jan'y	10	1704
Jo'n Millian Son To Do Born	Jan'y	16	1707
Eliz'a Morison Daug'r To Findly	May	18	1702
Findley Morison Son To Do Born	Oct'r	30	1709
And'w Murray Son To Wm Born	Dec'r	14	1702
Mary Mason Daug'r To Wm Born	Jully	29	1703
Jane Mason Daug'r To Do Born	May	25	1707
Janet Moon Daug'r To Mary Born	Feb'y	19	1707
Tho's Myars Son To Math'w Bap'd	July	3	1709
Eliz'a Moor Daug'r To Dav'd Bap'd	Oct'r	30	1709
Henry Mayes Son To Hen'y Bap'd	Oct'r	27	1709
Ja's Mortemore Son To Ja's Born	March	25	1704
Farigan Mortimore Son To Do Born	Nov'r	22	1707
Mary Morfoot Daug'r To Rob't Born	Oct'r	20	1708
Mary Murphy Daug'r To Hen'y Bap'd	Feb'y	21	1711

page 123   "M"

Sarah Moulder Daug'r To Ja's Bap'd	March	28	1711
Tho's Mahon Son To Tho's Born	Ap'l	12	1712
Mary McGown Daug'r To Ja's Born	Ap'l	12	1714
Tho's Meryday Son To Matthew Born	Feb'y	10	1716
Wm Melton Son To Rich'd Born	Oct'r	4	1713
Rich'd Melton Son To Do Born	March	11	1712
Tho's MoN all Son To Jo'n Born	Dec'r	28	1715
Eliz'a McDanell Daug'r To Denes Born	May	8	1718
Jo'n Murphy Son To George Born	Sep'r	30	1720

Wm Murphy Son To Do Born	Nov'r	22	1722
Wm Moor Son To Dav'd Born	Dec'r	21	1707
Wm Mackgown Son To Ja's Born	Dec'r	21	1707
Jo's McGown Son To Do Born	May	13	1710
Ja's McGown Son To Do Born	Jully	17	1712
Charles Meurow Son To Wm Born	Jan'y	1	1704
Jo'n Meath Son To Jo'n Born	June	13	1712
Sarah Mackmahon Daug'r To Tho's Born	Dec'r	2	1713
Mary Ann Mccormuck Daug'r To Fra's Born	Sept'r	10	1711
Elinor Mccormuck Daug'r To Do Born	Oct'r	31	1713
Nethon Meridey Son To Nathon Born	Dec'r	8	1710
Jo'n Meridey Son To Do Born	Jan'y	24	1712
Ann Meredey Daug'r To Do Born	Feb'y	14	1713
Eliz'a Mason Daug'r To Wm Born	Jully	22	1699
Margarett Mason Daug'r To Do Born	Dec'r	24	1700
Eliz'a Mason Daug'r To Do Born	Jan'y	24	1702
Henry Mason Son To Do Born	March	19	1705
Peter Mason Son To Do Born	Sep'r	23	1710
Wm Mason Son To Do Born	June	21	1713
Rodham Mason Son To Findley Born	Jan'y	18	1719
Tho's Morton Son To Ellias Born	Nov'r	25	1725
George McNall Son To Jo'n Born	Ap'l	4	1718
Wm McNall Son To Do Born	March	18	1723
Elliz'a Morheads Daug'r To Allx'r Born	Oct'r	31	1723
Ann Morehead Daug'r To Do Born	Oct'r	2	1726
Danill Murphey Son To Wm Born	Aug't	12	1728
Mary Morton Daug'r To Ellias Born	Sep'r	2	1728
Ja's Moor (or Moon) Son To Wm Born	Feb'y	10	1729
Ja's Mortmor Son To Ja's Born	Apl	13	1730
Judith Mash Daug'r To Ja's Born	May	9	1730
Mathew Morton Son To Ellias Born	Aug't	30	1730
Margaret Murphey Daug'r To Wm Born	Dec'r	24	1730
Winif'd Magee Daug'r To Wm Born	Nov'r	28	1730
Jiney Moore Daug'r To Wm Born	Dec'r	28	1724
Mary Moore Daug'r To Do Born	Feb'y	15	1730

page 124, headed "M".

Hannah Morrison Daughter of Leuen Morrison & Sary his wife was Born	October	20	1770
William Murfey Son of Wm & Alis his wife was born	February	12	1771
William Morrison Son of Richard Morrison Was Born	April	11	1771
Mary Murrey Daug'r of James & Elizabeth Murrey was Born	August	12	1770
William Martin Son of Bette Wornum was Born	January	3	1772
Lawson More son to John & Mary his wife was Born	Sep'r	13	1796
Randolph Mott son to Isaac Mott & Lucy his wife was Born	October	16	1793
Fanney Thornton Mott Daughter to Isaac & Lucy his wife was born	October	2	1795
Marten S Mott son to Isaac Mott & Lucy his wife was born	April	5	1801

page 125, headed "R".

John Rautt the son of Ruth Hall & Anthony Rout as She Says was Born (Imperfectly written, date may be 1769)	December	31	1779
John Reason Son of Luke Reason a desolate woman was born	December	6	1769
Tho's Robusson son of William & Syner his wife was born	May	11	1770
Winnefrit Rainger Daughter to Winefrit was born	May	8	1770
Anthony Sidner Rautt Son of John Rautt was born	February	2	1771
Nancey Richerson Daughter to Isaac Richerson & Margit his wife was Born	April	10	1771
George Rice son to William P. Rice & Caty his wife was Born	July	10	1796

page 125 (continued)

Samuel Pollard Roberts Son to Evin Roberts & Jean Roberts
his wife was Born   Oct   5 1797
Beckey Wildey Robertson Daughter to Joseph Robertson
& Judith his wife was Born   Oct'r   25 1797
Fanney Rice Daughter to William P. Rice & Catey his
wife was Born   July   17 1798

page 126, headed "T" and "S".

Molley Templemun Daug'r To James & Hannah his wife
was Born   April   10 1770
Ruth Ticer Daughter of Job Ticer & Margaret his
wife was Born   March   15 1770
Presley Townsin son of Hainnis & Bettey his wife
was Born   July   24 1770
John Conway Toulson Son of Tho's Toulson & Ann
his wife was Born   November 1 1770
James Trasee the Son of John Trasee & Marget his
wife was Born   January 31 1771
James Toulson Son of John Toulson & Elenner his
wife was Born   February 8 1771
John Trussill Son of William & Mary Trussill was Born March   6 1771
Bette Turner Daughter of Alis Turner was Born   January 12 1766
Mille Thomas daughter of James & Hannah Thomas
his wife was Born   June   16 1762
Nancy Thos Daughter of Do Born   February 11 1765
Sharlit thomas Daughter of Do was Born   february 14 1768
William Toulson Son of Sary Toulson was Born   february 22 1771
William Trase Son of Sammuel & Anne trayse his
wife was Born   April   26 1771
Gabril Ticer Son of Wm Ticer & Margit his wife
was Born   October   8 1771
Kennor Thomas Son of James & Hannah his wife was Born January   4 1772
Lucey Sebre Daughter to James & Bettey his wife
was born   March   30 1779
Elizabeth Short Daughter of Sary a bastard child
was born   May   15 1770
Woldrig Smith Son of Richard Smith was born   October   6 1770
Judah Sherley was Born   August   13 1770
Judah Smith Daughter of John & Sarahan Smith was born August   17 1770
Jesse Alexander Son of Jesse & Mary Alexander his
wife was Born   August   2 1770
Betsey Sutton Daughter of John & Mary his wife was Born October   3 1770
Ann Smith Daughter of Tho's Smith & Sary his
wife was Born   March   4 1771
Phiplip Sprittle Son of William Causse & Elizabeth
Sprittle Born   Decemb   29 1770
Ruth Shurley Daughter of Argeland & Elizabeth his
wife was Born   August   28 1771
James Straton Son of John & Elizabeth his wife
was Born   June   10 1771
Ephrum Williams Spy son of James & Sary his wife
was Born   January 25 1772
Elizabeth Schofield Daughter of Tho's & Sarah his
wife was Born   Feb   11 1777
Peter Smith Son of Richard & Deborah his wife
was Born   Nov'm   30 1777
Salley Lewis Shearlly daughter of Peter & Milley
his wife was born   April   8 1778

page 126 (continued)

Elizabeth Sanders Daughter to Edward & Jean his
    wife was born   July   8 1778
Mary Beacham Stuckey Daughter to Job & Mary his
    wife was born   Dec'm 31 1778
Fanney Scott Daughter to Thomas & Sarah his wife was born Dec'm 15 1778
Thomas Smoott son to Charles & Elizabeth his wife was born Jan'r 12 1779
Jean Lamkin Straughan Daughter to David & Salley his
    wife ws born   Jan'r   3 1779
John Short son to William & Sarah his wife was Born   Oct   22 1778
Jackey Swillivant son to John was born   March 15 1779
Nancey Schofield Daughter to Thomas & Sarah his wife
    was born   Feb   24 1779
William Swillivent son of Danniel & Hannah his wife born March 13 1778
page 127, headed "W".
Charles Brown Winsted Son of Sammuel Winsted & Elizabeth
    his wife was Born   Decembr 30 1769
Cateren Walker Daughter of Frances & Mary his wife was born March 1 1770
Phillip White Son of George & Elisabeth White Born   April 15 1770
James Wilson Son of John Wilson & Judah his wife was born December 12 1769
David Winsted Son of Sammuel Winsted Seener & Winnifret
    his wife was Born   May   21 1770
Griffin winsted Son to Sammuel & Rhode his wife was Born June   4 1770
Vinson Williams Son of Absolom & Winnefrit his wife was Born July 10 1770
Clarke Short Son of Mary Williams was Born   July   8 1769
Joseph Walker Son of Joseph & Hannah Walker was Born   August 10 1770
Hainnice Wilkins Son of William & Dorrity Wilkins his
    wife was Born   January 26 1771
Elizabeth wilkins Daughter of Sary Wilkins was Born   March 17 1771
William Williams Son of Moses Williams & Maryann his Wife
    Was Born   May   1 1771
Judith way Daughter of Richard Was Born   August 29 1771
Tho's Wornum Son of Wm & Betty his wife was Born   January 2 1772
James Winsted the son of James & Chloe his wife was Born Decembr 30 1771
Judith Welch Daughter of John & Bette Welsh his wife
    was Born   Decembr 29 1771
John McWherter the son of Andrew & Mary his wife was Born
    on Thursday the Eleventh of february about 1/2 after
    11 of clock att night   February 11 1772
Jeanney Winsted Daughter of Jeremiah & Winne his wife
    was Born   January 19 1772
Roston Deavenport Winstead son to James Winstead &
    Betsey his wife was Born   March 19 1793
Elizabeth Watts Daughter to Spencer & Bettey his wife
    was Born   Nov'm 11 1792
Richard Walker son to Thomas & Sarah his wife was Born Sept   7 1794
Prealv Cox Wilkins son to Daniel Wilkins & Milley his
    wife was Born   March   7 1796
Daniel Beacham Winstead son to John Winstead & Salley
    his wife was Born   Nov'm   4 1797
Elezebeth Deavenport Wilkins Daughter to Daniel Wilkins
    & Milley his wife was Born   April   2 1798
Benjamin Morgan Walker son to Richard Walker & Mary T
    Walker his wife was Born   April   3 1798
Betty Walker Daughter to William Walker & Nancy his
    wife was Born   Feb   28 1799
William Wilday son to William Wilday & Sarah his wife
    was Born   October 9 1808

page 128, headed "V".

George Vanlandingham Son to Henery & Elizabeth his
wife was born ...... february 11 1770
Lucey Vanlandingham Daughter to Frances & Sara his
wife was Born ...... August 3 1798

page 129, headed "M."

Benj'm Moris Son To Wm Born		Jan'y	20 1719
George Moris Son To Do Born		May	1 1721
Margaret Moris Daug'r To Do Born		Sep'r	16 1724
Betty Moris Daug'r To Do Born		Sep	12 1727
Jo'n Moris Son To Do Born		Mar	30 1729
Jo'n Maltemore Son To Ja's Born		Mar	30 1732
Jo'n Milton Son To Michell Born		Oct'r	14 1729
Wm Murphey Son To Wm Born		Jully	28 1733
Mary Butler Marton Daug'r To Eliz Born		Nov'r	1 1733
Winif'd Moon Daug'r To Wm Born		June	26 1733
Wm Meyson Son To Jo'n Born		Ap'l	18 1743
Peter Meyson Son To Do Born		Mar	30 1736
Josias Meyson Son To Do Born	(1738)	Sep'r	18 1738
Ja's McGowan Son To George Born		Feb'y	19 1749
Mary McGowen Daug'r To Tho's Born		Marc	15 1747
Jo'n McGowen Son To Do Born		Jan'y	4 1749
Judith Mayson Daug'r To Peter Born		-	- 1749
Betty Mote Daug'r To Mosley Bprn		Sep'r	5 1750
Cloye McGowen Daug'r To Tho's Born		Aug'r	2 1751
Bety McGowen Daug'r To George Born		Nov'r	9 1751
Wm McGowen Daug'r To Do Born (sic)		May	6 1753
John Mainall Son To William & Margaret was Born		Feb	9 1749
Judeth Mainall Daug'r To Do Born		July	9 1748
Hannah Mainall Daug'r To Do was Born		March	29 1751
Betty Mainall Daug'r To Do was Born		March	11 1754
Mary McGowne Bastard of Sarah Lindsay was Born		May	2 1755
Mary Mott Daug'r To Mosely was Born		Feb'ry	29 1755
Mary Maze Daug'r To Josiah & Marget was Born		Nov'r	24 1755
Ann Metcalfe Daug'r To Wm & Ann Born		Nov'r	19 1723
Betty Metcalfe Daug'r To Do was Born		Feb'y 14	1725/6
Thomas Morris Son To John was Born		April	26 1756
William McGaw Son To John & Sarah was Born		Feb'ry	18 1757
Billy Maltimore Son To Wm & Sarah Maltimore was born		April	28 1758
Mary Matthews Daughter To John & Mildred Matthews was born		Oct'r	24 1759
William Mason Son to John & Mary Mason was born		Jan'ry	1 1756
John Mason Son to John & Mary Mason was born		April	1 1758

page 130, headed "M".

Ann Mason Daughter to Peter & Mary Mason was born	Feb'ry	21 1762
John Matthews Son to John & Mildred Matthews was born	April	1 1763
John Mason Son to Peter & Mary Mason was born	Septem	27 1763
Isaac Mott Son to Randolph & Ann Mott was born	Novem	23 1765
George Matthews Son to John & Mildred Matthews was born	Novem	6 1766
Molly Matthews Daughter to Moses & Elizabeth Matthews was born	Decem	2 1766
Mary Thrift Daughter of William & Elizabeth Morgan was born	Feb'r	25 1767
Sally Eskridge Daughter of Ann Moon was born	Dec'r	18 1766
Reuben son of James & Elizabeth Murray was born	March	3 1767

page 130 (continued)

George Son of Adam & Phebe Menzies was born	Sep't	16	1755
Samuel Peachy son of Do & Do Was Born	Sep't	23	1759
Adam Son of Do & Do was born	June	26	1767
John Middleton Son of Jeremiah & Elizabeth his wife was Born	January	17	1770
Hulday Mash the son of Joseph & Judah his wife was Born	October	22	1771
James Mayson Son of Josias & Sary his wife was Born	April	6	1772
Nancy McKay Daughter of Dannel & hannah McKay his wife was Born	Aug't	10	1772
Frances Mayson Daughter of Mary Mason was Born	July	4	1772
Dannell Mealy son of Dannel & Ann his wife was Born	February	6	1773
Jeanny Morisson Daughter of Richard was Born	December	16	1772
Betsey Morgin Daughter William & Betty his wife was Born	Aprill	20	1773
Bottey Warenton Daughter of William Maltomore & Nancy his wife was born	March	10	1773
Salley Morgin Boattoy Daughter Jessey Beetley & Winny his wife was born	May	4	1773
Ann Middelton Daug of Jeromiah & Elizabeth his wife was born	December	3	1773
Peter Morris Son of John & Elizabeth his wife was Born	January	8	1774
Salley Richars Maskell Daughter to Thomas was Born	Sept'r	22	1774
James Mayson Son of Joseph & Sary his wife was Born	October	15	1774
Jese Mears Son of Jese & Rebecker his wife was born	June	16	1776
Richard Morris Son of John was Born	August	15	1775
Betsey Mattemore Daughter of Wm & Pegge was born	July	15	1775
Richard Monson Son of Molley Wildey was Born	July	13	1775
Bettey Mason Daughter to Josiah & Sarah his wife was born	May	29	1778
Randolph Mott son to Randolph & Ann his wife was born	Dec'm	26	1767
Lewoey Mott Daughter to Ditto & Ditto was Born	Sep't	6	1776
Ann Mott Daughter to Ditto & Ditto was Born	Dec'm	14	1777
Joseph Maurison son to William & Nancey his wife ws born	June	24	1778
Hannah Morrison Daughter to William & Nancey his wife was born	December	1	1787

page 131, headed "M".

Joseph Mott son of Randell & Ann his wife was Born	December	2	1772
Sary Mott Daughter to Randell & Ann his wife was Born	february	18	1775
William Mealey Son of James & Winnefret his wife was born	March	23	1775
Sammuel Mealey Son of Dannel & Nancy his wife was born	Jan	22	1775
John Mealey Son of James & Winnefritt his wife was Born	Febr	20	1777
George Mott son of Mosley & Jane his wife was Born	Apl	2	1777
Thomas Middleton son of Thomas & Judith his wife was Born	May	19	1777
Nancey Moltemore Daughter to William & Margett his wife was Born	Apl	3	1777
Judith Mason Daughter of Ann Mason was Born	May	9	1777
Elizabeth Morris Daughter of John Morris was Born	July	9	1777
Betsey More Daughter of William & Nancey his wife was Born	Sept	22	1777
John McCave son to Blackman McCave & - ws born	Augt	28	1778
Bettey Nelms Morrison Daughter to Richard & Salley his wife was born	Augt	16	1778
Elizabeth Mitchell Daughter to Isaac & Elizabeth his wife ws bn	Nov	8	1778
Susannah Pitman Daughter to Mitchell & Lucresha his wife ws bn	Mar	8	1779
Mary Maley Daughter to James & Winnefrit his wife was born	Nov'm	17	1779
James Mason son to James & Mary Bailey a bastard child was born	Augt	24	1779
John Math son to William & Lawranah his wife was born	Feb	4	1780
Ann Mathaney Daughter to William & Mary his wife was Born	Augt	21	1781
Bettey Maeth Daughter to Josse & Jemima his wife was Born	Feb	5	1782
William Meath son to William & Lucranah his wife was Born	March	7	1782
Thomas Payne Marskil son to Thomas & Kesiah his wife ws bn	Decm	3rd	1782
James Mealey son to James & Winnyfret his wife was born	March	13	1784
William Maith son to Jesse & - (the name Jemina erased in the original) his wife was born	Oct	20	1783

page 131 (continued)

Fanny Maskill Daughter to Thomas & Keziah his wife was born   Octr   18 1784
Rolley Minnis son to Elizabeth A B child was born   Feb   15 1785
Elizabeth Moss Daughter to Ebenezer & Hannah his wife was born April 3 1785
John Maith son to Jesse & Jemima his wife was Born   Jan'r 25 1788
Bettey Middleton Daughter to John & Hannah his wife was Born Jan'r 28 1789
Ezekiel Mors son to Ebenezer & Hannah his wife was Born   Augt   13 1789
John Mors son to Obadiah & Nancey his wife was Born   Augt   1 1789
Nancey Maurison Daughter to William & Nancey his wife was Born Feb 23 1790
Elizabeth Mason Daughter to Eli & Hethey his wife was Born March 22 1790
Fanney Meath Daughter to Jesse & Jemima his wife was Born   March 20 1790
Robert Middleton son to John & Hannah his wife was Born   Febr   17 1792
Mary More Daughter to John & Molley his wife was Born   Sept   27 1793
Salley Mason Daughter to Eli Mason & Catey his wife was Born Sept 30 1795

page 132, headed "N".
Betty Nickklis Daughter to Tery (or Jery) Nickklis and
    An his wife was Born   decembr 9th 1769
Betty Shapleigh Nelms Daughter of Charles & Bettey His
    wife was Born   October 8 1770
John Norman Son of Sammuel Partridge & Hannah his wife
    was Born   May   5 1771
Molley Nutt Daughter of Richard & Alse Nutt his wife was Born May 23 1764
John Nutt Son of Do was Born   June   6 1766
Rhodham Nutt Son of Do was Born   May   23 1771
Isaac Night the Son of George Night & Judith his wife was Born Novmbr 20 1771
Presley Neale son to Matthew Neale & Rebeckah his wife
    was Born   October 22 1802
Matthew Neale son to Ditto & Ditto his wife was Born   Feb   4 1805

page 133, headed "O".
Nathaniel oldham Son te Leroy oldham and Elinor his wife
    was Born   January 27 1770
Mary owens Daughter of William owens & Sary his wife ws born August 6 1770

page 134, headed "O".
            John Oldham Son To Ja's Born   Octr   17 1708
            Lindzey Opie Son To Lindzey Born   March   5 1714
            Tho's Opie Son To Do Born   March 25 1716
            Hannah Owen Daug'r To Hugh Born   Sep'r 23 1720
            Rich'd Son To Hugh Owen Born   Aug't 31 1716
            Winefd Owen Daug'r To Do Born   Feby   13 1722
            Lindzey Opie Son To Jo'n Opie Born   March   5 1714
            Tho's Opie Son To Do Born   Feby   25 1716
            Susana Opie Daug'r To Do Born   Feby   5 1719
            John Oldham Son To Jo'n Born   Jan'y 28 1664
            Abegal Oldham Daug'r To Do Born   March 27 1666
            Rich'd Oldham Son To Do Born   May   27 1671
            James Oldham Son To Do Born   Aug   11 1669
            Charles Onel Son To Arther Born   May   27 1694
            Ann Odethey Daug'r To Neel Born   Octr   2 1703
            Sarah Odethey Daug'r To Jo'n Born   Dec'r 10 1724
            Hanah Odothey Daug'r To Do Born   July   10 1726
            Ruth Owens Daug'r To Hugh Born   Sep'r 25 1727
            Wm Oldham Son To George Born   May   15 1732
            Jane Owen Daug'r To Hugh Born   Oct'r 14 1709
            Wm Owen Son To Do Born   Nov   25 1714
            Ann Owen Daug'r To Do Born   Sep'r 24 1718
            Sarah Owen Daug'r To Do Born   Feb'y 25 1726

page 134 (continued)

Mary Owens Daug'r To Owen Born	Dec'r	17	1733
Benj'n Oxendane Son To Jo'n Born	Apr	12	1733
Jenne Oxendane Daug'r To Do Born	Feby	14	1735
Eliza Owens Daug'r To Wm Born	Sepr	8	1735
Clark Oxendan Daug'r To Jo'n Born	Novr	28	1736
Jo'n Oxendane Sone To Do Born	June	10	1739
Wm Owens Son To Wm Born	Apl	28	1741
Rich'd & Dav'd Owens Twins To Do Born	Nov'r	26	1743
Jo'n Owens Son To Do Born	Sepr	1	1745
Nancey Owens Daug'r To Wm Born	Sepr	18	1747
Sarah Owens Daugr To Do Born	June	7	1750
Edmund Northen Nelms Son To Joshua was Born	March	5	1741
Primus Nelms Son To Do was Born	Dec'r	18	1751
Milly Nelms Daug'r To Do was Born	Sep'r	15th	1754
Nansey Oldham Daug'r To Rawleigh was Born	July	25	1755

page 135, headed "O".

George Pickren Owens Son To Wm & Sarah was Born	June	2nd	1755
James Oldham Son To Moses & Frances was Born	Oct'r	13th	1738
Spencer Oldham Son To Do was Born	Nov'r	16	1740
Peter Oldham Son To Do was Born	July	20	1743
Ann Oldham Daug'r To Do was Born	Nov'r	2d	1745
William Oldham Son To Do was Born	April	30th	1748
Eliza Oldham Daug'r To Do was Born	Feby	20th	1751
James Oldham Son To George & Jean was Born	Nov'r	25th	1751
Mary Oldham Daug'r To Do was Born	Sept	3d	1753
Hannah Oldham Daug'r To Do was Born	May	12	1757
John Ouldum Son of William & Ann ouldum his wife was Born	May	10	1772
Nancey Owen Daughter of William Owens & Sary his wife was born	March	24	1773
Richard Ouldum Son of Leroy & Elinor his wife was Born	february	3d	1773
Salley Oldhom the Daughter of William Oldhom Jun'r was born	Sept	18	1774
Grace Smith Oldham Daughter to tho's & Ann his wife was Born	Decemb	10	1775
Jenney Oldham Daughter to William & Ann his wife ws born	June	21	1778
Samuel Oldham son to William & ann his wife was born	March	22	1781
Nancey Oldham Daughter to Thomas & Ann his wife ws Born	Oct	4	1781
Thomas Oldham son to William & Nancey his wife was bn	Janr	28	1783
Peter Oldham son to George and Judith his Wife was born	June	11	1785
Lucey Oldham Daughter to Thomas & Ann his wife was Born	Sept	6	1785
Mary Oldham Daughter to Ditto & Ditto was Born	April	26	1778
Fanney Lawson Oldham Daughter to William Oldham & Nancey his wife ws Bn	April	6	1787
Nancey Oldham Daughter To William & Nancey his wife ws Bn	July	13	1787
John Oldham son to George & Judith his wife was Born	Feb'y	7	1788
William Oldham son to William & Nancey his wife was Born	March	7	1790
Neddy Oldham son to William Oldham & Nancy his wife was born	July	27	1790

page 136, headed "P".

Wm Pendergrass Was Born	May	14	1714
Robt Pendergrass Was Born	Dec'r	8	1711
John Perre Son of John Born	Feby	5	1718
Tho's Perre Son To Do Born	Sept	8	1720
Isaac Perre Son To Do Born	Octr	5	1723
Winef'd Perre Daug'r To Thos Born	June	11	1719
Eliza Pearsefull Daug'r To Mary Born	Sep'r	15	1731
Dav'd Peugh Son To Hen'y Born	Dec'r	22	1732
Lurene Pickrell Daugr Isaac Born	Aug'r	14	1735
Edward Pedley Son To George Born	June	13	1676
Jane Pedley Daug'r To Do Born	June	17	1672
Jo'n Porter Son To Tho's Born	June	23	1695
Wm Pickrell Son To Wm Born	March	6	1694
Jane Presley Daug'r To Peter Born	June	29	1664
Samuell Prewtt (or Prentt) son to Rosamond Born	Feby	1	1700
Grace Pierce Daug'r To Ralph Born	Oct'r	13	1706
Margaret Pursley Daug'r To Tobayas Born	Sepr	7	1707
Jo'n Parker Son To Ja's Born	July	23	1710
Wm Pearce Son To Ralph Born	Jany	13	1711
Wm Parker Son To Wm Born	Jany	19	1711
Ann Palmer Daugr To Eliz'a Born	Apl	4	1712
Jas Prett Son To Jas Born	March	16	1712
Mary Perrie Daug'r To Thos Born	Oct	3	1713
Mary & Catharin Pure Daugr To Jo'n Born	Feby	9	1714
Jane Parker Daug'r To Wm Born	Mar	30	1715
Wm Pema Son To William Born	March	22	1717
Tho's Pow Son To Jas Born	Octr	26	1717
Jo'n Peame Son To Wm Born	Apl	7	1700
Rich'd Parker Son To Wm Born	Nov	17	1702
Wm & Peter Twins To Thos Porter Born	May	28	1693
Mary Parker Daug'r To Ja's Born	Apl	28	1706
Charity Parker Daugr To Wm Born	Apl	29	1705
Isaac Pickrom Son To Wm Born	May	27	1705
Jo'n Perrie Son To Jo'n Born	Feby	5	1718
Winif'd Perrie Daug'r To Tho's Born	Jany	11	1719
Grace Peme Daug'r To Wm Born	Jully	15	1720
Eliza Porter Daug'r Wm Born	June	25	1718
Tho's Perrie Son To Jo'n Born	Sep'r	8	1721
Mary Philops Daug'r To Eliza Born	Nov'r	23	1721
Samuell Pean Son To Wm Born	Octr	15	1723

page 137, headed "P".

Elisha Peme Son To Jo'n Born	Sept	12	1724
Sarah Pickrom Daug'r To Wm Born	Dec'r	18	1718
Wm Pickrom Son To Do Born	Nov'r	24	1720
Ann Pickrom Daug'r To Do Born	Dec'r	28	1722
Dav'd Pickrom Son To Do Born	Feby	2	1725
Winef'd Pickrom Daug'r To George Born	Aug't	27	1725
Georg Pickrom Son To Do Born	Mar	18	1729
Spencer Pickrom Son To Wm Born	Aug't	22	1729
Winif'd Porter Daug'r To Wm Born	Octr	6	1725
Eliza Pickrom Daugr To Isaac Born	Mar	20	1728
Judeth Pickrom Daug'r To George Born	March	17	1730
Nelley Pickrom Daug'r To Wm Born	Jan'y	15	1732
Sarah Pickrom Daug'r To Isaac Born	Jany	22	1732
Joseph Power Son To Jo'n Born	Jan'y	25	1712
Ja's Power Son To Do Born	Jully	25	1717
Peter Power Son To Do Born	June	30	1727

page 137, (continued)

Jane Parker Daug'r To Wm Born	Aug't	16	1733
Daniell Pickrell Son To George Born	Sepr	14	1733
Mary Parker Daug'r To Wm Born	May	14	1735
Wm Prett Son To Jas Born	March	5	1737
Fra's Ann Prett Daug'r To Do Born	March	17	1739
Wm Parker Son To Wm Born	Jan'y	27	1737
Tolsun Parker Son To Do Born	Dec'r	27	1740
Jas Prett Son Jas Born	Apl	4	1741
Sarah Phillopes Daug'r To Jas Born	Oct'r	31	1731
Mary Ann Phelopes Daug'r To Do Born	Jany	1	1735
George Phelopes Son To Do Born	Feby	28	1738
Jo'n Pelmore Son To Jas Born	Octr	22	1746
Eliz'a Peugh Daug'r To Tho's Born	Dec'r	22	1745
Jo'n Pickrom Son To Wm Born	Apl	23	1746
Sarah Ann Power Daug'r To Joseph	May	9	1739
Mary Power Daug'r To Do Born	Nov	29	1741
Betty Power Daug'r To Do Born	Jully	31	1744
John Power Son To Do & ~ Born	March	30	1747
Jesse Patrige Son To Rich'd Born	Dec'r	29	1741
John Patrig Son To Do Born	Jully	20	1743
Kity Pickrom Daug'r To George Born	Nov'r	15	1748
Sarah Pealmer Daug'r To Jas Born	March	9	1748
Wine Peray Daug'r To Francis Ann Born	Dec'r	27	1749

page 138.

Wm Power Son To Joseph Born	Sepr	26	1749
Betty Palmer Daug'r To James Born	Nov'r	30	1749
Lucke Neel Perrie Daug'r To Winef'd Born	Ap'r	18	1748
Nansey Power Daug'r To Peter Born	Jany	24	1752
Sarah Ann Perrie Daug'r To Jo'n Born	March	28	1752
Salley Pritchett Daug'r To John & Grace was Born	Octobr	16	1754
Joseph Powers Son To Joseph & Sarah was Born	Jany	24	1754
Christopher Pritchett Son To John was Born	Dec'r	2d	1747
Susannah Pritchett Daug'r To Do was Born	Sep't	12th	1751
Sarah Pickron Daug'r To David was Born	April	9th	1747
Susannah Pickren Daug'r To Do was Born	Dec'r	29th	1749
David Pickren Son To Do was Born	Sept'r	15	1754
George Pitman Son To George & Winefred was Born	July	26th	1755
James Power Son To Peter & Lydda was Born	March	23d	1756
Nansy Pickril Daug'r To Wm was Born	Octr	4th	1753
Sarah Pickril Daug'r To Do was Born	Nov'r	7th	1756
Leannah Power Daug'r To Joseph was Born	Jan'ry	10th	1757
Betty Parry Daughter to John & Frances Parry born	Octob'r	20	1754
Thomas Parry Son to John & Frances Parry was born	March	5th	1758
Wm Pickrell Son to Spencer & Judith Pickrell was born	June	12th	1752
John Pickrell Son to Spencer & Judith Pickrell was born	Novem	28th	1753
Charles Pickrell Son to Spencer & Judith Pickrell was born	Decem	23d	1755
Winefred Price Bastard Daughter to Eliz Price was born	April	5th	1754
Winny Power Daughter to Joseph and Sarah Power was born	Septm	4th	1758
Betty Parsons Daughter to James and Ruth Parsons was born	March	11	1749
Molly Parsons Daughter to James and Ruth Parsons was born	Septem	12th	1757
Nancy Parry Daughter to John and Franky Parry was born	Octob	13th	1760

page 138 (continued)

John Phillips son to James Phillips Jun'r and Winefred his
    wife was born   March   2d 1763
Spencer Mattrom Pickrell Son to Spencer & Judith Pickrell
    was born   April   17 1763
Betty Pickren Daughter to William and Ann Pickren was born July   26 1760
William Pickren son to William and Ann Pickren was born   July   13 1762

page 139, headed "P".

John son of John and Elleanor Pittion (possibly Pillion although
    the ts are crossed) was born   July   19th 1763
William son of Jesse & Sarah Pitman was born   March   1st 1767
Judith Pullen Daughter of Le roy & Winnefrit his wife
    was Born   December 13 1772
William Hennery Pickrin Son of Spencer & Judith his
    wife was born   Novembr 23 1772
Winne Palmer Daughter of Sammuel & Easter his wife was Born December 4 1772
Nancy Pickrin Daughter of Isaac & Sary his Wife Was Born Octob'r 13 1772
Salloy Hayos Daughter of Richard Piper & Sary his
    wife was bn   August 13 1772
Elizabeth Parker Daughter to Toulson & Jean his wife
    was Born   february 12 1774
Juno Pitman Daughter of John & Juday his wife was born   Septembr 7 1773
Sharlotte fousho Daughter of Mary Price was Born   December 23 1774
Jean Pickrin Daughter of George Pickrin & bette his
    wife was Born   Aprill 25 1774
John Pickrin Son of John & Bette his wife was Born   Novembr 10 1773
John Power the son of William & Molle his wife was Born   December 21 1773
William Brabsill Son of Winnifret Price Bastard was Born   Aprill 17 1774
Clooy Phiplips Daughter of James & winne his wife was born August 18 1774
Bette Power the Daughter of William & Mary his wife was born february 6 1776
Thomas Pullin Son of Le roy and Winne his wife was born   August 20 1776
Minne Power Daughter of Joseph & Bettey his wife was born August 23 1776
Vinson Dickson Son of John and Bettey his wife was born   January 6 1776
John Pullin Son of Lory & Winne his wife was Born   October 9 1774
Thomas Pickrin Son of Isaack & Sary his wife was Born   March 5 1775
Molley Parmer Daughter of John & Elizabeth his wife born Nom'br 15 1774
David Piper Son of Richard & Sary his wife was Born   Septm'br 4 1774
Jean Parker Daughter of Tolson & Jean his wife was born   Feb 20 1777
Charlott Philipson Daughter of James & Winnefret his
    wife was Born   April 28 1777
Caty Curtis Piper Daughter of Richard & Sara his wife
    was born   March 18 1777
Elizabeth Prootor Daughter of Abraham & Bottey his wife Born May 16 1777
Fleet Potts son of Enock and Susannah his wife ws Born   March 1 1778
Rhodom Popwoll son of Mary ann Popwoll was Born   Sept 5 1777
Richard Pullin son of Nathan & Elizabeth his wife was born March 29 1778
John Peters son to John & - ws born   June 7 1778
Milley Pullin Daughter to Leroy & Winney his wife born   Aug't 10 1778
William Power son to William & Mary his wife was born   Jan'r 5 1779
Daniel Pickren son to Isaac & Sarah his wife was born   Decm 8 1778
Charles Henry Pickren son to John & Maryan his wife was born Nov'm 8 1778
Providonoo Orrings Pickren son to John & Bettey his
    wife ws bn   Nov'm 17 1778
Sarah Power Daughter to Joseph & Betty his wife ws bn   Ap'r 15 1779
Susannah Pitman Daughter to Mitchell & Lucreshe his
    wife ws bn   Mar 8 1779
John Power son to William & Mary his wife was Born   Dec'm 23 1781

page 139 (continued)

Bettey Power Daughter to Joseph & Bettey his wife was Born Janr 1 1782
John Phillips son to George & Sara ann his wife ws born April 14 1783
Mary Stonam Pullen Daughter to James & Betty his wife w b March 3 1783

page 140, headed "P".

Ailsey Prosser Daughter to William & Elizabeth his wife
was born April 3 1785
Beekah Swindell Power Daughter to Joseph & Bettey his
wife was born Octob'r 15 1784
James Pullin son to James & Betty his wife was born(1787 ?)Nov'm 25 178-
George Phillips son to George & Sarah ann his wife was born April 28 1787
James Power son to Joseph & Bettey his wife was Born Nov'm 24 1787
Welthe Regester Daughter to Salley Patridge a Bastard
child was Born Jan'r 3 1789
John Butler Pope son to Nathaniel Pope & Elizabeth his
wife ws Bn Jan'r 12 1790
Mary Pope Daughter to Ditto & Ditto was Born Jan'r 12 1792

page 141, headed "P".

Winne phillips Daughter of James and winne his wife was Born December 26 1769
Elizabeth persons Daughter to John Armstrong & Jean
his wife ws Born December 17 1769
  Children Born to Isaac pickrin & his wife Sarah
Judith pickrin Daughter to Isaac & Sarah his wife Born July 20 1762
John pickren Son to Isaac & Sarah his wife Born Januy 7 1764
Jean pickrin Daughter to Isaac & Sary his wife was Born Decembr 28 1766
Molley pickrin Daughter to Isaac & Sary his wife was Born March 31 1768
Isaac pickrin Son to Do & Sarah his wife was Born June 11 1770

Pollby parker daughter of toulson & Jean his wife was Born Novem'br 26 1770
Judith Taloe Pearsefull Daughter of Eligah Pearsefull
& Winnefrit was born February 13 1771
Elizabeth Pearsefull Daughter of Elijah Peasofull was Born February 5 1765
Sary Pickrin Daughter of George Pickrin & Bette his
wife was Born August 5 1771
Hulde pitman the Daughter of John & Judith pitman his
wife was Born docembor 19 1771
Lott Popler son of Maryan Popler Was Born Novenbr 20 1771
Harriot Lee Prosser Daughter to William Prosser & Elizabeth
his wife ws Born Septem'r 25 1794
William Prosser son to William Prosser & Sarah his wife
was Born March 24 1796
Suckey Pope Daughter to Humphrey Pope & Molley his
wife ws Born March 27 1796
John Pasquett son to William Pasquott & Elizabeth his
wife was Born Febr 10 1798
Richard Coelman Power son to William Power & Lucey R
Power his wife was Born August 12 1805
Elizabeth Sydnor Power Dau to William Power Lucey his
wife ws B March 6 1808

page 142, headed "W".

Linsey Parcer Winstead son to John Winstead & Salley
his wife ws born Nov'm 18 1795
Jeremiah Wildy son to William and Sarah Wildy his wife
was Born April 28 1801
Robert Alexander Welch son to Daniel Welch and Susan
his wife was Born January 6 1805

page 142 (continued)

James Wildy son to William Wildy & Sarah Wildy his wife was Born	June	16	1806
Thomas Coelman Walker son to Thomas Walker & Sarah his wife was Born	February	2	1797
Randolph Walker son to Thomas Walker and Sarah his wife was Born	June	1	1799
Frances Ann Walker Daughter to Thomas Walker & Sarah his wife was born	Septembr	30	1801
Sarah Walker Daughter to Thomas Walker & Sarah his wife was born	February	23	1804
William Walker son to Thomas Walker & Sarah his wife was Born	April	8	1806
Melinda Walker Daughter to Ditto & Ditto was Born	June	30	1808
Alice Walker Daughter to Do & Do was born	May	5th	1810

page 143, headed "Y".

John Nelms Yost son to Tobias Yost & Lucey Yost his wife was Born	October	12	1803

page 144, headed "J".

Hellen Johnston Daug'r To Rich'd Born	Dec'r	26	1666
Rich'd Johnson Son To Do Born	Apl	10	1671
Ann Johnson Daug'r To James Born	Sep'r	3	1669
Jean Johnson Daug'r To Do Born	Jully	26	1672
Mary Johnson Daug'r To Do Born	Oct'r	3	1674
Jane Joyce Daug'r To Abraham Born	Jany	29	1669
Eliz'a Joyce Daug'r To Do Born	Dec'r	14	1671
Dav'd James Son To John Born	Dec'r	26	1688
Mary James Daug'r To Wm Do Born	Nov'r	5	1681
Rebeckah James Daug'r To Do Born	Aug'r	20	1685
John James Son To Jo'n Born	Sep'r	12	1685
John Jones Son To Hugh Born	Apl	13	1662
Roger Jones Son To Do Born	Feby	14	1671
Elinor Jones Daug'r To Do Born	Aug't	12	1674
Mary Jones Daug'r To Do Born	Aug't	3	1676
Eliza Jones Daug'r To Do Born	Feby	15	1678
Eliza Jones Daugr To Wm Born	Sepr	17	1693
John Jones Son To Do Born	July	21	1695
Edward Jolins Son To Edward Born	Oot'r	22	1699
Margret James Daug'r To William born	Aug't	31	1691
Eliza Joanes Daug'r To Wm Born	Aug't	21	1707
Mary Jones Daugr To Edward Born	March	7	1707
Ann James Daug'r To Mered'th Born	Aug't	4	1706
Marg't James Daug'r To Tho's Born	Apl	14	1706
Eliz'a Jones Daug'r To Mary Born	July	10	1707
Charles Jones Son To Wm Born	July	16	1710
Jo'n James Son To Meridith Born	March	23	1711
Ann Jones Daug'r To Owen Born	June	13	1715
Allex'r Jackson Alis Son To Susana Born	May	17	1693
Mulrain Jackson Son To Do Born	Octr	14	1694
Jane Jameson Daug'r To Jo'n Born	Jan'y	29	1713
John Jameson Son To Do Born	Jany	4	1716
John James Son To Daniell Born	Apl	5	1717
Eliz'a Jaspor Daug'r To Edward Born	Aug't	11	1719
Johnson Jones Son To Francis Born	March	27	1720
Jemima Jones Daug'r To Wm	Jully	26	1720
Tho's James Son To Daniell Born	Aug't	30	1720
Winefred Jones Daug'r To Owen Born	Sep'r	20	1720
Wm Jones Son To William Born	May	12	1723

page 145, headed "J".

Brereton Jones Son To Robt Born	Jany	4	1716
Betty Jones Daug'r To Do Born	Jany	9	1718
Robt Jones Son To Do Born	Jany	26	1721
Wm & Tho's Jones Sones To Do Born	Oct'r	15	1723
Grace James Daug'r To Daniell Born	Aug't	30	1724
Fielding Jones Son To Owen Born	Jany	20	1731
Susana Jones Daug'r To Do Born	March	12	1724/5
Joseph Jones Son To Do Born	Feby	27	1724
Sarah Jones Daug'r To Do Born	Aug't	6	1728
Wm James Son To Jo'n Born	Ap'l	20	1735
Cloho James Daug'r To John & Jane was Born	Janry	9th	1754
William Jones son to Ambrus Jones & Bettey his wife	Octr	9	1729
Thomas Johnston Son To Thomas was Born	Janry	9th	1755
John Jones Son To Seymour was Born	Nov'r	28th	1754
Daniel James Son To Thomas & Sarah was Born	March	31st	1747
John James Son To Do was Born	Septr	17th	1749
Thomas James Son To Do was Born	May	9th	1752
Nancy James Daug'r To Do was Born	July	31st	1754
Thomas Crallie Jones Bastard To Mary was Born	March	26th	1756
Charles Jones Son to William & Ann Jones was born	Septemb	14th	1755
Swan Jones Son to William & Ann Jones was born	October	5th	1759
John Jones Son to Ambrose & Bettey Jones was born	June	20	1747
Charles Jones Son to Ambrose and Betty Jones was born	June	10	175-
Charles Jones the Son of William & Sarah his wife was Born	Septembr	6	1771
Hannah Jaqus the Daughter of William & Elizabeth his wife was born	May	1	1772
Ephroditus Jones the son of John and hannah his wife was Born	March	1st	1773
Charles Jones Son of James Jones & Keziah his wife was Born	february	4	1773
Winnefrit Jones Daughter of Charles Winefrit his wife was born	february	14	1774
Jesse Jones Son of William & Sayrah his wife was born	Octobr	6	1773
Elizabeth Jones Daughter of John & hannah born	March	3	1775
William Jones Son of John & Margit Jones his wife was born	February	12	1775
Elizabeth Jones daughter of John & Margrett his wife was born	March	9	1777
William Jones Son of Sammuel & Easter his wife born	March	19	1776
Lucey Jones Daughter of William & Sarah his wife was born	June	24	1777
Nancey Jones Daughter of John & Hannah his wife was Born	Nov'm	16	1777
Mary Jaques Daughter to William & Elizabeth his wife was born	Feb	12	1770
Ann Jaques Daughter to Ditto & Ditto was born	May	10	1774
Hill Jaques son to Ditto & Ditto was born	Sept	28	1776
John Jones son to John & Marget his wife was born	October	31	1778
Thomas Jones son to William & Sarah his wife was born	Octob	28	1768
William Jones son to Ditto & Ditto was born	June	6	1770

page 146, headed "J". Part of page torn away.

Mary Jaques Daughter of William and Elizabeth his wife Born	february	12th	1770
Dafne Jarrot Son of John Jarrot was born (sic)	Novembr	15	1770
John Jones the son of John & Hannah Jones his wife was Born	March	1st	1771
Joseph Jones Son of Charles & Winnefrit his wife was Born	June	27	1771
- - Jones son of James Jones was Born	October	27	1771
-ge Jones Son of John & hannah his wife was born	Aprill	10	1769
-iam Hill son to Ann Hill a Bastard child was Born	March	26	1791
-h Jopes Daughter to Hack B Jopes & Anna Jopes his wife was Born	March	1	1796

page 146 (continued)

-oey Cirk Jopes Daughter to Ditto & Ditto his wife was Born October 7 1797
-lley Hacky Jopes Daughter to Ditto & Ditto his wife
  was Born   Decemb 23 1799

page 147.
Elisha Payne Son To John & Grace died   March 31st 1755
Mary Power Daughter to Joseph Power Died   December 23d 1757
Leanna Power Daughter to Joseph Power Died   December 4th 1757
John Smith Departed this Life   July   29 1777
Easthor Abbey Departed this Life   August   25 1777

page 148.
Hannah Rogers Daug'r To Noah died   Aug'st 4th 1755
John Rice Died   June   6 1762

page 149.
John Smith Died   Dec'r   12th 1755
Jean Self Daug'r To William Died   Jan'ry 22d 1756
Stephen Stott Died   Octr   14   1757
The Rev'd Thomas Smith Died   March   16   1758
Thomas Self Died   Septem 10th 1758
Lucy Sibbalds wife to Robt Sibbalds Died   April   22d 1762

page 150.
Sarah Ann Barecraft Wife to John died   April   20 1755
John Barcraft Son To Do   April   21 1755
William Bailey Son To Wm Died   Oct'r   5 1766
Judith Beelley Died (sic)   May   9 1757
Francis Beckley Died   June   16 1757
Hannah Blackwell wife to John Blackwell Died May   13 1758
George Berry Died   Jan   3 1756
Wm Bush Son to John Bush Died   Novem   5 1759
Joseph Beekly Son to Francis & Judith Beekly Died March   1 1760
Charles Betts the Elder Died   March   14 1760
James Blincoe Died   March   22 1759
John Barecraft Son to John & Mary Barecroft Died May   12 1759
Elijah Blundell Died   Septem 29 1760
William Berry Died   July   25 1761
John Boyer Died   Novem   15 1761
Sam'l Blackwell Gen't Died   Octob   17 1761
Mary Boyer wife to John Boyer Died   Octob   12 1763

page 151.
John Conway Died   Sept'r 27 1755
Sarah Claughten Died   (Claughton)   Dec'r   5 1755
Robert Cristey Son To John Died   Feb'y   4 1757
Charles Son To Do Died   Feb'y   12 1757
Presly Cookaril Son to Presly & Sarah Cookaril Died Aug't   12 1756
Hannah Cookman Daughter to Sarah Cookman Died Septem   2 1758
John Claughton Died   Feb'ry 23 1760
Cap Edward Coles Died   Novem   21 1764

page 152.
Alice Dunaway Died   Feb'y   6 1758
Francis Davis wife to Barbee Davis Died   July   3 1761
Francis Davis Son to Barbee & Frances Davis Died Sep't   9 1761

page 153.

Hannah Eskridge Daug'r To Samuel Died	Oct'r	6	1754
George Eskridge Son To Do died	Nov'r	1	1754
Charlotte Foushee Eskridge Daug'r To Do Died	May	-	1756

page 154, headed "William McGoon Thomas Jones"

William Alverson Dr to three pound of tob'oo	December	5	1769

(Note: There appears to be no reason for this entry in the register, unless perhaps it is a fee for a grave digger or some small service for the parish.   B.F.)

page 155, headed "V".

Frances Vanlandingham Son To Mich'l Born	Dec'r	13	1666
Rich'd Vanlendengham son to Do Born	Aug't	6	1772
Ann Vanlendingham Daug'r To Do Born	Dec'r	3	1668
Benj'm Vanlandingham Daug'r To Do Born	Jan'y	31	1672
George Vanlanding'n Son To Frances Born	Oct'r	1	1718
Eliz'a Vanlandingham Daug'r To George was Born	Sep't	30	1756
Benjamin Vanlandingham Son To Benj'n was Born	Nov'r	23	1756
George Vanlandingham Son To Benj'n & Susannah Vanlandingham was born	August	6	1758
Thomas Vanlandingham Son To George & Mary Vanlandingham was born	Jan'ry	18	1759
Ezekiel Vanlandingham Son To George & Mary Vanlandingham was born	June	1	1762
Francis Vanlandingham Son To Benjamin & Susannah Vanlandingham was born	Novem	4	1763
Richard Litterill Vanlandingham Son to Benj'n Vanlandingham was born (son to Benj'n & Mary Vanlandingham)	August	6	1767
Ann Vanlandingham the Daughter of Hennery & Elizabeth his wife was born	April	24	1772
Ann Vanlandingham the Daughter of Frances & Winnefrit his wife was Born	Novem'br	29	1773
Elizabeth Vanlandingham Daughter of George Addams & Becky his wife was Born	April	23	1774
William Vanlandingham Son of Hennery & Elizabeth his wife was Born	February	21	1775
Mary Vanlandingham Daughter of George & Beckey his wife was Born	October	16	1775
Benjamin Vanlandingham Son of hennery & Elizabeth his wife was Born	October	20	1776
Jean Vanlandingham Daughter of James & Clarkey his wife was Born	March	23	1777
Elizabeth Vanlandingham Daughter of Tho's Vanlandingham & Mary Vanlandingham a bastard child was Born	October	6	1777
Kenner Vanlandingham son to Geo Adams Van'd & Beckey his wife ws bn	July	17	1778
Ellender Rodgarster Vanlandingham Daughter to James & Clark his wife ws bn	Oct'r	25	1778
George Brown Vanlandingham son to Henry & Elizabeth his wife was born	Jan'r	23	1779
William Vanlandingham son to Benja'n & Sarah his wife was born	Feb	27	1779
Elizabeth Brown Vanlandingham Daughter to Winney Vanlandingham Born	Oct	15	1778
Betsey Haynie Vanlandingham Daug'r To John & Nancey his wife was born	Jan'r	8	1780
Beckey Vanlandingham Daug'r to George A & Beckey his wife was born	March	8	1781

page 155 (continued)

Betsey Hail Vanlandingham Daughter to Hennery P Vanlandingham ws Born	May	13	1781
Lewis Vanlandingham Son to Benjamin & Salley his wife was Born	Oot	29	1781
William Haynie Vanlandingham son to John & Ann his wife was born	Jan'r	24	1782
Easter Brumbley Vanlandingham Daughter to Ezekiel Va'n & Betty his wife was born	April	30	1782
Salley Vanlandingham Daughter to Henry & - his wife was Born	July	10	1783
George Vanlandingham Son to George & Rebeokah his wife was born	Oot	12	1783
Haynie Vanlandingham son to John & - his wife was born	Jan'r	25	1784
Oliver Vanlandingham son to Ezekiel & Betsey his wife was born	March	6	1785
Spenoer Vanlandingham son to Henry P & Elizabeth his wife was Born	Ap'r	28	1787
Betsey Oliver Vanlandingham Daughter to Ezekiel & Betsey his wife was Born	Aug't	4	1788
Samuel Vanlandingham son to Thomas & Molley his wife was Born	Sept	7	1789
Thomas Vanlandingham Son to Ditto & Ditto was Born	Nov'm	4	1793
Joel Vanlandingham Son to Francis & Sarah his wife was Born	January	26	1803
& Baptized the 5th Day of May 1804			

page 156, headed "W".

Phebey Walter Daug'r To Jo'n Born	Ap'l	10	1664
Mary Walters Daug'r To Do Born	Jan'y	3	1666
Hester Walters Daug'r To Do Born	March	30	1673
Nathaniel Walters Son To Do Born	Oot'r	2	1665
Jo'n Walters Son To Do Born	July	3	1671
Wm Walters Son To Do Born	Sep'r	11	1679
Tho's White Son To Lur'y Born (sio)	Ap'l	20	1680
Mary White Daug'r To Lurenia	Jan'y	18	1683
Wm Warriok Son To Wm Born	Nov	26	1690
Ann Warreok Daug'r To Do Born	Aug't	1	1682
Mary Warreok Daug'r To Do Born	Feb'y	4	1685
Sarrah Warreok Daug'r To Do Born	May	2	1688
Ja's Warreok Son To Do Born	March	20	1693
George Warreok Son To Do Born	Aug't	5	1703
Frances Wadingtown Son To Ralph	Feb'y	3	1679
Jo'n Wadingtown Son To Do Born	July	19	1691
Rob't Wadingtown Son To Do Born	May	24	1687
Hanah Wadingtown Dau To Do Born	July	23	1693
Eliz Wornam Daug'r To Jo'n Born	Aug't	22	1681
Jo'n Wornam Son To Do Born	Dec'r	29	1685
Ann Wornam Daug'r To Do Born	Jan'y	11	1682
Mary Wornam Daug'r To Do Born	Mar	4	1687
Tho's Wornam Son To Do Born	Mar	4	1689
Jo's White Son To Joseph Born	Oot'r	31	1661
Jo'n White Son To Do Born	Oot'r	16	1679
Ja's White Son To Do Born	Nov'r	30	1681
Wm Wildey Son To Wm Born	July	28	-
Jo'n Wey Son To Rioh'd Born	July	18	1671
Tho's Webb Son To Sam'll Born	May	6	1685
Wm Webb Son To Do Born	Nov	26	1693

page 156 (continued)

Rich'd Webb Son To Do Born	Oct	11	1696
Jon Webb Son To Ja's Born	Oct	16	1686
Emanuel Walker Son To Emanuel Born	Ap'l	23	1692
Fra's Walker Son To Do Born	Ap'l	15	1694
Mary Walker Daug'r To Do Born	Jan'y	5	1695
Rich'd Walker Son To Do Born	May	8	1690
Jo'n Walker Son To Do Born	Ap'l	10	1701
Ralph Wadington Son To Ralph	Jan'y	31	169-

page 157, headed "W".

Wm Woodlin Son To Wm Born	Feb'y	10	1694
Jo'n Williams Son To Jo'n Born	March	4	1693
Priscala Williams Daug'r To Do Born	June	22	1700
Wm Wildey Son To Wm Born	June	11	1694
George Wadingtown Son To George Born	March	3	1694
Rich'd Wey Son To Jo'n Born	Oct'r	27	1695
Wm Wilkins Son To Edw'd Born	Aug't	16	1695
Tho's Wilkins Son To Jo'n Born	Oct'r	20	1684
Jo'n Wilkins Son To Do Born	July	1	1689
Cha's Wilkins Son To Do Born	Apl	15	1692
Peter Wilkins Son To Do Born	Nov'r	12	1694
Mary Wilkins Daug'r To Rich'd Born	Aug't	10	1697
Mottley Wildey Son To Wm Born	Jully	31	1698
Cernitie Will'ms Daug To Dav'd Born	Octr	8	1702
Grace Will'ms Daug'r To Do Born	Nov	25	1703
John Woolridge Son To Edw'd Born	Oct'r	9	1701
Samuell Winsteed Son Saml Born	Octr	25	1701
Jo'n West Son To Jo'n Born	Feby	2	1695
Obedayah Wigintown Son To Jos Born	Feby	16	1707
Ann Wilson Daug'r To Jo'n Born	May	16	1708
Bethena Wadingtown Daugr To Mary Born	Feb	20	1710
Mary Wadingtown Daug'r To Jo'n Born	Apl	4	1712
Mary Ann Woode Daug'r To Wm Born	Aug't	27	1712
Margaret Whitt Daugr To Symon	Nov'r	14	1712
Wm Wilkins Son To Hen'y Bern	Decr	30	1713
Mary Watte Daugr To Rich'd Bo'n	Nov'r	14	1713
Winef'd Welsh Daug'r To Silvester Born	Dec'r	8	1714
Ann Wilson Daug'r To Robt Born	July	27	1711
Elinor Wilson Daug'r To Do Born	March	22	1712
William Wood Son Wm Born	Octr	1	1714
Tho's Wilkins Son To Peter Born	Octr	15	1715
Ann Wilkins Daug'r To Do Born	Nov'r	12	1716
Jane Wilkins Daug'r To Jo'n Born	Dec'r	26	1716
George Wilkins Son To Jo'n Born	Aug't	15	1716
Jean Wilkins Daug'r To Chas Born	July	17	1717
Griffin White Son To Simon	July	8	1717
Frances Ann Warrick Daug'r To Wm Born	March	2	1717
John Wilkins Son To Peter Born	March	17	1713
-nard Walker Son To Nathl Born	Aug't	-	1717

page 158, headed "W".

Jo'n Whithead Son To Tho's Born	Feby	15	1706
Eliz Walker Daug'r to Emaniell Born	Feb'y	23	1703
Mary Waters Daug'r To Tho's Born	July	22	1705
Hannah Williams Daug'r To Dav'd Born	Feby	16	1705
Wm Wilkins Son To Jo'n Born	Jan'y	4	1719
Sarah Wornam Daug'r To Jo'n Born	May	18	1707
Jo'n Wornam Son To Do Born	Nov'r	5	1709

page 158 (continued)

Edward Wornam Son To Do Born	June	21	1712
Tho's Wornam Son To Do Born	Nov'r	26	1714
Samuell Wornum Son To Do Born	March	30	1717
Jane Wornam Daug'r To Do Born	Ap'l	22	1720
Eliz'a Wornam Daug'r To Do Born	May	11	1725
Wm Webb Son To Wm Born	Sep'r	23	1719
Peter Wilkins Son To Peter Born	Octr	8	1719
Ann Wilkins Daug'r To Hen'y Born	Jany	21	1719
Bety Winsteed Daug'r To Samuell Born	June	23	1720
Grace Webe Daug'r To Tho's Born	Nov'r	19	1710
Thos Webb Son To Do Born	Oct'r	2	1712
Eliza Webb Daug'r To Do Born	Sep'r	18	1714
Jo'n Webb Son To Do Born	Mar	31	1717
Wm Webb Son To Do Born	May	11	1717
Wenef Webb Daug'r To Do Born	Dec'r	11	1721
Rich'd Warrick Son To Wm Born	Feby	1	1719
Jo'n Wilkins Son To Jo'n Born	Apl	28	1721
Sarah Wilkins Daug'r To Peter Born (sic)	Mar	27	1721
Sarah Wilkins Daug'r To Peter Born (sic)	Marc	19	1721
Hanah West Daug'r To Jo'n Born	Apl	19	1721
Daniell Winsted Son To Samuell Born	Sepr	16	1721
Winef'd Warrick Daug'r To Wm Born	Jany	13	1721
Rich'd Waters Son To Jo'n Born	June	22	1713
Jo'n Waters Son To Do Born	June	19	1715
Chas Wilkins Son To Charles Born	Feb'y	12	1722
"LElackga" (?-illegible) Wilkins Son Peter Born	Apl	19	1723
Hen'y Watkins Son To Hen'y Born	Apl	7	1723
Samuell Winsteed Son To Sam'll Born	July	10	1723
Hanah Williams Daug'r To Dav'd Born	Jany	13	1706
Lazuras Williams Son To Do Born	Feby	8	1708
Mary Williams Daug'r To Do Born	Jan'y	8	1709
Absalim Williams Son To Do Born	Feby	24	1715
Dav'd Williams Son To Do Born	Jan'y	8	1713
Eliz'a Williams Daug'r To Do Born	Jully	31	1717
Ann Williams Daug'r To Do Born	Sep	21	1720
Wm Williams Son To Do Born	Jany	9	1722
George Wilkins Son To John	Sep	18	1723
John Walker Son To Fra's Born	Sep'r	14	1724

page 159.

Jo'n Williams Son To Dav'd Born	Nov'r	11	1724
Edward White Son To Simon Born	June	20	1726
Jo'n Williams Son To Rich'd Born	Dec'r	15	1707
Jane Wilkins Daug'r To Peter Born	Jany	15	1725
Mary White Daug'r To Simon Born	Jany	27	1720
Mergarie White Daug'r To Do Born	March	20	1722
Simon White Son To Do Born	Aug't	22	1724
Thos Wilkins Son To Chas Born	March	14	1724
Winef'd Welsh Daug'r To Silvester Born	Aug't	22	1721
Benj'n Welsh Son To Do Born	Jany	1	1723
Samuell Wilkins Son To Jo'n Born	Octr	26	1725
Joseph Wilkins Son To Peter	Dec'r	15	1726
Jane Wilkins Daug'r To William	Jully	15	1727
Mary Wildie Daug'r To Mettley Born	May	12	1728
Cha's Wilkins Son To Jo'n Born	May	28	1728
Judith Wilkins Daug'r To Wm Born	Aug't	3	1728
Isaac Waten (Water ?) Son To Jas Born	July	26	1729
Sarah Wooff Daugr To Hen'y Born	May	6	1730

124

page 159 (continued)

Clarke Wilkin Son To Peter Born	Jan'y	13	1730
Elinor Walas Daug'r To Joseph Born	Nov	8	1730
Bety Wilkins Daug'r To Jo'n Born	Jan'y	5	1730
James Winsted Son To Samuell Born	Nov'r	26	1730
Eliz'a McNall Daug'r To - Born	Oot'r	11	1717
Wm Wildey Son To Joseph Born	May	3	1730
Eliz'a Wildey Daug'r To Do Born	May	23	1731
Wm Walker Son To Tho's Born	Dec'r	1	1731
Neme Woode Daug'r To Jo'n Born	Nov'r	15	1729
Mary Woode Daug'r To Do Born	Jan'y	10	1731
Jo'n Wilkins Son To Cha's Born	Nov'r	22	1731
Jo'n Wildey Son To Motley Born	Jan'y	15	1732
Moses Wildey Son To Do Born	Oot'r	4	1730
Sinah Wildey Daug'r To Wm Born	Jan'y	27	1729
Jo'n Welsh Son To Silvester Born	Aug't	17	1727
Silvester Welsh Son To Do Born	Oot'r	1	1729
Daniell Welsh Son To Do Born	Feb'y	18	1732
Winif'd Wildey Daug'r To Wm Born	Jan'y	11	1732
Winif'd Wilkins Daug'r To Jo'n Born	Nov'r	-	1733

page 160, headed "W".

George Winsted Son To Samuell Born	May	13	1733
Lurena Welsh Daug'r To Silvester Born	Dec'r	6	1733
Jo'n Wildey Son To Motley Born	Sep'r	28	1734
Sarah Webb Daug'r To Tho's Born	March	15	1735
Jo'n Woode Son To Jo'n Born	May	4	1736
Eliz'a Wey Daug'r To Jo'n Born	Nov'r	15	1729
Judith Wey Daug'r To Do Born	March	12	1731
Rich'd Wey Son To Do Born	Ap'l	7	1735
Eliz'a Williams Daug'r To John Born	Feb'y	5	1733
Spencer Williams Son To Do Born	Oot'r	13	1734
Eliz Wey Daug'r To Rich'd Born	Dec'r	26	1728
Winif'd Wey Daug'r To Do Born	May	3	1731
Simon Wey Son To Do Born	May	5	1734
Daniell Wilkins Son To Jo'n Born	Ap'l	5	1736
Mary Ann Wey Daug'r To Rich'd Born	Dec'r	16	1736
Bety Woode Daug'r To Jo'n Born	May	7	1737
Susana Winsted Daug'r To Sam'll	Ap'l	18	1736
Tho's Wornum Son To Tho's Born	Oot'r	19	1736
Winif'd Wildey Daug'r To Motley Born	Dec'r	17	1737
Unity Wilkins Daug'r To Sarah Born	Jan'y	30	1738
Rich'd Webb Son To Mariann Born	Jan'y	18	1739
Jo'n Williams Son To Lazarus Born	July	18	1737
Peter Winsted Son To Sam'l Born	Jan'y	20	1739
Rich'd Watts Son To Thomas Born	Feb'y	5	1736
Tho's Wats Son To Do Born	May	5	1739
Wm Webster Son To Winif'd Born	Marc	11	1737
Shadrick Wildey Son To Motley	Dec'r	24	1739
Nancy Welsh Daug'r To Silvester	Oot'r	18	1740
Samuell Walker Son Joseph Born	Sep'r	15	1740
Frances Williams Daug'r To Lazarus	Dec'r	25	1739
Jo'n Span Webb Son To Jiles Born	Sep'r	8	1738
Lucey Webb Daug'r To Do Born	Ap'l	3	1741
Samuell Walker Son To Joseph	Sep'r	15	1740
Boty Watts Daug'r To Tho's Born	Aug't	11	1741
Mary Williams Daug'r To Dav'd Born	Jan'y	15	1742
Josoph Wildey Son To Jo's Born	July	22	1733
Jane Wildey Daug'r To Do Born	Ap'l	3	1735

page 160 (continued)

Lucretia Wildey Daug'r To Do Born	Feb'y	15	1738
Judith Wildey Daug'r To Do Born	Nov'r	1	1740
Motley Wildey Son To Wm Born	Aug	5	1736

page 161, headed "W".

Eliz'a Wildey Daug'r To Wm Born	Feb'y	20	1734
Sarah Wildey Daug'r To Do Born	Aug't	15	1738
Hanah Wildey Daug'r To Do Born	Jan'y	23	1739
Leanah Wildey Daug'r To Do Born	July	30	1741
Meekeek Wildey Sone To Motley Born	March	14	1742
Jo'n Wood Son To Jo'n Born	Aug't	14	1742
Tho's Walker Son To Tho's Born	Oct'r	15	1736
Bety Walker Daug'r To Do Born	March	15	1739
Joseph Walker Son To Jos'h Born	Marc	6	1743
Letee Watts Daug'r To Tho's Born	Dec'r	16	1743
Epram William Son To Dav'd Born	Ap'l	13	1744
Nathanel Walker Son To Emaniell Born	Sep'r	10	1741
Sam'll Webb Son To Wm Born	Feb'y	16	1745
Jo'n Webb Son To Wm Born	Ap'l	25	1745
Chloe Wildey Daug'r To Motley Born	Jan'y	12	1745
Judith Walker Daug'r To Jos'h Born	Dec'r	25	1744
Wm Woode Son To Jo'n Born	Dec'r	29	1745
Nathaniell Walker Son To Lenard Born	March	18	1745
Sarah Wilkins Daug'r To Wm Born	Dec'r	28	1744
Grace Wilkins Daug'r To Ja's Born	Oct'r	16	1741
Jiles Webb Son To Jiles Born	Sep'r	13	1743
Eliz'a Williams Daug'r To Absolum Born	June	29	1746
John Webb Son To Wm Born	Oct'r	20	1746
Jo'n Wornam Son To Tho's Born	Oct'r	23	1739
Leanah Wornam Daug'r To Do Born	May	7	1744
Sarah Williams Daug'r To Epraham	Jan'y	25	1742
Letie Williams Daug'r To Do Born	Aug't	8	1747
Joseph Wood Son To Jo'n Born	Jan'y	19	1748
Hanah Williams Daug'r To Laz'us Born	Jan'y	4	1748
Jo'n Walker Son To Joseph Born	April	8	1747
Jo'n Wilkins Son To Wm Born	Oct'r	19	1748
Agathie Williams Daug'r To Ephram	June	14	1748
Mary Williams Daug'r To Absolem Born	Feb'y	28	1749
Eliz'a Webb Daug'r To Jo'n Born	Jan'y	29	1739
Sarah Webb Daug'r To Do Born	Oct'r	4	1741
Lucretia Webb Daug'r To Do Born	Jan'y	3	1746
Jo'n Webb Son To Do Born	Feb'y	22	1748

page 162, headed "W".

Winy Webb Daug'r To Jo'n & Hannahbeth Born	Feb'y	9	1749
Eliz'a Walker Daug'r To Lenard Born	Nov'r	2	174-
Grace Wood Daug'r To Jo'n Born	Nov'r	4	1749
Tho's Wornum Son To Tho's Born	Jan'y	8	1748
Wm Wornum Son To Do Born	Ap'l	3	1751
Sarah Walker Daug'r To Tho's Born	May	9	1750
Lazuras William Son To Laza's Born	Feb'y	8	1751
Denis White Son To Simon Born	Dec	16	1748
Mary White Daug'r To Do Born	August	19	1751
Tho's Webb Son To Jo'n Born	Ap'r	20	1751
Wm Wayatt Son To James Born	Sep'r	26	1746
Jo'n Wyatt Son To Do Born	Feb'y	24	1749
Ja's Wyatt Son To Do Born	Jan'y	16	1752

page 162 (continued)

Joseph Wood Son To Jo'n Born	Nov'm	23	1751
Eliz'a Webb Daug'r To Jiles Born	Oct'r	13	1746
Winif'd Webb Daug'r To Do Born	July	25	1749
Maley Webb Daug'r To Do Born	June	25	1752
Eliz'a Webb Daug'r To Wm Born	Jan'y	15	1750
Wm Webb Son To Do Born	March	11	1751
Wildey Webb Son To Do Born	March	6	1753
Isaac Wabb Son To Jo'n Wabb (sic)	May	31	1753
Susana Walker Daug'r To John Was Born	Sep'r	25	1754
John Williams Son To John & Winifred was Born	Octob	5	1754
Susannah Walker Daughter To John was Born	Sep'br	21	1754
Elizabeth Williams Daug'r To Tho's & Katherine was Born	April	20	1741
Joseph Williams Son To Do was Born	July	23	1743
Katherine Williams Daug'r To Do was Born	Nov'r	26	1745
Thomas Williams Son To Do was Born	Aug't	12	1748
Jane Williams Daug'r To Do was Born	Aug't	11	1751
Molley Williams Daug'r To Do was Born	Feb'y	23	1754
Rhoda White Daug'r To Edward & Ann was Born	October	30	1749
William Walker Son To Robert was Born	Sep'r	23	1750
Travise Walker Son To Do was Born	Aug't	5	1753
Hannah Webb Daug'r To John & Hannah was Born	July	3	1747
William Webb Son To Do was Born	Feb'y	18	1748
Lucy Ann Webb Daug'r To John & Winnefred was Born	Sep'r	14	1751
John Webb Son To Do was Born	Jan'y	1	1754
Nansy White Daug'r To Simon was Born	April	9	175-

page 163, headed "W".

Ann Walker Daug'r To Rich'd & Rachel was Born	Aug'st	17	1742
Richard Walker Son To Do was Born	January	20	1745
John Walker Son To Do was Born	Feb'ry	15	1747
Winifred Walker Daug'r To Do was Born	Feb'ry	20	1749
Elisabeth Walker Daug'r To Do was Born	Feb'ry	22	1751
Milley Walker Daug'r To Do was Born	April	9	1753
Jane Walker Daug'r To John & Mary was Born	Jan'ry	11	1754
Nancy Walker Daug'r To George & Winefred was Born	April	16	1753
Betty Walker Daug'r To Francis & Mary was Born	Aug't	21	1751
Grace Walker Daug'r To Do was Born	May	21	1753
William Waters Son To John & Sarah was Born	May	21	1755
George Webb Son To William was Born	June	1	1755
James Webb Son To James was Born	May	18	1755
Bettie Walker Dau'r To John & Mary was Born	Sept'r	4	1755
Nancy Webb Daug'r To Giles & Elizabeth was Born	July	29	1755
George Walker Son To George was Born	Dec'r	7	1755
Opie Waters Son To John & Elizabeth was Born	Dec'r	6	1755
John Welsh Son To Benjamin & Judah was Born	Jan'ry	17	1751
Anna Welsh Daug'r To Do was Born	July	27	1753
Silvester Welsh Son To Do was Born	Nov'r	21	1755
Charles & Sarah Wilkins Son & Daughter To John & Ann were Born	May	10	1755
Samuel Winstead Son To Daniel was Born (1749)	Sept	25	1749
Mary Winstead Daug'r To Do was Born	Jan'ry	28	1752
Elisabeth Winstead Daug'r To Do was Born	April	23	1754
Mosly Walker Son to Rich'd was Born	Feb'ry	6	1756
Risdon Walker Son to Francis & Mary was Born	April	24	1756
Cuthbert Williams Son To Absolom & Mary was Born	Janry	19	1756
Wm Williams Son To John & Joannah was Born	Jan'ry	21	1756

page 163 (continued)

Willoughby Walker Son To John was Born	June	7	1757
James Webb Son To John & Winifred was Born	Feb'y	10	1757
Sam'l Wornum Son To Thomas was Born	May	5	1757
John Wilkins son to John & Ann was Born	Nov'r	2	1757
Mollie Walker Daug'r To Rich'd & Mary was Born	Sept'r	5	1757
William Walker Son To Thaddeus & Ann was Born	Janry	3	1758
Churchill Watts son to Ewell & Mary Watts was born	Feb'ry	18	1758

page 164, headed "W".

Molly Walker Daughter to John & Mary Walker was born	June	1	1758
Sally White Daughter to Simon & Mary White was born	January	20	1757
Frances Winsted Son to Samuel Winsted was born	Nov'm	19th	1758
Sally Webb Daughter to Giles & Eliza Webb was born	Septm	30th	1758
Thomas Wilkins Son to John & Ann Wilkins was born	Octobr	10th	1759
Shapleigh Waddy Son to Benj'a and Judith Waddy was born	Septem	14	1758
Benjamin Waddy son to Benjamin and Judith Waddy was born	Janry	23d	1760
John Walker Son to John & Mary Walker was born	Feb'ry	21	1760
William Walker son to Fran's Walker Jun'r and Mary was born	July	18th	1760
Betty Fallin White Daughter to Simon and Mary White was born	January	20	1761
Motley Wildy Son to Frederick & Leannah Wildy was born	October	1st	1760
Richard Way Son to Richard Way and Judith his wife was born	Novem	5th	1758
Griffen Warmoth Daughter to Tho's and Betty Warmoth was born	Octob	14th	1761
Jordan Webb Son to John and Winefred Webb was born	Oct'o	13th	1761
William and Nancy Walker Twins to John and Sarah Walker was born	March	1st	1762
Thomas Walker Son to John and Mary Walker was born	April	12th	1762
Absolom Williams Son to Absalom and Winefred Williams was born	April	25	1762
Betty Watts Daughter to Rich'd and Mary ann Watts born	June	12	1762
Peter Wilkins son to John and Ann Wilkins was born	Decem	1st	1761
Molly Walker Daughter to Franc Walker Jun'r & Mary his wife was born	Feb'ry	15	1763
Winefred Winsted Daughter to Samuel Winsted was born	May	3	1762
William Wilson Son to William and Mary Wilson was born	Decemb	29th	1760
Griffin White son to Simon and Mary White was born	May	3d	1763
Sarah Wildy Daughter to Joseph and Judith Wildy was born	Septm	2d	1758
William Wildy son to Joseph and Judith Wildy was born	April	9th	1760
Molly Wildy Daughter to Joseph and Judith Wildy was born	Septm	14	1761
Judith Wildy Daughter to Joseph and Judith Wildy was born	March	17	1763
Lucy White Daughter to Edward and Ann White was born	Septem	30	1763
Molly Wornom Daughter to John & Betty Wornom was born	Decem	31st	1763
Nanny Williams Daughter to Absalom and Winefred Williams was born	Febru'ry	12	1764

page 164 (continued)

Reubin Williams Son to John and Winefred Williams was born	April	6	1764
Thomas Winsted Son to Samuel and Winnefred Winsted was born	June	14	1764
William Wildy son to Frederick and Leannah Wildy was born	Novembr	18	1761
Tunstall Wildy son to Frederick and Leannah Wildy was born	Septemb	15	1764
John Coles Wise son to Spencer and Elizabeth Wise was born	March	2	1759
Edward Coles Wise son to Spencer and Elizabeth Wise was born	June	7	1760
Spencer Wise Son to Spencer and Elizabeth Wise was born	March	7	1763
Katy Watts Daughter to Richard and Mary ann Watts was born	Octob	1	1764
William Walker son to John and Mary Walker was born	June	29	1765
Katy Wilkins Daughter to John and Ann Wilkins was born	May	24	1761
Nancy Wilkins Daughter to John and Ann Wilkins was born	Septem	16	1765
Judith Hutching Walker Daughter to Francis Walker Jun'r and Mary was born	Novem	22	1765

page 165, headed "W".

Judith Walker Daughter to John and Sarah Walker was born	October	26	1765
Thomas Warnom Son to John & Betty Warnom was born	Septemb	30	1765
George Wilkins Son to Daniel & Mary Wilkins was born	May	21	1764
Sally Webb Daughter to John & Molly Webb was born	March	27	1766
Frankey Watts Daughter to Richard & Maryann Watts was born	October	21	1766
Alice Daughter of Samuel & Betty Winstead was born	March	9	1767
Ellis son of Absalom & Winifred Williams was born	Jan'r	29	1767
Winifred Warnom Daughter to John & Betty Warnom was born	Decemb	9	1767
John Webb Son to John & Judith Webb (Smiths point) was born	October	4	1763
Elizabeth Webb Daughter to John & Judith Webb (Smiths point) was born	August	24	1767
Williams Watts Son Richard & Maryan Watts was born	Octob	12	1768
Attanling (? -Stalaning ?) Wildey Sun to Fradrick Wilday and Leaner Wilday was Borne	Novenbr	20	1766
Ann Way Daughter to Richard & Judith way his wife was Born	May	28	1763
Devenport Way son of Do was Born	Nov	1	1765
John way Son of Do was Born	June	3	1768
Ellis Watts Daughter of Richard Watts & Maryann his wife	June	24	1771
Jeanne Warmuth Daughter of Thomas & Elizabeth his wife was born	March	28	1772
Bettey Winstead Daughter of Cuttance & Caty his wife was born	March	20	1772
John Williams Son of John & fanney his wife was Born	Novembr	26	1771
Hannah Winsted Daughter to Samuel & Winnifrit was Born	March	19	1772
Rebeckah Lewis Winsted Daughter to John & Cloey his wife was Born	Octo	26	1772
Sary Welsh Daughter of Benjamin & Mary his wife was born	Septembr	20	1772
Thomas Walker Son of tho's & Frances his wife was born	September	3	1772
Sammuel Walker Son of Joseph & Hannah his wife was born	January	18	1773
Lazarus Webb Son of Lazarus was Born	January	14	1773

page 166, headed "W".

Richard Walker Son of tho's & frances his wife was Born	Septmbr	3	1772
Tho's Wilkins Son of William & Doley Was Born	Septmbr	5	1772
Ailsey Wood Bridg Daughter of Mary harford Bastard Was born	March	16	1773
Mary Ann Watts Daughter of Richard & Mary ann was born	May	10	1773
Samuel Winstead son to Sammuel & Roda his wife ws born	August	7	1778
Nancey Webb Daughter to Charity Webb was born	July	19	1778
William Webb son to Ellender Webb was born	Sept	9	1778
Nancey Wilkins Daughter to Thomas & Nancey was born	Aug't	30	1778
Bettey Webb Daughter to William & Millicent his wife born	Sep't	19	1778
Joseph Wood son to Joseph & Winnefret his wife was born	Oct	18	1778
William White son to George & Elizabeth his wife was born	Novm	27	1778

page 166 (continued)

John Williams son to Raughley & Beckey his wife was born	July 26	1778
Hannah Welsh Daughter to John & Bettey his wife was born	Jan'y 14	1779
Bettey Wornum Daughter to William & Bettey his wife was born	Dec'm 2	1778
Sarah Walker Daughter to Richard & Sarah his wife was born	Jan'r 8	1779
Thomas Warnum son to William & Bottey his wife was born	Jan'r 2	1772
John Wornom son to Ditto & Ditto was Born	Sept 27	1776
Winnah Haynie Winstead Daughter to Jeremiah & Winnah his wife was Born	March 17	1779
John Haynie Winstead son to James Winstead & Chloe his wife was Born	Octobr 11	1779
Mary Kenner Williams Daughter to Joseph & Mary K. his wife was born	Jan'r 6	1780
Edward Wall son to Edward & Marget his wife was born	Febry 16	1780
Samuel Wroe son to John & - (wife's Name omitted) was born	June 17	1780
Thomas Webb son to William & Millisent his wife was born	August 18	1780
Francis Winstead son to Francis & Cathorine his wife was born	Nov'm 25	1780
George Walker son to Thadda & Elloner his wife was born	March 23	1781
Cathorine Williams Daughter to Joseph & Mary* his wife was born	July 5	1781
Chloe Winstead Daughter to John & Chloe his wife was born	June 23	1781
Samuel Williams son to Rawleigh & Rebecca his wife was born	Oct 27	1781
Salley White Daughter to George & Elezabeth his wife was born	Jan'ry 6	1782
Eroell Winstead son to Sammuel & Rhodæ his wife was born	Sept 3	1782
Botty Williams Wall Daughter to Edward & Margot his wife w.b.	March 27	1783
Sara Williams Daughter to Joseph & Mara K. his wife was born	April 6	1783
Mary Ann Bails Wilkins Daughter to Mary Wilkins was born	Jan'ry 27	1781
Samuel Winstead son to James & Chloe his wife was born	Sept 17	1783
Bommoy Dick Walker son to Sammuel & Mary his wife was bn	Oct 17	1783
Thomas Wroe son to William & Salley his wife was born	Dec'm 26	1783
Susannah Haynie Walker Daughter to William & Catharine his wife was born	Feb 9	1784
William Warren Son To John Warren & Elizabeth his Wife was Born	March 4	1784
Fanney Warren Daughter To Do & Do Twins was Born	March 4	1784
Rhoda Winstead Daughter to Sammuel & Rhoda his wife was born	Jan'ry 20	1784

page 167, headed "W"

Ann Smout Winstead Daughter of Sammuel & Rhoda his wife was Born	January 22	1773
Joseph Woodley Son of francos & Elizabeth his wife was Born	April 17	1773
Elias Winsted Son of Susanner Winsted a bastard child was Born	July 8	1773
Ezekial White Son of George & Elizabeth his Wife Was Born	January 19	1773
Marthew Williams Daughter to Peter & winnefrit his wife was Born	January 24	1774
Ann welsh Daughter of John & Bottey his wife Was Born	December 20	1773
Elizabeth Walker Daughter of Randul & Bottey his wife Was Born	May 2	1774
Millekent Wornum Daughter of William & Betto his wife Was Born	June 12	1774
William Walker son of Tho's & francos his wife was Born	May 24	1774
Elizabeth Wilson Daughter of John & Judah his wife was Born	June 27	1773
Elizabeth Worrick Daughter of Obediah & Ann his wife was Born	July 13	1773
Botto Wordrup Daughter of William was B orn	June 13	1774
Bette webb Daughter of John & Molle his wife was Born	February 15	1774
William Way Son of Richard Was B orn	Octobr 13	1773
Hulday Wilkins the Daughte r of Sary Wilkins Was Born the	April 29	1774
Lucy Webb Daughter of Lazarus & Leanner his wife was B orn	febry 8	1775
Presley Williams Son of Ephram & winne his wife was Born	December 20	1774

* Joseph & Mary Kennor Williams

Molley white Daughter to Dennis & Winne his wife was Born March   17   1775
Zekiel hill Winsted Son of frances & Catey his wife
   was Born   November 26   1775
Jeremiah Winsted Son of Jeremiah & Winnefrit his wife
   was born   December 14   1775
George White Son of George & Elizabeth his wife was Born March   14   1776
Salley Winstead the Daughter of John & Chloe winstoad February   4   1776
Richard Yates Walker Son of hennery & Elennor his wife
   was born   feb'ry   22 1777
Phebe Peachy Daughter of Sammuel Winsted & Rhode his wife
   was born   May   22 1776
Wilday Wilkins Son of William & Dolley his wife was born Agust   10 1774
Elias & Heathey Walker Son & Daughter to James & Hannah
   his wife was Born   January   8   1776
John Wood Son of Joseph & Ann his wife was born   Novmbr   13 1775
John flint webb Son of Elindor was born   May   23 1776
William Winsted Son of James & Clory his wife was Born Septmb   21 1775
Pegge Wilkins Daughter of Betty was Born   Feb'ry   9   1775
Thomas Williams Son of John & fanne his wife was Born March   4   1775
Elezebeth Webb Daughter of Sarah Webb was born   Janu'r   11 1777
William Webb Son of Lazarus & Leanner his wife was Born Decem   17 1776
James Whealey son of Thomas & Marget his wife was B orn April   1   1777
Randal Walker son of Randal & Bettey his wife was Born March   14 1777
Edwin Way son of Richard and Winnah his wife was B orn October   19 1777
Hannah Wilkins Daughter of William and Dolley his wife
   was Born   Nov'm   25 1777
Winney Fallen White Daughter of Dennis and Winney his wife
   ws Born   Dec'm   24 1777
Elizabeth Kenner Williams Daughter of Joseph and Mary
   Kenner Williams his wife was born   April   7   1778
Spence Walker son of John & Winneyfrit his wife was born Mar   19 1778
Salley Winstead Daughter to Frances & Catey his wife was born June 21 1778
Thomas Way son to Richard and Winney his wife was born Nov'm   16 1775
Holland Haynie Winstead son to John & Chloe his wife was born July 11 1778
Bettey Efford Winstead Daughter to Ditto and Ditto was born July   11 1778

page 168
Barbery White Daughter to George & Elizabeth his wife ws bn July 13 1784
Matthew Winstead son to Francis & Catherine his wife was Born July 26 1784
Molley Everitt Williams Daughter to Raw'l & Becca his wife
   ws B orn   Nove'm   28 1784
Henry Warmoth son to Thaddeus & Winney his wife was born Jan'r   10 1785
George Winstoad Son to Daniel &--(wife'sname omitted) his
   wife was born   Dec'm   9   1786
Risdon Walker son to William & Catherine his wife was born April   9   1786
Rebeckah Walker Daughter to William & Catherine his
   wife was Born   July   13 1787
Thomas Williams son to Willaughby & Magdalen his wife
   was Born   March   23 1788
Ann Webb Daughter to William & Winneyfret his wife ws Bn June   28 1788
Jean Winstead Daughter to Samuel & Rhoda his wife was Born March 29 1788
John Lewis Winstead son to John & Chloe his wife was Born July   18 1788
Neuton Walker son to William & Catherine his wife was Born Oct   28 1788
Ewel Self Wobb son to Rachel Webb A bastard child was born April 25 1789
Chittester Walker son to William & Catherine his wife
   was Born   January   25 1791
Jean Corbin Wilkins Daughter to Daniel Wilkins & Milley
   his wife was born   October   8   1792

page 169.
| Farnifold Nutt Died The Elder | May | 4 | 1762 |

page 170.

Mary Kenner Daug'r To William Died	Nov'r	16th	1756
Molley Keeve Daug'r To Beverley Keeve Died	Novem	2	1766
Thomas Kesterson Son To William & Eliz'a Kesterson Died	Novem	29	1768
Beverley Keeve Died a friday Night a little after Dark	Octobm	6	1769
Elizabeth Knott Wife to Peter Died	July	22	1775

page 171.
| Mary Lamkin wife to Lewis Died | Jan'ry | 30th | 1758 |

page 172.

John Leach Died	Nov'r	1st	1755
Nanny Lawless Wife to Dennis Died	Dec'r	9	1755
George Lex Died	March	9th	1757
Betty Coelman wife to Thomas Coelman Departed this life December the 14th 1788 & in the 49th year of her age & Liv'd in a married state 30 years & six months	December	14	1788

page 173.

Samuel Moore a Parishioner Died	Jan'ry	3	1755
Josiah Mayes a Parishioner Died	Nov'm	5	1755
John Maltemore a Parishionor Died	Jan'ry	10	1756
Sarah McGown Wife to John Died	March	2	1757

page 174, headed "St. Stephans Parrish in Northumberland County in Virginia".

Cap't Griffin Fauntleroy Died	Octob'r	28	1755
Swan Fauntleroy Died	Septem	24	1756
Dennis Fallin Died	July	13	1765
Richard Claughton Senor Died	July	24	1773

page 175.

Daniel Struton Gill Died	Nov'r	15	1756
Jese Gaskins Died	June	27	1757
Cap't Ellis Gill Died October the 27th day	Octob	27	1760
Elizabeth Gibson wife to George Gibson Died	June	29	1761
Thomas Gill (Potomack river) died	October	12	1765

page 176, headed "Y".

Samuell Yop son to Jo'n Born	Ap'l	18	174-
Jeremie Yopp son to John & Winefred Yopp was born	Novemb	25	1759
Molly Yopp Daughter to John & Winefred Yopp was born	Feb'ry	23	1762

page 177.

Sam'l Wornom Son to Tho's & Winefred Died	Nov	4	1757
Elizabeth Webb Died about 2 'ccl in the evening wife to Giles	June	22	1759
Nancy Walker Daughter to George Walker Died	Decemb	1	1762

page 178.

| Elizabeth Vanlandingham Died | - | - | - |

(Finis)

INDEX

There should be no need for an index for this register. The names
are grouped alphabetically and in general order of date. It is an
index in itself. However since the pages of the original are disordered and a few names out of place, it is best that a very general index
be added. Also in entries where the child's father may or may not be
shown, it is difficult to decide just what name was actually used for
the child. A number of these are entered below, but it must be under-
stood that those are, to me, uncertain. There may never have been
any such persons.   Beverley Fleet.

A. 1. 2. 3. 4. 5. 6. 7.
Abbey, Easther 119.
Alexander (entered as Ellixander,
   Elexander, etc.)
   Angus, 46
   Dorcas, 47. 84.
   Haddeway Hanie, 47.
   Jesse, 46
   John, 84
   Judah, 84.
   Mary, 43. 46.
   Rawle (Raleigh) 43.
   Robert, 46.
   Shapley, 84.
   William, 47. 84.
Ayres (entered as Heirs)
   James, 73.
   James Williams, 73.
   Rebeccah, 73.

B. 7. 8. 9. 10. 11. 12. 13. 14.
   15. 16. 17. 18. 19. 20. 21.
   22. 23. 24. Deaths, 119.
Bailey, Mary, 110.
Beacham, Ann, 71.
   John West, 71.
   John West, Junior, 71.
Beatley (Beekley ?)
   Jessey, 110
   Salley Morgin, 110.
   Winny, 110
Beekley (?) Elisha Paine, 68.
Boggess, John, 6.
          Winnefred, 6.
Bransill (Price ?) Wm. 115.
Bray, Isaac, 73. 95.(duplicate
   entries)
Bray, Isaac, Junior. 73. 95.
Bridg (?) Ailsoy Wood, 128.
Brown, Charles, 55.
       George, 55.
       Susannah, 55.

C. 24. 25. 26. 27. 28. 29. 30.
   31. 32. 33. 34. 35. 36.
   Deaths. 119.

Claughton, Priscilla, 102.
   Richard, 102.
   Sarah Lewis, 102.
Coelman, Betty, 131.
          Thomas, 131.
Cookman (Kookman) Anna, 99.
   George, 104.
   Hannah, 99. 104.
   Rice, 99. 104.

D. 36. 37. 38. 39. 40. 41.
   42. 43. Deaths 119.
Davis, Nancy, 95.
   Richard, 95.
Dickson, Betty, 115.
   John, 115.
   Vinson, 115.

E. 43. 44. 45. 46. 47. 48.
Edwards, Millison, 51.
Elleston, Bottey, 84.
          John S. 84.
Eskridge (Mason ?) Sally, 109.

F. 48. 49. 50. 51. Deaths 131.

France (?) Shapley, 85.

G. 51. 52. 53. 54. 55. 56.
   Deaths 131.
Garner (?) Rachel, 86.
Gill, Salley, 68.
Gill (?) Rhodham Hudson, 68.
Gill, Salley, 35.
   James Claughton, 35.
Glasscook, Grigg Blackorby, 20
   Nance Blackeby, 16.
   Thomas, 16.
Golds Bery, Margit, 19
   Robert, 19.
   William, 19
Gordon, George, 85.
   Sharlotte, 85.
Grayham (?) Charles, 86.
Grimes, James, 41.

H. 56. 57. 58. 59. 60. 61. 62,
  63. 64. 65. 66. 67. 68. 69.
  70. 71. 72. 73. 74.
  Deaths 89. 92.
Hagdon (Haydon ?) Nanny Dimsdel 38
  Zachariah, 38.
Hall, Ruth, 106.
Hambelton, George Sanford, 86.
Handley (prob. Standley) Jno. 80.
Harford, Mary, 128.
Harris,Wm. of Westmorland Co. 67.
Hill, Ann, 118.
  William, 118.

J. 95. 117. 118. 119.
Jones, Abishai, 66

K. 95. 96. 97. 98. 99. 104.
  Deaths 131.
Kelley, Mary, 50.
Kennon, John, 30.
  Nancy, 30.
  Sarah, 30.
  Thos. 30.
  Wm. 30.
Kesterson (Hesterson) Eliz'a 67.
  James, 67.
  Wm. 67.
Knight (Night) George, 111.
  Isaac, 111.
  Judith, 111.

L. 99. 100. 101. 102. 103. 104.
  Deaths, 92. 131.
Lamkin, Lewis, 131.
  Mary, 131.
Lindsay, Sarah 109.

M. 105. 106. 109. 110. 111.
  Deaths, 131.
Martin, Sarah, 97.
Mason, William, 58.
McClanham, Elizabeth, 34. 35.
  James, 34. 35.
  Peter Griffin, 34.
McDaniel, George, 43
  Judith, 43.
  Salley, 43.
McKarter, Fanne, 98.
  Mary, 98.
  Richard, 98.
McNall, Elix'a. 124.
McWherter, Andrew, 108.
  John, 108.
  Mary, 108.
Metcalf, Ann (marriage) 53.
Middleton (?) George, 84.

Morris, Esther, 61.
  John, 61.

N. 93. 94. 95. 111.
Nelms, Aron, 5.
  William, 5.
  Edmund Northen, 112.
  Joshua, 112.
  Milly, 112.
  Primus, 112.
Nutt, Farnifold, 131.

O. 111. 112.

P. 113. 114. 115. 116.
  Deaths, 119.
Partridge, Hannah, 111.
  John Norman, 111.
  Sammuel, 111.
Phipps (Fipps) John, 48.
  John, Junior, 48.
Pitman, Lucresha, 110.
  Mitchell, 110.
  Susannah, 110.

R. 74. 75. 76. 77. 78. 79. 106.
  107.
Regester (Patridge ?) Welthe,116.
Rice, Jno. 119.
Roe (Whroe,Wroe) Jean, 73
  John, 129.
  Salley, 129.
  Samuel, 129.
  Thomas, 129.
  William, 129.
Rogers, Hannah, 119.

S. 79. 80. 81. 82. 83. 84. 85.
  86. 87. 107. 108.
  Deaths 119.
Sanders, Darcus, 43.
  Ewel Ellik, 43.
  William, 43.
Seebree, Jossey, 41.
  John, 41.
  Winnean, 41.
Senette, Cathorine Fauntleroy, 49.
  Mary, 49.
  William, 49.
Short (Williams ?) Clark, 107.
Simmons, Ann, 89.
Smith, George, 54.
  John, 119.
Smith (Kesterson ?) Jno. 97.
Straughan (?) Ann, 99.

T. 87. 88. 89. 90. 91. 92. 107.
Tiffy, Austin, 7.
   Rebecca, 7.
Thomas, Catesby, 31.
   Darous, 31.
   Thom, 31.

V. 109. 120. 121.
Vanlandingham, Elizabeth. 131.

W. 107. 108. 116. 117.121. 122. 123.
    124. 125. 126. 127.128. 129. 130.
    Deaths, 131.
Webb, John, 33.
   Lucresha Cottrell, 33.
   Molle, 33.
Wilday, Molley or Motley, 110.
Williams, Aaron, 88.
   John, 88.
Wornum, Bette, 106.

Y. 117. 131.

www.ingramcontent.com/pod-product-compliance
Lightning Source LLC
Chambersburg PA
CBHW021832020426
42334CB00014B/600